The Mystical Teachings
of al-Shadhili

SUNY Series in Islam
Edited by Seyyed Hossein Nasr

The Mystical Teachings of al-Shadhili

Including His Life, Prayers, Letters, and Followers

— —

A Translation from the Arabic
of Ibn al-Sabbagh's
Durrat al-Asrar wa Tuhfat al-Abrar
by Elmer H. Douglas

Edited with an Introduction
and a Bibliography
by Ibrahim M. Abu-Rabi'

— —

STATE UNIVERSITY OF NEW YORK PRESS

Published by
State University of New York Press, Albany

For information, address State University of New York Press,
State University Plaza, Albany, N.Y., 12246

Production by Cathleen Collins
Marketing by Theresa A. Swierzowski

Library of Congress Cataloging in Publication Data

Ibn al-Ṣabbāgh, Muḥammad ibn Abī al-Qāsim.
  [Durrat al asrār wa-tuḥfat al-abrār. English]
  The mystical teachings of al-shadhili : including his life, prayers,
letters, and followers : a translation from the Arabic of Ibn al-
Sabbagh's Durrat al-asrar wa tuhfat al-abrar / by Elmer H. Douglas;
edited with an introduction and a bibliography by Ibrahim M. Abu-Rabi'
    p. cm. — (SUNY series in Islam)
  Includes bibliographical references (p.) and index.
  ISBN 0-7914-1613-5 — ISBN 0-7914-1614-3 (pbk.)
  1. Shādhilī, Abū al-Ḥasan ʿAlī ibn ʿAbd Allāh, ca. 1196–1258.
  2. Sufis—Egypt—Biography. 3. Shādhilīyah—Biography.
  I. Douglas, Elmer H. II. Abu-Rabi', Ibrahim M. III. Title.
  IV. Series.
BP189.7.S52I2413 1993
297'.4'092—dc20
[B]   92-33632
                                                                    CIP

10 9 8 7 6 5 4 3 2 1

For Meltem with affection

Contents

Preface

The subject of this book is the life and thoughts of the North African Sufi and saint Abu al-Hasan al-Shadhili. It was partially translated by the late Elmer Douglas of Hartford Seminary in 1945. In 1970, Professor Douglas completed the translation, and, in 1990, just a few months before his death, his translation was accepted for publication by the State University of New York Press.

Born in Morocco in the latter part of the twelfth century, al-Shadhili studied under Shaykh Abu Madyan. He traveled through Algeria to Tunisia, and later to Egypt where he began to form an independent mystical movement in Islam.

Establishing residence in Alexandria, his renown as a Sufi master attracted a large following. Eventually, brotherhoods claimed authority of his name and way, and developed in many Muslim countries where they are known today. Al-Shadhili died on pilgrimage in 656/1256.

The author, Ibn al-Sabbagh, divides his book into five chapters. Chapter 1 recounts the story of al-Shadhili's career. Chapter 2 reveals correspondence with his disciples. Chapter 3 contains litanies and prayers attributed to al-Shadhili. Chapter 4 the longest, is composed of the master's teachings that resemble, in general, those of early Muslim mystics—for example, al-Qushayri. Chapter 5 indicates al-Shadhili's death, and relates many deeds and teachings of his Epyptian successor, Abu al-'Abbas al-Mursi.

The author, who was writing a little more than six decades after al-Shadhili's death, received his information from the master's disciples in Tunisia, from members of al-Shadhili's family, and from companions and friends of his companions in Egypt and Tunisia. There is, likewise, internal evidence that the author borrowed much from the *Lata'if al-minan* of Ibn 'Ata' Allah al-Iskandarani, a disciple of al-Mursi, the reputed founder of the Shadhiliyya order.

Al-Shadhili was a Sunni. In theology, he was orthodox, an opponent of Mu'tazilism, and he was given to an esoteric interpretation of the *Qur'an* and Islamic beliefs. He is reputed to have been learned in all the religious sciences. Yet, he gave precedence to intuitional knowledge over that received through intellectual processes.

The text of *Durrat al-asrar*, which was used as a basis for this translation, was printed in Tunis in 1304/1887. This has been collated with several manuscripts and with the printed text of Ibn 'Ata' Allah's *Lata'if al-minan*.

I should like to thank Mrs. Eva Douglas of Florida and Professor David Kerr of Hartford Seminary who encouraged me to edit this translation. I would like also to thank Irfan Omar of Hartford Seminary and Barbara Zingg of Barrytown, for the many hours they spent typing the manuscript.

Ibrahim M. Abu-Rabi'
Hartford, Connecticut
November 1992

Editor's Introduction

Paul Nwyia identifies three distinct phases in the development of Islamic mysticism during the first seven centuries of Islam.[1] The first period, beginning with Hasan al-Basri[2] (d. 110/728) and ending in the fourth century, was "the moment of the birth of the mystical experience in Islam—a moment in which the Muslim world shaped itself culturally."[3]

Muslim theologians and mystics consider this period—which is, historically speaking, the closest to the Prophet's time, as the purest in terms of its religious and spiritual expression. Many a thinker debated newly emerging religious, mystical, philosophical, and social questions in the spirit of the Qur'an—a spirit that was responsible for the development of Sufi technical terms, which, in turn, have shaped the entire spiritual life of Islam.

The second period began in the second half of the fourth/tenth century. During this phase, the center of political and cultural gravity of the Muslim Empire was slowly moving out of Baghdad. Nwyia calls this period "the phase of the composition of the manuals of sufism."[4] He maintains that it was the most sublime spiritual phase in Islam, mainly because some of the best minds dedicated themselves to the study of sufism with the hope of showing its perfect orthodoxy and its roots in the most traditional aspect of Islam. The following classical manuals of Sufism appeared in this period: *Kitab al-luma' fi'l tasawwuf* by Abu Nasr al-Sarraj (d. 378/987)[5]; *Kitab al-ta'arruf fi madhhab ahl al-tasawwuf* by al-Kalabadhi (d. 380/990)[6]; *Qut al-qulub* by al-Makki (d. 386/995)[7], and *Tabaqat al-sufiyyah* by al-Sulami (d. 1021).[8]

The third period, according to Nwyia, witnessed the rise of two perhaps competetive types of Sufism: elitist and intellectual on the one hand, and populist on the other. In his famous refutation of philosophical and intellectual sufism, al-Ghazali paved the way, somewhat, for the rise of the latter type.[9] Al-Shadhili, as Ibn al-Sabbagh shows clearly in his biography, attempted a compromise in his thought and action between both types of sufism. Although he was not as theoretically inclined as was al-Suhrawardi (d. 1191),[10] for instance, he preached contemplation and absolute devotion to God. Further, he argued that action in society was a necessary outcome of contemplation.

The Shadhiliyya order originated in the Maghrib, which is roughly present-day North Africa. The meeting of the Arabo-Islamic culture with the indigenous Berber culture led to outstanding religious results, one of which was the flourishing of different Sufi brotherhoods in North Africa. Mackeen attests to this by arguing that, "The growth of sufism in the Maghrib [prior to al-Shadhili] forms an integral part and is largely a direct result of the development of Islam in Barbary, displaying features characteristic of a heterogeneous Muslim Society. The Muslim West produced results which, while maintinaining a general uniformity with those of the East, reflected the color of its own surroundings."[11] The rise of the Shadiliyya *tariqa* should be seen in the historical context of North Africa, especially Egypt, in the sixth and seventh centuries of Hegira. The disintegration in the fifth and sixth centuries of the Fatimid (Shi'ite) Empire, which had ruled over a large portion of the Arab world, inaugurated the conservative Sunnite reaction against philosophy and any form of sufism associated with it. Further, the Muslim world was characterized by many political divisions that resulted in the crusaders' invasion of Syria and Egypt. Mustafa, for example, maintains that people resorted to sufism at the time as an escape from a harsh political and social reality.[12] But in addition, the proliferation of Sufi brotherhoods in North Africa and Egypt before the rise of Shadhiliyya gave rise to new religious and mystical movements in Islam. Mackeen maintains that, "By the twelfth century A.D. the impact of the Sufi movement had been sufficiently absorbed by society to pave the way for the emergence in the succeeding centuries of the powerful Sufi orders which left their imprint on the history of the land. One such order of great consequence and fame was that of the Shadhiliyya."[13]

Little is known about the early life of al-Shadhili while he was in North Africa. His biographer, Ibn al-Sabbagh, relates the events that led to his migration to Egypt and his settling permanently there.[14] Arriving in Egypt shortly after 1227, al-Shadhili was confronted with a disturbing political reality in which the Ayubid dynasty, established by Salah al-Din in 1169, was under political and military pressure of the Mamluks, or soldier-slaves, who became the real force in Egypt after 1250.

Ibn al-Sabbagh does not delve into politics in his biography. From our standpoint as modern readers, however, this biography itself must be understood against the tumultous events of North Africa and Egypt of the thirteenth century. In spite of the tense political situation for al-Shadhili, he "must have found great animation in intellectual and religious circles, for, in spite of turmoil within the realm and strife on the frontiers, among both Fatimid and Ayubid sovereigns, as among the Mamluks of a later date, there were some whose concern was the cultural advancement of their people."[15]

Against the turbulent political situation and the rich intellectual life of Egypt in the thirteenth century, the Shadiliyya order was formed and assumed a major religious role that enabled it to expand well beyond the boundaries of Egypt. Mackeen suggests that the Shadiliyya assumed historical significance only after its main seat of activity shifted to Egypt because, "In Tunisia the [Shadhiliyya] movement was essentially in a state of incubation during which al-Shadhili was primarily concerned with gathering the nascent forces with a minimum of doctrine."[16]

Ibn al-Sabbagh gives the following biographical data about al-Shadhili.[17] He was born in the region of Ghumara[18], in today's Morocco, around A.H. 583 or A.D. 1187. He embarked on a spiritual journey in search of a genuine Sufi shaykh or the *qutb* [pole].[19] As a result, he travelled to Baghdad which was still famous as a theological and intellectual center. There, he was told by an Iraqi Sufi shaykh to go back to the West, to his homeland, because the *qutb* was there. 'Abd al-Salam Ibn Mashish (d. 622/1225) was this *qutb*. Ibn al-Sabbagh says that Ibn Mashish was a strict follower of the *Qur'an* and the *Sunna*. He applied them in his life and encouraged his disciples to do so. Douglas postulates on the meeting between al-Shadhili and Ibn Mashish by saying that, "Early in life al-Shadhili went to [Ibn] Mashish to take him as his spiritual guide. The venerable teacher recognized the 'saintly' qualities of the young man and gave him his final injunction to refrain from men and to depart to Tunisia."[20] Ibn Mashish "was by far the most important of al-Shadhili's teachers, one to whom he owed his instruction in the Sufi way."[21] Ibn Mashish also laid the foundations of "the future life of Abu al-Hasan al-Shadhili."[22]

Al-Shadhili's stay in Tunisia marks the beginning of his career as a saint and theologian. It is on the basis of Ibn al-Sabbagh's biography that we can determine with some accuracy al-Shadhili's life in Tunisia and his struggle to form an independent Sufi movement. The account given by Ibn 'Ata' Allah in his biography does not shed as much light on the Tunisian phase of al-Shadhili as does Ibn al-Sabbagh's writings. Later authors of Shadhiliyya's *Tabaqat* base their narratives on Ibn al-Sabbagh's biography. Al-Shadhili's departure to Egypt, as already mentioned, marks the second phase in his career, which had a lasting effect on the future development of the Shadhiliyya order.

Ibn al-Sabbagh devotes a major section of his biography to a discussion of al-Shadhili's various travels in search of the *qutb*. He also assumes that the *qutb* plays a crucial role in sufism because he transmits the *baraka* (blessing) of the Prophet. One may argue that "Sufi realization" depends upon this *baraka* which, in turn, is transmitted through a shaykh, who is part of a *silsila* leading back to the Prophet of Islam. In that sense, *tasawwuf*, as spiritual training and method, cannot be learned from books and sophisticated theories about God and the universe. Spiritual initiation is attained only with the help of a Sufi shaykh.

'Abd al-Halim Mahmud [d. 1977], a leading modern Shadhili disciple and former rector of the Azhar University, enumerates three essential conditions for attaining spiritual inititiation. The first is a natural readiness on the part of the would-be disciple. The second condition is the necessity of belonging to a genuine *silsila* (chain) that traces its origin back to the Prophet, and the third, after being blessed by a shaykh, is the need to engage in the greater *jihad* which is self-discipline, spiritual contemplation, and asceticism. Al-Shadhili was part of this genuine *silsila* into which he was initiated by Ibn Mashish.[23]

The meeting with Ibn Mashish played a pivotal role in the al-Shadhili's intellectual and spiritual formation. Feeling comfortable with his spiritual achievements after this encounter, al-Shadhili decided to move to the nearest urban center—the city of Tunisia—where he settled for several years before his permanent departure to Egypt. During his stay in Tunisia, he attracted many followers, who perceived in him great human and spiritual qualities, and who considered him to be on the side of the poor and downtrodden in society. This popularity, however, won him the envy and the hatred of Ibn al-Bara' the chief *qadi* of Tunisia, who, according to Mackeen, charged al-Shadhili "with Fatimid leanings."[24] However, a modern biographer of al-Shadhili, 'Abd al-Halim Mahmud does not portray the Shadhiliyya order as a dissident movement, but as a movement that was favored by the sultan, Abu Zakariyya al-Hafsi (625/1228–647/1249). In spite of the political support of the sultan, however, al-Shadhili decided to move to Egypt where his *tariqa* grew quickly. He died in 656/1258 in Egypt on the way back from one of his pilgrimages to Mecca.

During his lifetime, al-Shadhili had disciples who were dispersed in North Africa, especially in Tunisia and Egypt. The real strength of his movement was derived from the disciples whom he attracted in Egypt. Ibn 'Ata' Allah, for example, highlights the emphasis which al-Shadhili laid on the disciples' training and intellectual growth. Al-Shadhili is reported to have said, "My disciples are my books [that I leave behind]."[25]

Ibn al-Sabbagh recounts the life of a number of important Shadhiliyya disciples who became leaders in their own rights. One of them is the Spanish disciple of al-Shadhili, Abu al-'Abbas al-Mursi, who became the first shaykh of the *Tariqa* after death of al-Shadhili in 656/1258. Ibn 'Ata' Allah (d. 709/1309–1310), the famous author of *The Book of Wisdom*[26] and *Lata'if al-minan*, became the second shaykh of the order after the death of al-Mursi in 686/1287. Therefore, in its gestation phase, the Shadhiliyya order was formed against the background of "an urban surrounding not necessarily in revolt against it but as an outcome of the existing patterns of politic-religious and economic life."[27] The Shadhiliyya, as well as other renowned orders in Islam such as Badawiyya and Dasuqiyya, continued to expand and flourish after the thirteenth century. The Shadhiliyya, in particular, assumed new organizational structures and won new adepts in both Egypt and North Africa.

Ibn al-Sabbagh's Reconstruction
of al-Shadhili's Sufi Theories

The historical evolution of the term *tasawwuf* in the first few centuries of Islam reflected the deep Qur'anic roots and religious meaning of sufism. Al-Shadhili was keen about distilling his Sufi philosophy from the *Qur'an*. In this regard, Paul Nwyia agrees with Ibn al-Sabbagh's contention that al-Shadhili had a deep knowledge of the Sufi teachings of the Eastern doctors, as well as a personal experience of spiritual realities. Al-Shadhili possessed qualities of spiritual discernment and knew how to extract from his personal experiences what was valuable to others.

Opposing Paul Nwyia's thesis that al-Shadhili formed no intellectual system, 'Abd al-Halim Mahmud maintains that the Shadiliyya *tariqa* has been characterized, since its inception, by both intellectualism and social action. Mahmud claims that al-Shadhili started learning the religious sciences while still young and earned himself the best education.[28] While young, he memorized the *Qur'an* by heart and studied the Sunna. Ibn al-Sabbagh does not relate anything about the intellectual and theological environment of the Azhar, established in A.D. 972 as a Shi'ite educational institution, and the impact it may have had on al-Shadhili. Nevertheless, he insists on the importance and genuineness of mysticism as an Islamic science. In fact he considers it to be superior to acquired— or (non-revealed) science, such as philosophy and historiography. Ibn al-Sabbagh argues that al-Shadhili saw no contradiction between *shari'a* and *haqiqa*, nor between the exoteric and esoteric in Islam. In short, the emphasis which al-Shadhili laid upon learning became part of the rules of his *Tariqa*. Disciples were accepted only after they were versed in the sciences of the *Shari'a* and *fiqh*.

One may argue that al-Shadhili's mystical aspiration was shaped by his understanding of the *Qur'an* and his deep awareness of the Divine presence in the universe. The vision of the divine being (*hudur ilahi*) stirred him to the depth of his soul, and implanted in him the perennial bonds of love of God (*mahaba*) and gnosis (*ma'rifa*). Although he was intellectually oriented, al-Shadhili associated *mahaba* with *ma'rifa*, and took the heart to be the locus of this association. In Qur'anic symbolism, the heart signifies the connection between mercy and comprehension as well.[29] Al-Shadhili, then, pondered the all-encompassing nature of Sufi knowledge in the following manner:

> Mystical knowledge (*ma'rifa*) is a disclosure of the sciences along with the veil. When the veil is removed, we call it certainty (*yaqin*). He who has access to the divine realities is drawn away in rapture. He who has mystical knowledge is carried away (*maslub*) from himself. The mystical sciences are garnered treasures, and the illuminations (*anwar*) are spiritual insights (*basa'ir*). Mystical knowledge is divine amplitude (*si'a*); unity

(*tawhid*) is sincerity (*sidq*); wisdom is instruction; light is clarification (*bayan*). The object of knowledge is of two kinds: one derived from divine bestowals (*mawahib*) and one from acquisitions (*makasib*). Acquisitons are of two kinds: one coming by way of instruction and the other by specualtion.[30]

Therefore, in order to know God intimately, a true Sufi must lose himself in God and attempt to annihilate any distance or chasm that may separate him from God's treasures of mercy. This is not to say that, according to al-Sadhili, Man is God and God is Man. Man is conscious of his imperfection and often attempts to reach perfection by manifesting the divine presence in his life. To al-Shadhili, true servantship (*'ubudiya*) is strengthened by persisting in neediness, impotence, weakness, and lowliness before God. He said, "The opposites of these are the attributes of Lordship, and what have you to do with them? So hold fast to your attributes while depending on the attributes of God. Then say as an expression of genuine neediness: 'O Sufficient One, whom has the needy but Thee?' As an expression of weakness, say: 'O Powerful One, whom has the weak but Thee?' "

As E. H. Douglas says, al-Shadhili's concept of *tawhid*, "is not identical with the metaphysical conception of the oneness of being...It is an experience of witnessing or contemplating Allah, of the soul's uniting in rapture with Allah...The real unitarian is he who allows Allah to have complete sway over his life."[31] From al-Shadhili's perspective, sufism (*tasawwuf*) is training the self in servantship and restoring it to the rules of lordship. Therefore, to him, the true Sufi is one who does not turn his attention to mankind (*khalq*) and who has relied on nothing except the promises of the True One (Haqq).

According to Martin Lings, for example, there is a strong connection "between mercy and comprehension" in the Qur'an.[32] In Qur'anic language, mercy can thus be synonomous with rain, comprehension, and revelation—symbols that are embodied in the Islamic archetype of *umm al-kitab* (the Mother of the Book). In view of Ibn al-Sabbagh, al-Shadhili pondered the intricate connections between his external praxis and the inner meanings of mercy and comprehension as portrayed by the Qur'an. Thus, he achieved the status of a Qutb only after he embodied all these transcendent qualities in his personal life and behavior.

Al-Shadhili's search for certainty and divine knowledge brings to mind the famous journey which al-Ghazali (d. 1111) embarked upon as a restless and anxious teacher and theologian. Both al-Shadhili and al-Ghazali were enchanted by the mystery of the Divine and the meaning of existence. Both travelled to distant lands to achieve personal calm and alleviate their senses of anxiety. Although in his autobiography, *al-Munqidh min al-dalal*, al-Ghazali seems to be more intellectually oriented in his endeavors, he nevertheless reaches conclusions similar to those of al-Shadhili. The final aim of mysticism in their views is "the purification of the heart completely from what is other than God."[33] Moreover, mysticism cannot be attained by study or pure intellectual comprehsion, but by immediate experience or Sufi taste (*dhawq*). In sum, to both al-Ghazali and al-Shadhili, "certainty reached by demonstration is knowledge ('*ilm*); actual acquaintance with that 'state' is immediate experience (dhawq); the acceptance of it as probable from hearsay or trial (or observation) is faith (iman). These are three degrees. 'God will raise those of you who have faith and those who have been given knowledge in degrees!' " (Q.58:12)[34]

Throughout the biography, one gets the clear sense that, in addition to its intellectualism, al-Shadhili's *tasawwuf* was socially oriented. It propagated the values of family life, competitiveness in the economic sphere, and hard work. This pragmatic attitude toward life was shown by al-Shadhili toward the end of his life when the Crusaders invaded Egypt.

Reflecting the religious and intellectual concerns of his age, Ibn al-Sabbagh highlights the importance of piety in Islamic life and thought. He argues that, as a man trying to perfect himself in the image of the Islamic ideal, al-Shadhili was continuously searching within himself for the supreme qualities that God implanted in man. Al-Shadhili comments on the ideal Sufi by saying that he must have four essential qualities: being characterized by the characteristics of God, abiding closely to the commands of God, relinquishing the defense of one's self out of shame before God, and holding to the practice of spiritual converse by truly abiding with God.

It could be argued that the model of al-Shadhili as an active, learned, and ascetic person is still relevant to modern-day Muslims. Theoretically speaking, asceticism is more than curbing one's desires or evil motives. It is a process or a movement that aims at achieving ethical balance and total integration of man in this world. Integration is the the only answer to spiritual alienation and estrangement. As Seyyed Hossein Nasr said, "To be dissipated and compartmentalized . . . is to be removed from that state of wholeness which our inner state demands of us."[35] Above all, the doctrine of integration "can hardly be overemphasized, especially for modern man, who is over-cerebral, thinking too much and often wrongly."[36] Al-Shadhili was a perfect model of this integration because, "He represented the genuine Muslim personality that God prefers everyone would choose."[37] Ibn al-Sabbagh contends that Islam introduced many doctrines of which the purpose was to benefit both the society and the individual. Those duties can, however, become a burden on those who have never tasted divine union.

To Ibn al-Sabbagh, metaphysics is the means *par excellence* which can lead man to attain the perfect understanding of the principles of knowledge. The esoteric and metaphysical doctrines of Islam, which are universal in nature, affirm the genuine nature and traditional character of the past messengers who have carried essentially the same message. He affirms that the manifestations of the universal

Divine message were many, corresponding to different historical and geographical circumstances. However, from a metaphysical point of view, the Principle is One.

Metaphysical knowledge is the supreme condition which any human being could achieve because eternal and universal truths are the backbones of such knowledge. Ibn al-Sabbagh shows, therefore, that the true value of human culture resides in the integration of these universal principles and truths with the multiplicity of social forms of culture and ethics. He says that the metaphysical doctrine is, in principle, no more than the science of reality (*'ilm al-haqiqa*). This science distinguishes between the Principle and the manifestation—or between God and the world. Therefore, in the final analysis, *tasawwuf* is the knowledge of metaphysics. This knowledge is not a closed system of theoretical concepts that can be merely comprehended rationally. A higher stage, whose source is divine, can allow the gifted to relate to it through their intellectual intuition.

As did all traditional thinkers who have written on the subject of sufism, Ibn al-Sabbagh considers Islam to have three complementary dimensions. First, there is *islam* or the complete submission to God who is the One and the Real. Second comes *iman*, the belief in the major metaphysical doctrines of Islam as verified in the *Qur'an*; and third is *ihsan* or excellence, which is the spiritual path leading to the recognition of the One.

Ibn al-Sabbagh relates a story about al-Shadhili that explains these three notions. Al-Shadhili is reported to have said, "In al-Qayrawan, I was ill, and I saw in a dream, the Prophet who said, "Cleanse your raiment of defilement and you will obtain the help of God with every breath (*nafas*)." I asked, "What is my raiment, O Apostle of God?" He replied,

> God has clothed you with the vestment (*hulla*) of mystical knowledge, then with the vestment of love, then with the vestment of belief in the divine unity (*tawhid*), then with the vestment of faith (*iman*), and then with the vestment of submission (*islam*). If anyone knows God, everything becomes of little importance for him; if anyone loves God, everything becomes contemptible for him; if anyone asserts the unity of God, he associates nothing with Him; if anyone has faith in God, he is safe from everything; if anyone is resigned to God, rarely does he disobey Him; if he disobeys Him, he begs of Him to be excused; if he begs of Him to be excused, his excuse is accepted. With these words I understood the meaning of His saying, 'And thy garments keep from stain.' " (Q. 74:4)

Ibn al-Sabbagh, following in the footsteps of the great mystics in Islam, contends that *tasawwuf* is both a path or *tariqa* and a goal or *ghaya*. *Tasawwuf*, which is the sanctification or purification (*safa'*) of the self, is man's direct means to get closer to the Divine. There are different paths that may lead man to achieve such a sanctification. The final goal and the supreme state to be achieved is the dissolution of the individual self. Through this process man becomes part of the center and resides permanently in the essence of God. In the final analysis, *tasawwuf* is the combination of both the *tariqa* and the *haqiqa*.

The role of ethics and asceticism do have a place in Ibn al-Sabbagh's view of *tasawwuf*. Thus, he considers *tasawwuf* as a *weltanschauung*, and a system of life. Ethics is one of the cornerstones of sufism. It is al-Shadhili's view that *tasawwuf*, as a science, could lead to an exemplary ethical and social behavior. The starting point of *tasawwuf* is *'ilm* or religious science. Its middle point is action, and its end is divine gift.

In Ibn al-Sabbagh's view, ethics is the foundation as well as the fruit of *tasawwuf*. However, *tasawwuf* is not only ethics nor is it asceticism or worship. It is also a complete metaphysical and behavioral doctrine that aims at transforming the conduct of man in society. As a metaphysical doctrine, sufism is not detached from life and its transient complexity. As one Sufi thinker says, "since it [sufism] is based on the social and juridicial teachings of Islam, sufism is meant to be practised within society and not in a monastic environment outside the social order."[38] The strong social aspect of Sufism is based on both the Qur'anic conception of social integration and the *Shari'a's* social injunctions and prohibitions. People are requested to believe in God, His angels, and the Day of Judgment, and they are prohibited from the display of arrogance, hypocrisy, and jealousy.

Author and Text

Muhammad Ibn Abi al-Qasim al-Himyari, known as Ibn al-Sabbagh, author of *Durrat al-asrar wa tuhfat al-abrar*, was born in North Africa. He became a devotee of the Shadhiliyya order at an early age in his life. He mentions in his biography that he embarked on a spiritual and intellectual journey to document with detail the life, thoughts, and work of the Shaykh Abu al-Hasan al-Shadhili. Pursuing accuracy and as much information as possible about al-Shadhili, Ibn al-Sabbagh traveled to Egypt, Iraq, and Hijaz. His chief source of information was, however, al-Shadhili's closest disciples, especially the ones residing in Egypt.

The text of *Durrat al-asrar* used by Elmer Douglas as a basis of this translation was printed in Tunisia in 1304/1887. This is the same text which was used in editing the translation.

Ibn al-Sabbag divides his work into five chapters. The first chapter deals with al-Sahdhili's career and his encounter with the chief *qadi* of the city of Tunis. The second chapter contains informative letters which the shaykh wrote to some of his disciples in North Africa. Chapter 3 is composed of devotional material attributed to al-Shadhili. Chapter 4, the longest of all, discusses at length the religious teachings and epistemological principles of al-Shadhili's *tasawwuf*. This chapter sheds an important light on the importance which Islamic mysticism of the thirteenth century attached to theology, philosophy, and rationalism in general. Chapter 5 relates the circumstances attending the death of al-Shadhili. It continues with the story of the attainments of his disciple and successor, al-Mursi, along with numerous anecdotes and testimonies of apparently miraculous events.

The Translator

The late Elmer H. Douglas was born on 12 January 1903 in Kensington, New York. After graduation from Ohio Wesleyan University (B.A.) and Drew University (B.D.), he began Arabic and Islamic Studies at Hartford Seminary where he received a Ph.D. in 1945. For many years, Mr. Douglas was a professor of Islamic Studies at Hartford Seminary and the editor of its chief journal, *The Muslim World*.

In addition to the present translation, Professor Douglas translated a number of important works relating to Islamic mysticism. He collaborated with Dr. Howard Yoder in translating Miguel Asin Palacios's *The Mystical Philosophy of Ibn Masarra and His Followers* (Leiden, 1979).

Professor Douglas died on 5 October 1990. *Rahimahu Allah.*

Ibrahim M. Abu-Rabi'

Author's Introduction to the Pearl of Mysteries and the Treasure of the Righteous

Concerning the virtues of the one possessing eminence and lofty and illustrious nobility, the greatest *Qutb*[1] and the most celebrated *Ghawth*,[2] my master 'Ali Abu al-Hasan al-Shadhili, may God be pleased with him, a literary work by the scholar and erudite, my master Muhammad ibn Abi al-Qasim al-Himyari, known as Ibn al-Sabbagh,[3] may God Who is exalted, have mercy on him. Amen.

In the name of God the Compassionate, the Merciful, may God bestow His blessing upon our lord and master Muhammad. Praise be to God Who, through His eternal Word, does not cease to be praised; the Compassionate, the Merciful, Who by His mercy has stirred up in us gratitude for His manifold blessings upon us, and has inspired us to praise and glorify Him. The compass of His beneficences and the bounds of praise were enlarged when He promised to those grateful for His bounty still more (blessings), and He spread out wide the carpet of spiritual converse with Him to those who invoke Him.

He is too exalted to possess corporeal attributes, and places do not enclose Him. He has brought into subjection all things according to His wisdom and decree, as He willed, by His power, so that by His authority, the mover remains still and the quiescent moves. "He is the First and the Last, the Evident and the Hidden," (Q. 57:3) the Controller of expansion (*bast*) and contraction (*qabd*).[4] "[He is the knower] of the unseen, from Whom is not hidden the least little atom in the heavens or on earth" (Q. 34:3).

We praise Him with the praise of those who know Him with real knowledge of Him. We give thanks to Him with expressions of gratitude of those who acknowledge the all-comprehensiveness of His beneficence and favor. We bear witness that there is no god but God alone, Who has no associate, with an

— 11 —

affirmation to which no trace of doubt is attached, and in the face of which no door closes [to prevent] one's acceptance. We testify that our master Muhammad is His servant and apostle chosen from the mine of pure nobility, selected from the family of honor whose virtues profusely spoken homage fails to describe. May God bless him and grant him peace, with a blessing that will bring us to him and gather us about him on the day of confrontation and reckoning. May God be pleased with his family, his helpers, his descendants, the people of his household, his devoted companions, the best of comrades, as long as a star shines, a new moon rises, and the clouds spread out over the face of the earth.

Now the most excellent production in which the tongue can be employed and for which, when it is published and diffused, the heart can rejoice, is but the commemoration of those deeds and narratives which characterize the saints, the favorites of God, of those supplications (*da'awat*) and devotional recitations (*adhkar*) which they uttered with all sincerity, of their particular states and stations, and of those supernatural powers (*khawariq*) and divine gifts (*karamat*) that have been attributed to them.

Among God's favors to me and my predecessors have been the pursuit of whatever authoritative narratives may exist of our master the shaykh, the saint (*wali*), the utterly sincere (*siddiq*), gnostic (*'arif*), adept in the mystical sciences (*muhaqqiq*), Ghawth, Qutb, Sharif of the family of al-Hasan,[5] Abu al-Hasan, known as al-Shadhili, and a recording of whatever supplications (*da'awat*) and devotional recitations (*adhkar*) are ascribed to him. I was wont to search for them, to strive to gather them together, and to be zealous to go to anyone who might be acquainted with them. So some of them I received directly in Tunis from the righteous Shaykh Abu al-'Azai'm Abu Madi ibn Sultan, pupil and servant of Abu al-Hasan. Some of them I secured in the eastern lands, of Abu 'Abd Allah Muhammad, called Sharaf al-Din,[6] son of Yaqut al-Habashi. Some of them I received from still other devotees of the Sufi Path of our shaykh and from companions of his companions from among the people of the East and the West, until there was brought together in my possession material the hearing of which is a source of delight, and the collection of which is something rare. Some of the brethren desired me for the sake of God to compile all that in a text for him, in order that the benefit to be derived therefrom might accrue to the future in every place. So, I consented to do that out of desire for that great reward gained from it that I could hope to receive, and in order that it might preserve for me what was in my mind and be a reminder to me whenever I should read it over.

I have divided it into five chapters. Chapter 1 concerns his noble lineage, his origin, his receiving instruction in the Way and authority from his teacher, his travels from the Maghrib[7] to the Province of Ifriqiya[8] and to the land of the East, and his attainment there to the rank of *Khalifa*[9] and *Qutb*.

Chapter 2 concerns his correspondence with his disciples in the Province of Ifriqiya.

Chapter 3 contains an account of his supplications (*da'awat*), his devotional recitations (*adhkar*), and his prayers or orientation (tawajjuhat).

Chapter 4 treats his opinions, his teaching on sufism and the inner reality (*haqiqa*) of the faith, and his injunctions upon his companions.

Chapter 5 speaks of his death and his prior appointment of my master Abu al-'Abbas al-Mursi as his successor, of whom I shall recall some splendid anecdotes.

I have entitled the work *Durrat al-asrar wa tuhfat al-abrar [The Pearl of Mysteries and the Treasure of the Righteous]*, concerning the states and stations, extraordinary powers and divine gifts, supplications and devotional recitations that have been attributed to our master, the shaykh, the saint, the gnostic, the one with true knowledge, the trustworthy, the *Qutb*, the *Ghawth*, Abu al-Hasan 'Ali, in order that its appellation may be in accord with the work indicated by the name and conformable to its significance.

From God, I hope for approval and the attainment of the object of my expectations, because He is the preserver from error in narration and the One who brings felicity by His help in lucidity of expression. There is no Lord at all other then He, and no good except His.

Chapter One

— —

His Noble Lineage, Travels and Rank

With reference to his noble lineage, it is: 'Ali ibn 'Abd Allah ibn 'Abd al-Jabbar ibn Tamim ibn Hurmuz ibn Hatim ibn Qusay ibn Yusuf ibn Yusha' ibn Ward ibn Battal ibn Idris ibn Muhammad ibn 'Isa ibn Muhammad ibn al-Hasan ibn 'Ali ibn Abi Talib. His birthplace was in Ghumara.[1] He entered the city of Tunis when a young lad, turned toward the East, performed many pilgrimages, and went into Iraq.

He related,

> When I came to Iraq, I met the Shaykh Abu al-Fath al-Wasiti,[2] the like of whom I have not seen in Iraq. My quest was for the *qutb*. One of the saints said to me, "Are you searching for the *qutb* in Iraq while he is in your country? Return to your land and you will find him.

So, he returned to the Maghrib where he met his teacher, who is my master the shaykh, the saint, the gnostic, the trustworthy, the *qutb*, the *ghawth*, Abu Muhammad 'Abd al-Salam ibn Mashish al-Sharif al-Hasani.[3] He related,

> When I drew near him, while he was living in Ghumara in a lodge on the top of a mountain, I bathed at a spring by the base of that mountain, forsook all dependence on my own knowledge and works, and went up toward him as one in need. Just then he was coming down toward me, wearing a patched cloak, and on his head a cap of palm leaves. "Welcome to 'Ali ibn 'Abd Allah ibn 'Abd al-Jabbar," he said to me, and repeated my lineage down to the Apostle of God. Then he said to me, "O, 'Ali, you have come up to us destitute of your knowledge and works, so you will receive from us the riches of this world and the next."

He (al-Shadhili) continued,

> Awe of him seized me. So I remained with him for some days until God awakened my perception, and I saw that he possessed many supernatural

powers (*kharq al-'adat*). For example, one day as I sat before him while a young son of his played with him on his lap, it came into my mind to question him concerning the greatest name of God. The child came to me, threw his arms about my neck, and shook me, saying, "O Abu al-Hasan, you desired to question the master concerning the greatest name of God. It is not a matter of importance that you should ask about the greatest name of God. The important thing is that you should be the greatest name of God, that is to say, that the secret (*sirr*) of God should be lodged in your heart." When he had finished speaking, the shaykh (Ibn Mashish) smiled and said to me, 'Such a one has answered you for me.'

He was, then, the *Qutb* of that time.

Then he said to me, "O 'Ali, depart to the Province of Ifriqiya and dwell there in a place called Shadhila, for God will name you al-Shadhili. After that you will move to the city of Tunis where charges will be brought against you before the authorities. Then you will move to the East where you will inherit the rank of *qutb*."

I said to him, "O my master, give me your spiritual bequest." So he replied, "O 'Ali, God is God and men are men. Keep your tongue from the mention of them, and your heart from inclining before them, and be careful to guard the members (*jawarih*) and to fulfill the divine ordinances; thus the friendship (*wilaya*)[4] of God is perfected in you. Have no remembrance of them except under obligation that duty to God imposes on you; thus your scrupulousness is perfected. Then say: O God, relieve me from remembrance of them and spare me disturbances from them. Save me from their evils, enable me to dispense with their good through Thy good, and as a special favor assume Thou care of me among them. Verily, Thou art mighty over all things."

He related,

When I entered the city of Tunis as a young man, I found there a great famine, and I came upon men dying in the market places. I said to myself, "Had I wherewith to buy bread for these hungry people, I would surely do it." Then I was instructed inwardly: "Take what is in your pocket." So I shook my pocket and, lo, there was silver money in it. So I went to a baker at Bab al-Manara[5] and said to him, "Count up your loaves of bread." He counted them for me. Then I offered them to the people who took them greedily. I drew out the pieces of money and handed them to the baker. He found them to be spurious and said, "These are Moroccan, and you Moroccans practice alchemy."[6] So I gave him my *burnus*[7] and small bag as a pawn on the price of the bread, and turned toward the gate. Right there by the gate stood a man who said to me, "O 'Ali, where are the pieces of money?" So I gave them to him, and he shook them in his hand, then returned them to me, saying, "Pay them to the baker, for they are genuine." So I paid them to the baker who accepted them from me, saying, "These are good." I took my *burnus* and bag and then looked for the man, but did not find him.

Consequently, I remained for some days inwardly perplexed until, on Friday, I went into the Zaytuna mosque,[8] near the reserved section on the east side of the mosque, and performed two cycles of the greeting of the mosque and pronounced the salutation. Suddenly, I saw a man on my right. I greeted him and he smiled at me, saying, "O 'Ali, you say, 'Had I wherewith to feed these hungry people, I should surely do it.' You would presume to be more generous than God toward His creatures. Had He willed it, He would surely have fed them, for He is more cognizant of their welfare than you."

Then I said to him, "O my master, by God, who are you?" He replied, "I am Ahmad al-Khidr.[9] I was in China and I was told, 'Go and look for my saint 'Ali in Tunis.' So I came hurriedly to you." When I had performed the Friday worship, I looked about for him, but did not find him.

Testimony of Ibn Futuh: Alchemy, and Divine Protection

In his book on *The Virtues of My Master Abu Sa'id al-Baji*, the Shaykh Abu Faris 'Abd al-Baji related of Abu al-Hasan that he said,

> When I entered the city of Tunis in the beginning of my spiritual life, I went to the Sufi masters who were there, for I had a certain matter that I wished to present to someone for clarification. But no one among them could clarify for me a certain mystical state, until I came upon Abu Sa'id al-Baji.[10] He informed me of my state before I revealed it, and discussed my secret thoughts. So I recognized that he was a true saint of God, and I remained close to him, profiting much from him.

According to the narrator, and often did I hear him tell it, he (al-Shadhili) related,

> In the beginning of my career I was wont to pursue the science of alchemy and would make petition to God regarding it. I was told, "Alchemy is in your urine. Put into it whatever you will and it will become what you desire." So I heated a pickax, quenched it therewith, and it turned into gold. Then my presence of mind returned to me and I exclaimed,

"O my Lord, I petitioned Thee for a certain thing, but I obtained it only by the use of unclean devices, and the use of unclean devices is unlawful." Then I was told, "O 'Ali, the world is filth, and, if you desire it, you will not obtain it except by filth." I replied, "O my Lord, deliver me from it." I was then told, "Heat the pickax and it will return to iron." I heated it and it became iron.

He related,

One night in the beginning of my period of wandering, I lodged in a place where there were many wild beasts. The beasts began to growl at me. So I sat down on a high hill and said, "By God, I will invoke blessings on the Apostle of God. Surely he said, 'If anyone blesses me once, by that act the blessing of God will be upon him tenfold'; and, if the blessing of God be upon me, I shall pass the night under His protection." So I did thus and feared nothing. At dawn I went to a pool of water to perform ablutions for the morning prayer. Before it was a mass of reeds from which partridges emerged with a great flutter of wings. Fear overcame me and I drew back. Then I was summoned within me with the words, "O 'Ali, when you passed last night under the care of God, the growling of the wild beasts at you did not frighten you; but when you arose today under your own care, the flutter of partridge feathers has caused you to be afraid."

He related,

One night in my period of wandering, I came to a cave to pass the night there. Within I heard the voice of a man praising God. I said, "By God, I will not trouble him this night." So I passed the night at the mouth of the cave. About dawn I heared him say, "O God, verily some people have besought Thee that men should be brought in their presence and be subject to them. O God, I pray Thee for their removal from me and for their shunning of me that I may have no refuge except in Thee."

When it became light, he came out, and, lo, he was my teacher. Thereupon I said to him, "O my master, last night I heard you say so and so." He replied, "O 'Ali, which is better for you, that you should say, 'Be Thou for me,' or 'Cause the hearts of Thy creatures to be submissive to me'? For whenever He is for you, you have all things."

Story of the Woodcutter

When he left his teacher, who had instructed him to move to Shadhila and proceed to the Province of Ifriqiya, he came to the city of Tunis, near the place where the prayer of the "Two Feasts"[11] is performed. There he met a woodcutter who belonged to the people of Shadhila, as his teacher had instructed him. The woodcutter forgot his business at the market and turned back directly to attend to it, leaving his donkey with him (al-Shadhili). When he had started, he said to himself, "This is a stranger who will run away from me with the donkey and I shall be left deprived of it."

The shaykh called him, and he turned back to him. Said he, "O my son, take your donkey while I wait for you until you return to me, lest I run away from you with your donkey and you remain deprived of it."

The woodcutter wept and said, "By God, no one was informed of this except God, may He be exalted." So then he recognized that he was a saint, and began to kiss his hands and ask him to pray for him.

Then he left to attend to his business and returned to him. He (the woodcutter) begged him to mount the donkey. So he (al-Shadhili) mounted and made him ride behind him. The woodcutter exclaimed, "By God, the donkey was wont to carry me only with great effort, on account of its weakness and scanty food."

The woodcutter went on to say, "We had proceeded about a mile when the teacher dismounted. We were beside the stream on the edge of Shadhila. Having become filled with dismay, I looked hard at him and said, "O my master, I am afflicted with poverty. I gather wood and sell it, and succeed in gaining a livelihood only with great effort."

I had in my sack some barley which I had bought as a provision of food for my family and fodder for the donkey. Then he said to me, "Bring me that barley." So I untied the sack and he inserted his hand, saying to me, "Put that barley in a basket, close it up, insert your hand, and eat of it. As long as you live you will never complain of poverty. I shall ask God to provide a sufficiency for you and your children." So to the present time no one of his progeny has been seen in poverty. He said, "So I proceeded to insert my hand, take out some of the barley, and eat of it. I plowed with the donkey, sowed some of it, and obtained an excellent harvest. I opened it, measured it, and found it about as it had been. When I went to him, he said to me, 'Even if you had not measured it, you would surely earn of it as long as there remains any of it in your possession.'"

Al-Habibi, First Companion

The first one to become his companion in Shadhila was my master, the worthy shaykh, the saint, the "revealer" (*mukashif*)[12] Abu Muhammad ʿAbd Allah ibn Salama al-Habibi, of the people of Shadhila. In Tunis, he used to attend the assembly of our master, the worthy shaykh, the mystic, the excellent Abu Hafs al-Jasus, who was wrapped in a woolen mantle and of whom our shaykh would say, "high personage in lowly garb."

He (al-Habibi) said,

> One day I seized his hand (that of al-Jasus), saying to him, "O my master,
> I choose you to be my shaykh." To this he replied, "O my son, await
> your teacher until a sharif of the family of al-Hasan,[13] a great saint, arrives
> from the Maghrib. He is your teacher and to him will you claim your
> spiritual kinship."

He (al-Habibi) awaited him, and whatever poor devotee (*faqir*) from the Maghrib
he saw he would take as a companion. Finally, the shaykh drew near to Shadhila
and he joined him. That was, for him, a token of honor and a harbinger of good.
So it was that he (al-Habibi) became his companion, remained with him, traveled
with him to Mount Zaghawan,[14] worshipped with him, practiced mortification
for a long period, and related concerning him many charismatic phenomena
(*karamat*).

Among those that he related about him was the following:

> One day on Mount Zaghawan he recited the *Al-An'am* chapter [of the
> Qur'an) as far as the saying of God, "If it [that is, the soul] offered every
> ransom, none will be accepted" [Q. 6:70]. Then a mystical state
> overwhelmed him, and he began to repeat it and to tremble. As often
> as he leaned to one side, the mountain leaned in like manner, until the
> mountain became still.

Testimony of al-Ibri: Mount Zaghawan, Birds, and the Spring

The worthy teacher Abu al-Hasan 'Ali al-Ibri, known as al-Hattab, related to us,

> One day I said to my master, Muhammad al-Habibi, "Tell me something
> of what you have seen concerning my master Abu al-Hasan." He replied,
> "I have seen many things regarding him, some of which I shall relate
> to you. I remained with him on Mount Zaghawan for forty days, feeding
> on herbs of the fields and laurel leaves until the inside of my cheeks
> became sore. Then he said to me, "O 'Abd Allah, it seems that you
> desire food." I replied, "O my master, my looking at you enables me to
> do without it." So he said to me, "Tomorrow, if God wills, we shall go
> down to Shadhila and some divine gift will come to us on the way."

He continued,

> So the next morning we descended and, while walking through a valley,
> he said to me. "O 'Abd Allah, if I should leave the road, do not follow
> me."

He went on to say,

> An intense mystical state fell upon him, and he departed from the way until he was some distance from me. Then I saw four birds about the size of a stork come down from the sky and spread their wings over his head. Each one of them came and conversed with him, and then flew away. Among them were birds about the size of swallows which flew around him between the earth and the horizon, hovering in circles about him. When they had disappeared from sight, he returned to me, saying, "O 'Abd Allah, did you see anything?" I told him what I had seen and he explained to me. "The four birds are some of the angels of the fourth heaven which came to question me concerning knowledge (*'ilm*), and I answered them thereon. The birds which had the form of swallows are the spirits of the saints which came to receive a blessing from our arrival."

He remained on Mount Zaghawan a long time and God caused to flow for him a spring of fresh, running water. There he had a cave in which to dwell. At present, the call to prayer is heard from the base of the mountain at the hours of worship, and people go up to the cave but find no one, and no one inhabits it except the believing *jinn* who were his companions.

He said,

> I was told, "O 'Ali, go down to the people in order that they may receive some good from you." I replied, "O my Lord, deliver me from other men. I have no capacity to mingle with them." Then I was told, "Descend, for We have caused security to accompany you and We have withdrawn blame from you." I said, "O Lord, if Thou commit me to men, I must eat by their pittances." Then I was told, "Spend, O 'Ali, for I am the Provider, if you wish from your pocket (*jayb*) or if you wish, from the unseen (*ghayb*)."

So he entered the city of Tunis and resided in a house by the Balat Mosque.[15] There, he had as companions a group of noble men. Among them were the Shaykh Abu al-Hasan 'Ali ibn Makhluf al-Siqilli, Abu 'Abd Allah al-Sabuni, the Shaykh Abu Muhammad 'Abd al-'Aziz al-Zaytuni, his servant Abu al-'Aza'im Madi, Abu 'Abd Allah al-Bijai' al-Khayyat,[16] and Abu 'Abd Allah al-Jarihi. They were all endowed with miraculous powers (*karamat*) and blessings (*barakat*). May God give benefit by means of all of them.

Intervention of Ibn al-Bara' and Abu Zakariya

He remained there some time, until a large number of people joined him and the jurist Abu al-Qasim ibn al-Bara' heard of him. At that time, he was chief judge. Taken with envy of al-Shadhili, he turned toward him to dispute with him, but he was unable to gain the mastery over him. So he said to the Sultan, "Here is one of the men of Shadhila, a donkey thief, who claims to be a sharif. A great crowd had joined him and, alleging that he is al-Fatimi,[17] is stirring up your land against you."

The shaykh related,

> So I said, "O my Lord, why hast Thou named me al-Shadhili, when I am not of the village Shadhila?" I was told, "O 'Ali, I did not call you by the name al-Shadhili. You are *al-Shadhi-li*, meaning that you are set apart uniquely for my service and love."

Abu Zakariya was then Sultan.[18] Ibn al-Bara' assembled a group of jurists in the palace (*qasaba*), the Sultan being seated behind a screen while the shaykh was present before them. They questioned him a number of times regarding his genealogy, and the shaykh continued to reply to them while the Sultan listened.

They discussed with him all the sciences, and he answered in a manner that silenced them. Meanwhile, they could not answer him on the basis of the intuitive sciences. The shaykh would converse with them about the acquired sciences, and, in these, he participated equally with them.

The Sultan said to Ibn al-Bara', "This is a man who is one of the greatest of the saints. You have no power over him." "By God," replied Ibn al-Bara', "indeed, if he should go out now, the people of Tunis would certainly come in against you, and they would cast you out from among them, for even now, they are gathered at your door."

The jurists withdrew. The Sultan commanded the shaykh to sit down. "Perhaps one of my companions will come in," said al-Shadhili. So it was that one of his companions entered and said to him, "O my master, the people are talking about you and reporting that you are being treated so-and-so with various kinds of disciplining," and he wept before him.

The shaykh smiled and said, "By God, if it were not that I am disciplined to act in accordance with the law, I would surely go out here or here," and in whatever direction he pointed his finger the wall split. Then he said, "Bring me a pitcher, some water, and a prayer carpet. Greet my companions and tell them that we are absent from them today only and that we shall not observe evening worship except with them, if God wills." The companion brought him what he ordered. Then al-Shadhili performed ablutions and turned his face toward God.

Al-Shadili said,

> I felt strongly inclined to pray against the Sultan, but I was told, "God will not be pleased with you if you pray with anxiety about a creature." So I was inspired to say, "[O Thou Whose] Throne doth extend over the heavens and the earth; He feeleth no fatigue in guarding and preserving them. For He is the most High. The Supreme in glory" [Q. 2:255]. I pray thee for faith in Thine upholding, a faith by which my

heart will remain undisturbed from anxiety for sustenance and from fear of men. Draw near to me with Thy power so close that Thou dost remove from before me every veil which Thou didst remove from before Ibrahim, Thy friend. He had no need of Gabriel, Thy messenger, nor of asking Thee, and Thou didst shield him on that account from the fire of Thine enemy. How should not one whom Thou didst remove from the benefits of friends be shielded from the harm of enemies? Nay, I ask Thee that Thou shouldst remove me by Thy nearness to me, until I neither see nor feel the nearness of a single thing, nor even its remoteness from me. Assuredly Thou art mighty over all things.

The Sultan had a female slave who was the dearest to him of his women. An illness befell her, and she died at once. He was grieved because of her. She was washed in a room of his dwelling, and people attended to the washing and shrouding of her, and carried her out for the prayer. They forgot a censer in the room and the fire blazed up without their being aware of it until everything in the room was consumed including bedding and clothes, plus other valuable objects. The Sultan knew that his affliction had come from the influence of this saint (al-Shadhili).

The Sultan's brother, Abu 'Abd Allah al-Lihyani, heard of it while he was in his garden outside the city, and he hastened to him. He was a great believer in and frequent visitor of the shaykh. So he said to his brother, "What is this matter into which Ibn al-Bara' has plunged you? He has plunged you, by God, into ruin, you and all who are with you." Then he went in to al-Shadhili. "O my master," he said to him, "my brother lacks knowledge of the extent of your power, but it was Ibn al-Bara' who inveigled him into the like of this."

He began to kiss his hands and to ask pardon for his brother. Al-Shadhili replied, "By God, your brother possesses for himself no authority over good or evil, death or life, or the resurrection. How then does he possess authority over them for others? That is recorded in the Scripture."[19]

Abu 'Abd Allah al-Lihyani went out accompanying the shaykh to his house. The latter remained there some days and then disposed of his quarters which were by the Balat Mosque, and instructed his companions to travel to the land of the East. He went to Ibn al-Bara' and said, "You see that I am leaving to you the whole city of Tunis."

Narration of Madi

The Shaykh Abu al-'Azai'm Madi, his servant, related to us,

One day the shaykh met Ibn al-Bara' and greeted him, but he shunned him and did not return the salutation. Just then appeared the jurist,

Abu 'Abd Allah Ibn Abi al-Husayn, chamberlain of the Sultan, who, on seeing the shaykh, alighted from his she-mule, hastened to the shaykh, and began to kiss his hands, to weep, and to solicit him to ask God's favor upon him. Al-Shadhili invoked God's favor on him and departed. When the shaykh entered his house, he said, "I have just received a message concerning these two men, for I was told, 'O 'Ali, the marking (*wasm*) of a person with ill fortune is according to the foreknowledge of God, and he is blind to it, though he be very learned; and the marking of a person with bliss is according to the foreknowledge of God, and it comes to him, do what he may.' "

Abu al-'Azai'm said,

The shaykh was not heard to imprecate Ibn al-Bara', and he did not even mention him in any way until we were by 'Arafat,[20] when he said, "Say 'Amen' to my supplication, for just now I have been commanded to imprecate Ibn al-Bara'." So he said, "O God, lengthen his life, make his knowledge to be of no avail to him, bring him tribulation through his offspring, assign him at the end of his life to be a servant of the tyrants."

When al-Shadhili left Tunis, the Sultan heard of it, and was vexed because of his departure from the country, and sent to have him brought back. The shaykh said, "I left with the sole intention to perform the pilgrimage, if God, may He be exalted, wills. But when God will have ordained my affair, I shall return, if God wills."

Abu al-'Azai'm continued,

When we journeyed eastward and entered Alexandria, Ibn al-Bara' wrote an attestation sworn to by witnesses saying, "This man who is coming to you has stirred up our country against us and will do likewise in your land." So the Sultan of Egypt[21] ordered that he be detained in Alexandria, and we remained there a number of days.

The Sultan had levied a tax upon certain chiefs of the country's nomadic tribes, and, when they heard of the shaykh, they came to him to seek his supplication. He said to them, "Tomorrow, if God wills, we shall journey to Cairo and discuss your case with the Sultan."

So we started our journey and left by the Gate of the Lotus Tree.[22] The guards and the governor were there, and every person entering or going out was being examined, but no one spoke to us or was aware of us.

Arriving in Cairo, we came to the Citadel. Audience for him having been requested of the Sultan, the latter said, "How is this, since we have ordered that he be detained in Alexandria?" So he was ushered in before the Sultan, the judges, and princes, and he sat down with them while we kept our eyes on him. The King questioned him, "What have you to say, O shaykh?" He replied, "I have come to intercede before you in favor of the tribes." The King said, "Intercede for yourself. This is a sworn attestation against you which Ibn al-Bara' has sent from Tunis with his signature." He handed it to him. Thereupon al-Shadhili said, "You and I and the tribes are in the grasp of God." The shaykh arose to go. When he had walked about twenty paces, they shook the Sultan, for he neither moved nor uttered a sound. They hastened to the shaykh and began to kiss his hands and beg him to return. So he returned to the Sultan and shook him with his hand so that he moved, descended from his throne, and began to ask his pardon and solicit his supplication to God for him. Then the Sultan wrote to the Alexandria governor that he should remove the impositions from the tribes and restore all that he had taken from them. We remained some days with him in the Citadel, and the Egyptians were stirred up because of us until we set out on the pilgrimage.

On returning to the city of Tunis, the shaykh occupied, within the Bab al-Jadid[23] on the Shar'iya Square, a house opening toward the north. There he remained for a long time until there came the shaykh and saint Abu al-'Abbas al-Mursi who eventually inherited his station, mention of whom will be made, if God wills, after having come from Andalusia when very young with his brother, Abu 'Abd Allah Muhammad, who became a teacher of boys in Alexandria. When the shaykh met him and looked into his face, he exclaimed, "No one has brought me back to Tunis except this young man." So he raised him, instructed him in the Sufi Path, and traveled with him to the East.

Al-Shadhili said, "I saw the Prophet in a dream and he said to me, 'O 'Ali, migrate to Egypt and there raise and instruct forty disciples.'" It was in the season of summer and intense heat. So I said, "O my master, O Apostle of God, the heat is intense." He replied, "Clouds will overshadow you." Then I added, "I fear thirst." He said, "The sky will rain for you every day before you." So he promised me seventy miraculous gifts on my journey.

Directing his companions to start out, he journeyed toward Egypt. Among those who accompanied him on the journey was the shaykh, the worthy saint Abu 'Ali ibn al-Sammat. May God grant us the boon of the blessing of both of them in this world and the hereafter.

Testimony of Abu 'Abd Allah, the Copyist

My father related to me that the worthy shaykh and Qur'anic reader, Abu 'Abd Allah, the copyist, recounted thus to him,

I journeyed together with these two [Abu 'Ali and al-Shadhili] in the service of Abu 'Ali and, on reaching the city of Tripoli, the Shaykh al-Shadhili said, "Let me travel along the road of the interior." But the Shaykh Abu 'Ali chose the coast road. The latter saw the Apostle of God who said to him, "Abu 'Ali, you are a saint of God and Abu al-Hasan is a saint of God, and God will never arbitrate between two saints in the matter of a road to follow. Take the road which you have chosen and let him proceed along the road which he has chosen." So we went our separate ways until we met on the road near Alexandria.

When we had performed the morning prayers, the Shaykh Abu 'Ali approached the tent of the Shaykh Abu al-Hasan, we being in his company. He entered into his presence, sat down before him, and behaved toward him in a way which was not customary with him. He conversed with him in speech of which we understood not a word. When he was about to depart, he said, "O, my master, extend your hand so that I may kiss it." So he kissed his hand and departed weeping. We were amazed at his conduct with him.

When Abu 'Ali was well on his way, he turned toward his companions and said, "O Yunus, Abu al-Hajjaj al-Qusuri was in the land of Egypt and he was the *Qutb* of his time. Last night, he died and God caused him to be succeeded by Abu al-Hasan al-Shadhili."

So I went to al-Shadhili and gave allegiance to him as one possessing the office of *Qutb*. When we reached Alexandria, and the people came out to meet the party of travelers, I saw Abu 'Ali strike with his hand the forepart of the saddle and say weeping, "O people of this region, if you knew who it is who is advancing toward you in this caravan, you would kiss the feet of his camel, which, by God, have brought you the blessing."

Abu 'Abd Allah Muhammad, the copyist, also said,

I was walking behind Abu al-Hasan who was riding in a litter, and I saw two men walking under its shade. One of them said to the other, "O, so-and-so, I saw such a one treat you in an unfriendly manner and you were cordial to him." "He is a compatriot," he replied, "and I shall say, as the poet has said, Majnun saw in the desert a dog to which he was lavish in showing kindness. People censured him for what he did, asking, 'Why have you bestowed favor upon the dog?' He replied, 'Cease blaming me, for my eye saw him once in the quarter of Layla.'"

The shaykh extended his head from the litter and said, "Repeat what you said, O, my son." So he repeated his words and the shaykh became agitated in the litter and uttered, "Cease blaming me, for my eye saw him once in the quarter of Layla." He went on saying it over and over.

Then he threw to him a wine-colored mantle, saying, "Take this and put it on, for you are more worthy of it than I. May God reward you, O my son, with good according to the excellence of your covenant ('*ahd*)."[24]

I made a sign to him and said, "Let me have it." So I took it and embraced it. Thereupon I took a considerable sum of money and offered it to him, but he said, "By God, if you should give me enough gold to fill it, I would not sell it for that amount. This, by God, is a treasure that has fallen to me and that I will certainly use for my shrouding. By God, I walk under the shade of this litter only that perchance God may show mercy toward me through the hearing of whatever invocations he may utter. I know that mercy is poured out upon him, So perhaps I shall receive a portion of it." Thus, I recognized that he knew al-Shadhili better than I.

Al-Shadhili related,

> When I drew near to Egypt, I was told, "O 'Ali, the days of trial have gone and the days of felicity have come nigh, the difficult succeeded by the easy, following the example of your ancestor."

His dwelling in Alexandria was one of the wall towers that the Sultan had set aside as a religious bequest for him and his children. I entered it in the year A.H. 715. In its lower part were a large cistern and places for tying animals. In the middle part were dwelling places for the poor and a large mosque. The top-most part contained upper rooms for the dwelling of himself and his family. He married there and children were born to him. Among them were the Shaykh Shihab al-Din Ahmad, and Abu al-Hasan 'Ali, and Abu 'Abd Allah Muhammad Sharaf al-Din, the latter of whom I came upon in Damanhur[25] where he was residing. Among his daughters were Zaynab, who had children, some of whom I have seen, and 'Arifat al-Khayr, whom I met in Alexandria. I knew none except these. If God wills, I shall hereafter mention whatever blessings have come to my knowledge through them. So he continued for years. One year he sould go on pilgrimage and other years he would remain at home.

'*Izz al-Din and the Pilgrimage*

One in whom I have confidence related to me,

> In the year in which he went on pilgrimage there took place the movement of the Tatars[26] against Egypt. As the Sultan was occupied with operations against them, he did not prepare the military escort for the caravan of pilgrims. The shaykh sent out his tent to al-Birka [where

the pilgrims make a halt outside of Cairo] and certain people followed him. So the people met with the jurist, judge, and Mufti 'Izz al-Din ibn 'Abd al-Salam, and questioned him regarding the journey.

"The journey," he replied, "undertaken presumptiously and lacking an escort, is not allowable." The people informed the shaykh of that. "Let me meet with him," he responded. He met him in the mosque on Friday. A large crowd gathered around the two. "O jurist," he asked, "is it your opinion that, if a man had the whole world reduced to the size of a single step for him, he would be permitted to undertake a journey amidst dangers or not?"

The judge replied, "If anyone should find himself in such a circumstance, he would be beyond the bounds of a legal pronouncement (fatwa) or anything of the sort." "By God, beside Whom there is no other god," the shaykh said to him, "I am of those for whom the entire world has been made into the size of a single step. Whenever I see something that causes men to fear, I walk with them to a place of security. For you and me, there is no escape from standing before God [on the Day of Judgment] that He may question me concerning the truth of what I have told you."

So al-Shadhili departed and many charismatic events attended him on the way. The following is one of them. Thieves would attack the caravan by night, and they would find a wall built around it, as if it were a city. At the break of dawn, they would come to him, inform him of their deeds, repent to God, and travel in the company of the shaykh on the pilgrimage to Mecca.

The pilgrimage accomplished, he returned and entered Cairo the first of the people. His pilgrimage companions related to others the miracles he [Abu al-Hasan] had performed.

Then the jurist 'Izz al-Din went out to meet him at al-Birka, which is a place about six miles outside of Cairo. On entering into his presence, al-Shadihili said to him, "O jurist, by God, were it not for the training that I have received with my ancestor the Apostle of God, I would have taken the caravan on the Day of 'Arafa and I would have stepped over with it to 'Arafat."

"I am resigned to God," the mufti exclaimed. Thereupon the shaykh added, "Look at the reality of that." So everyone present looked at the Ka'ba. The people cried out and the jurist lowered his head between his hands and said, "You are my shaykh from this very hour." "Rather," the shaykh replied, "you are my brother, if God wills."

The Shaykh Watches over Madi

The worthy Shaykh Abu al-'Azai'm Madi related to me,

The shaykh discoursed on the real significance of a Sufi master in his dealings with his disciples. He said that his hand would be upon them to preserve them wherever they might be. I made objection to that in my mind, and I said, "That cannot be except with God."

When morning came, I was depressed, and I went out of Alexandria and sat on the seashore the entire day. After performing afternoon worship, I leaned my hand upon my knees, [that is, he drew his head into the collar of his mantle]. Suddenly, something shook me and I thought it was one of the devotees who was jesting with me. I raised my head from my mantle and, lo, there whe was, a beautiful woman garbed in lovely clothes and ornaments.

"What do you wish?" I asked.

"You," she replied

"I take refuge with God," I uttered.

"By God" she said, "I will not leave you."

Then I pushed her away from me. She grasped me to her bosom and played with me as a child plays with a sparrow, and I had no control over myself. She forced me to herself and my lower self (*nafs*) desired her.

Suddenly, a hand took hold of me by the collar, and I heard the shaykh saying to me, "O Madi, what is this into which you are falling?" Then he cast me away from her. I supposed that the shaykh had passed by that place, but, on raising my head, I found neither the shaykh nor the woman.

I marvelled at that, and recognized that I had been stricken by my opposing him. So I asked pardon of God, performed ablutions, and recited the evening prayer.

I came to the Green Gate,[27] for already the city gates had been closed, all of them. On approaching it, it opened of itself and I entered the city. Then it closed. Now this gate is opened only after the Friday worship when the *Amir* and the people pass through it to go to the seashore, after which it is closed.

So I came to the Citadel and entered my room, hiding myself from the devotees. Customarily when the shaykh had performed the last evening worship, he dismissed the people. Every night he would hold a meeting to which men from the surrounding country would come to listen to his teaching. Then al-Shadhili entered the retreat (*khalwa*) and asked, "Where is Madi?" They replied, "We have not seen him today." He ordered, "Look for him in his room." So they came to me, and I said, "I am ill." This was so, for I had gotten into a distressing state.

"Carry him between you," al-Shadhili ordered. So they carried me to him and brought me into his presence. Then he ordered them to depart. I sat down weeping before him and he spoke. "O Madi, yesterday, when I said so-and-so, you made objection to me. Where was my hand

with regard to you today when you were on the point of falling into
the act of disobedience? Whoever is not able to do that is not a shaykh."

Madi also related to us,

We were in Damanhur al-Wahsh and, after performing the afternoon
worship, al-Shadhili gave me a letter to take to the Shaykh and Jurist
Fakhr al-Din ibn al-Fa'izi of Alexandria, by reason of some need which
he happened to have. "O my master," I said, "tomorrow, if God wills,
I shall start out early in the morning, for that place is a day's journey
by horse." "This night," he said, "you will start out and return to me
with the reply, God willing."

I girded on a dagger which I had, went out directly, arrived in
Alexandria in the shortest time possible, delivered the letter, and returned
to him before the yellowing of the sun. On the way, I had passed by
the hills of al-Hajir in which I heard a noise and the sound of walking.
I supposed that thieves were there who would attack me at daybreak.
So I drew the dagger and waited expectantly. But, in fact, I saw no one.

When I sat down before al-Shadhili, he smiled at me and said, "O
Madi, you drew your little dagger to encounter the thieves. The sound
which you were hearing was the rustling of the angels. By God, you did
not pass out of my hands until eighty thousand angels became answerable
for you, protecting you by the command of God, until you reached
Alexandria and returned to us."

Again the aforementioned Abu al-'Azai'm related to us,

The shaykh sent me from Alexandria to Dumyat for something which
he needed. With us was a man of the people of that city who desired
to travel with me. Having asked permission of the shaykh, he granted
it for the journey. On approaching the Gate of the Lotus Tree, one of
the gates of Alexandria, the man took out some money with which to
buy bread and condiments. "You need nothing," I said. "Shall we find
the shop of anyone in the desert?" he asked. Then he pointed to the
shop of a confectioner in Alexandria. I replied, "We shall find something
better, God willing." I had been accustomed, whenever journeying, to
take no provision of food with me.

When I became hungry, I would hearken to al-Shadhili's words behind
me saying, "O Madi, go to your right and you will find tasty food and
fresh water.

So we left Alexandria and walked with haste on the journey until
the day was advanced. Then he said to me, "O Madi, give me something
to eat, for I am hungry." Instantly came the voice of the shaykh according
to custom saying, "O Madi, your guest is hungry. Go off to your right

and you will find something with which to feed him." So going off the right side of the road we found a pot full of sweet cakes imbued with musk and rose water, and we ate until we were filled. The man wept and was amazed by what he saw. "Which of the two is more tasty," I asked, "this food or that to which you pointed in the shop of the confectioner?" He replied, "By God, I have not seen the like of this, and such as this has never been made in the palace of a king."

He desired to gather up the remnants, but I prevented him and left them as they were. When we had walked on a short distance, we became thirsty. Instantly, the voice of the shaykh came to me. "O Madi, go toward your right and you will find water." We found a pool of fresh water in the sand, drank of it, and reclined for a while. On arising, we found not a drop of water. "Where is the water that was in this place?" the man asked. I replied, "I know nothing about it."

Then the man commented, "That shaykh is very powerful. By God, I will not return to my people until I obtain what this teacher has obtained, or die in the mercy of God." So he left his fur-lined mantle with me and walked off into the desert exclaiming, "God, God."

When I finished my journey and returned to al-Shadhili, he said, "O Madi, you have lost your guest." I replied, "You are the one who has lost him whom you fed with the sweet cakes in the desert and whose thirst you quenched with the water in the sand." Then he added, "He has passed on with those who are betaking themselves to God."

Again the Shaykh Madi related to us,

One year, I went on pilgrimage with his permission. When I had completed the rites of the pilgrimage and came to the farewell rite of circumambulating (*tawaf*)[28] the *ka'ba*, the people of Mecca rose up against those pilgrims who remained in the holy place and plundered them. As I had articles belonging to other people that had been left in my care, I entered the *hijr*[29] and stood under the waterspout. "If I go out," I said, "I shall be plundered. If I remain, I remain with the property of the people." Troubled in my predicament, I summoned the shaykh and, lo, there he was standing at the Bab al-Nadwa [one of the gates on the Western side of the mosque] beckoning to me. I hastened toward him, but he turned to go away from me. I followed him, without being able to catch up with him, until he entered the caravan. Entering the caravan myself, I searched but did not find him. On reaching Egypt, I came to him and greeted him. He questioned me regarding my experience. "O Madi," he said, "when the situation became critical for you and you summoned us, we came to you and saved you from your predicament."

Madi and al-Shadhili Visit the Tomb of the Prophet

Again my master Madi related to me,

> I went on pilgrimage with him one year and, on our arrival in the holy city of Medina, he stood before the door of the Mosque of the Apostle of God seeking permission to enter. "This is a place," he said, "regarding which God has spoken. 'O ye who believe, enter not the Prophet's houses until leave is given you.'" [Q. 33:53]. He stood there until leave to enter was granted him. Then he entered and stood before the face of the Apostle of God.
>
> Uncovering his head, he uttered, "The blessings of God, His angels, His messengers, His prophets, and of all His creatures from the inhabitants of His heavens and His earth be upon thee, O our master, O Apostle of God, and upon all thy companions." He went on repeating that over and over, as he was in a state of ecstasy, until the ecstasy subsided. Sitting on one side of the sanctuary, he said, "When I was in the act of greeting him with peace, I had a revelation of him wherein I was greeting him and he was returning to me the salutation with his forefinger."
>
> At that moment Abu Muhammad 'Abd al-'Aziz al-Zaytuni came in. He was supervisor of the food of the devotees. He said, "O my master, one of our camels has died and his load remains on the ground." "By God," he answered, "I have at this moment neither gold nor silver." The shaykh ordered him to sit down, and he sat with us who were in a circle about him. Then he drew his head within his mantle for a time.
>
> On raising his head he said, "O 'Abd al-'Aziz, come near me." He drew near. The shaykh ordered, "Put your hand into my pocket and take what is there." So he inserted his hand and withdrew it full of gold. The shaykh said, "Look at it. By God, a minter has not minted it and a goldsmith has not fashioned it. I was simply told, 'Take, O 'Ali, what is in your pocket.'" Then he instructed 'Abd al-'Aziz to buy a camel and whatever provisions he needed for the devotees.

Abu Muhammad 'Abd al-'Aziz was one of the most important of his companions. The shaykh, making supplication one day on 'Arafat, singled out Abu Muhammad to say "Amen" after his supplication, and him alone. The supplication completed, Abu Muhammad said, "By God, he has just supplicated Thee as a *badal*[30] and a *khalifa*." Then he asked the shaykh, "O my master, who is the *badal*, and who is the *khalifa*?" He replied, "You are the *badal*, and I am the *khalifa*."

Testimony of Jamal al-Din: Worship and Works

The worthy Shaykh, Jurist, and Mufti Jamal al-Din Yusuf al-'Iraqi related to me in the city of Cairo in the year A.H. 715,

> I heard my master the Shaykh and Saint, the one having mystical knowledge of God, Abu al-'Abbas al-Mursi, say, "I prayed behind my master the Shaykh and teacher Abu al-Hasan during the morning worship and he recited the Shura chapter [of the *Qur'an*]. When he came to His words—'He bestows (children) male or female according to His Will (and Plan), or He bestows both males and females, and He leaves barren whom He will: For He is full of knowledge and power' [Q. 42:49–50]—there occurred to my mind something in the way of its meaning. So, when the shaykh brought his worship to a close, he said to me, 'O Abu al-'Abbas, He gives to whom He will females, that is, religious duties ('*ibadat*) and social actions (*mu'amalat*); and He gives to whom He will males, that is, mystical states, sciences and stations; or He pairs them, male and female, bringing them together in whomsoever He will of His servants; and He makes whom He will to be childless, that is, without knowledge and without works.' As I was amazed at that, he said, 'By God, nothing has occurred in the mind of anyone in that worship without God having made it known to me.' "

Drunkenness of the Shaykh's Son

The worthy Shaykh Abu al-'Azai'm Madi related to me,

> The shaykh had a son named 'Ali. I met him in Alexandria drunk with wine. So I brought him to his home and beat him so severely that he grabbed onto his mother. I dragged him away with such force that he pulled out with his hands the cords of her hair. She cried aloud and wept, and the shaykh came in to her and asked, "Why do you weep?" Then she told him the story, but she did not inform him of the son's drunkenness.
>
> At that the shaykh became troubled. Entering the *zawiya*, he asked me, "O Madi, why have you done so-and-so?" I replied, "Because I found him drunk with wine. By God, even if he had clung to you, I would have flogged him according to the legal stipulation." His face was perturbed. "Thus, it is," he muttered. Then he went on a retreat for an hour and called for me. When I went in to him, I found him glad and rejoicing. "O Madi," he said, "I entered this place intending to imprecate my son, but I was told, 'O 'Ali, what is this between you and my saint?

Let him be until that which I have decreed for him shall be accomplished.'" A short time later he went out as a wandering ascetic (*siyaha*), appeared in the land of the Maghrib, and thus his sainthood became apparent.

Shihab al-Din before the Shaykh

One in whom I have confidence related to me,

> When the son of Abu al-'Abbas Ahmad, called Shihab al-Din, reached maturity, his mother said to him [that is, al-Shadhili], "O my master, my son Ahmad has come to manhood." He said to her, "Bring him to me that I may give him my injunction and teach him those rights of God which are incumbent upon him."
>
> She summoned her son, and he sat down before him. He looked at him intently for a moment, scrutinized him, and then turned his gaze away from him. "Arise, O my son," he said. "May God guide you." He made abundant supplication to God for him.
>
> When he had departed, his mother said to the shaykh, "O my master, I did not hear you give him your injunction or even address a word to him." He replied, "When he sat down before me, God allowed me to see the secrets of his future life, and I found nothing in his conduct against which to enjoin him. So I felt ashamed before God of speaking to him."

Testimony about 'Arifat al-Khayr

His grandson—I am in doubt about his name, but he is the son of the daughter of the shaykh—related to me in Cairo at the Azhar Mosque saying,

> When my mother was born to the shaykh, my father, who was 'Ali al-Damanhuri, went in to the shaykh to congratulate him because of her. "She is your wife," the shaykh said to him. At that time my father was very old. So he said to himself, "How can that be, and I at this age?" The shaykh said, "Yes, and there will be born to you so-and-so," reckoning for him the number of children. Then he added, "God has informed me of that."

So 'Ali al-Damanhuri married her and there was born to him what the shaykh had announced to him. Then he died in Alexandria. The author (Ibn al-Sabbagh) said,

In Alexandria I met his worthy and virtuous daughter 'Arifat al-Khayr, surnamed al-Wajhiya, who at that time was blind. I questioned her concerning her name, "Why were you given two names?"

This was her reply,

When I was born, my father was in Cairo. He wrote to my mother to say, "While praying in my retreat (*khalwa*), I was informed that a daughter had been born to me, and I have been ordered to name her 'Arifat al-Khayr."

On his arrival in Alexandria, he asked my mother, "Where is the daughter who has been born to me?" My mother lifted me up to him. He placed me on his bosom and put saliva into my mouth, saying, "Welcome to al-Wajhiya," that is, the one of whom he learned while performing the prayer of orientation (*tawajjuh*).

This woman was one of the saints of God, one of those after whom the *Qur'an* was recited, according to the seven modes of reading, from behind a screen, and a gracious lady was she.

The worthy Shaykh Abu 'Abd Allah Muhammad, son of the Shaykh and Saint Abu 'Abd Allah Muhammad ibn Sultan, related to me that one from Alexandria, in whom he had confidence, told him this,

I was present at the burial of the noble and gracious 'Arifat al-Khayr in Alexandria. Now, when she had been lowered into her grave, one of her relatives descended in order to place her in the lateral niche (*lahd*)[31] and he came up from the grave smiling. "When I uncovered her face to place her in the lateral niche," he explained, "she turned to me and laughed. I asked her, 'Why so?' She replied, 'Because of what I have seen of the bounties of God upon me, and I inform you that you will join me after three days.'" After three days, he died. Now, at the time of her death, a herald continued to cry out in Alexandria, "Come to prayer for the noble and gracious 'Arifat al-Khayr who went out into the world on three occasions, from the womb of her mother, to the home of her husband, and to her grave."

The Shaykh Settles a Dispute with Berbers

Among his companions in Tunis was the Shaykh, Saint, and Mystic Abu 'Ali, my master Salim al-Tabasi whose dwelling was in al-Misran. I heard the Shaykh Madi say,

My master Salim had a son named 'Ali. In al-Misran,[32] a disturbance occurred between the townsmen and a group of Berbers[33] who were tent dwellers and settling near them. Abu al-Hasan 'Ali, son of the Shaykh Salim, came along with a cane in his hand to intervene. The cane entered the eye of one of the Berbers and put it out.

So they gathered about him intent on killing him. Abu 'Ali, my master Salim, came out and said to them, "Tomorrow morning, God willing, my brother Abu al-Hasan will come to judge the matter between him and you." On the morning of the following day, there was the Shaykh Abu al-Hasan 'Ali al-Shadhili coming toward them. They spread before him a rug by the door of the room where my master Salim was living. The Shaykh Salim came out to him, and al-Shadhili said, "I have come for the sake of your son 'Ali."

So all assembled before the two men, and Abu al-Hasan addressed them. "Choose whether you will take my brother Salim as bloodwit (*diya*) for the eye of your companion or whether you will accept five hundred dinars."

They answered, "We will accept five hundred dinars, provided that we have them in our hands before leaving."

To that, the shaykh responded, "You speak as if you considered the poor devotees (*fuqara'*) unable to produce the money." Then he put his hand under the rug which, by God, had been spread out upon the ground while I was looking at it, and proceeded to take out and give to them the pieces of money. They counted until they had received the full five hundred dinars, and then they departed.

Thereupon, he turned to my master, Salim, and said, "O my brother, they have sold you for a few carats. If they had taken you, indeed they would have procured wealth of this world and the next. But, by God, before the end of this month their money will have departed from them, and they will be in need of the poor devotees."

So the Berbers departed from al-Misran, were plundered, and returned there poor and needy, begging from the lodge wherewith to clothe themselves.

When this blessed shaykh, my master Salim, died in al-Misran, we went out accompanying the shaykh to attend his funeral. On entering the house where he was, the shaykh said, "Peace be upon you." Salim responded from behind the veil (*hijab*), "And upon thee be peace, O my brother, with mercy and blessings of God." Before us was a small lad, grandson of the Shaykh Salim, who went outside saying, "My grandfather, by God, is alive. He returned the salutation upon the Shaykh Abu al-Hasan."

The shaykh washed him with his own hands and shrouded him. Then he kissed him between the eyes and said, "O my brother, by God, beware lest you forget the agreement that was between you and me." I saw him, by God, open his eyes and he replied, "Yes, O my brother."

When we had recited the prayer over him and buried him, I asked the shaykh, "O my master, what is the agreement between him and you?" He replied, "We had made an agreement before God that whoever should die before the other should be for him a means of access (*wasila*) before God."

He was buried in al-Misran. May God have mercy on him and bring benefit by the blessing of both of them.

Argument with a Group of M'utazila

One in whom I have confidence related to me that he heard the worthy Shaykh Abu Marwan 'Abd al-Malik, known as al-Qassat, say,

When I journeyed to Egypt and entered Alexandria, I went to the shaykh and found him sitting with a company of men with whom he was arguing about knowledge ('*ilm*). When I had greeted him and sat down before him, he asked, "What is your name, from whence have you come, and what doctrine do you profess?" I informed him of my name, my city, and that my preoccupation was the Book of God. "Recite to me," he said, "a verse from the Book of God." So I invoked the protection of God, and He set my tongue free to say, "So put your trust in God, for thou art on [the Path of] manifest Truth" [Q. 27:79], as far as His word, "And the word will be fulfilled against them, because of their wrongdoing, and they will be unable to speak [in plea]" [Q. 27:85].

The face of the shaykh brightened. Then he turned to those present and said, "After a clear explanation of God, no explanation is necessary." So I knew that they were a group of the M'utazila and the shaykh had been arguing with them concerning their system of beliefs. God had caused to flow from my tongue those words from the Book of God which would rightly guide them to the truth. They abandoned their way of thinking, repented before him, and returned to the truth and the *Sunna*.

Al-Shadhili said to me, "Ask of me what you will." So I told him three things: "That you clothe me, that you direct me to someone with whom I shall learn to recite the Book of God, and that you invoke upon me some good." Accordingly he gave me fine clothing, directed me to an outstanding teacher by the name of Ibn al-Dahhan, and said to me, "May God incline the hearts of the chosen ones toward you. May He bless you in whatever He gives you, and may He bring you bliss in the end." By God, I have seen the fulfillment of the first two supplications, and I am hopeful about the third.

True Asceticism

My master Madi recounted to me,

> The shaykh was discoursing one day in his assembly (*majlis*) on asceticism (*zuhd*) with regard to the world. In the assembly was a poor man wearing worn-out garments, while the shaykh was dressed elegantly. The poor man commented, "How is it that the shaykh discourses on asceticism while wearing those garments? I am the ascetic with regard to worldly goods."
>
> The shaykh answered, "O you disputer, your garments are the garments of worldly desire (*raghba fi'l-dunya*) that bespeak pursuit [to acquire] and poverty; but our garments, these bespeak self-restraint (*ta'affuf*) and sufficiency [*ghina*]." Then the poor man stood up before the people and declared, "I, by God the Mighty, am the one who says likewise in my heart, and I beg pardon of God and turn to Him in repentance." Then the shaykh bade me clothe him with elegant garments.

A Litigation

Another person whose authority I trust related to me,

> Among those who followed his teaching in the city of Tunis were the two excellent jurists, Ibn Sawdan and Ibn al-Rimah. One of them was secretary for the Qadi Abu Zayd ibn Nafis, chief justice at that time, and was constantly in his presence. The other attended to the food storehouse that required his daily presence. Now, when the shaykh journeyed to the East, one of them said to his companion, "How shall we do? If we go out to send him on his way, we shall fail to discharge our duties, for our presence is indispensable. If we remain behind, we shall be deprived of his favor and blessing (*baraka*)."
>
> So we accompanied the shaykh as far as Radis [six miles East of the city of Tunis]. While we were sitting with him, a man came reclaiming from him the payment of a certain sum in favor of some merchant. "Indeed," said the shaykh, "we did not leave before settling his account." The man said, "You will go to court with me."
>
> The shaykh named one of his companions as deputy (*wakil*) and said to me, "Record my appointing him as my deputy." I looked at my companion and said, "This is difficult, because he did not volunteer to witness [on behalf of the shaykh]." But he instructed both of us, "Give your testimonies for I have constitued you two notaries." So we wrote out the act of deputation, and in it, we testified to him.

When the deputy proceeded to the carrying out of his trust for the one who deputized him, he told the story to the merchant. The latter rebuked him for that, and informed him that the shaykh had not departed without paying him. Therefore, there was no need of sending a deputation. The merchant departed hastily to go to the shaykh, overtook him, put his mind at ease, and informed him that he had not sent anyone to him.

Then, in the words of the secretary,

> We went to the merchant to ask, "Has anyone sought us?" "No one has sought you," he replied. So no one had raised a question about our absence and, before the close of that month, we were constituted to the office of legal witness.

Miraculous Multiplication of Sheep and Grain

The worthy Shaykh Abu 'Ali 'Umar, son of Abu Yahya al-Jabbari, related to me that his father had related to him what Ya'qub ibn Sa'id al-Jundubi and his brother Muhammad had recounted to him.

> The shaykh drew near to us one night while we were in a small fort. We had ten sheep which we had taken on loan for the gain to be realized therefrom. We slaughtered for him one of the choicest of the flock. "Why have you done this?" he asked. We replied, "This is for the blessing, if God wills."
>
> Then he said, "This sheep will be worth a thousand sheep, God willing." "With them a thousand measures [of grain] for us to store up?" asked one of the two brothers. "And with them," he replied, "a thousand measures, if God wills."
>
> My father added, "So only a short time elapsed before we had acquired a thousand sheep and a thousand measures stored up." "I was present," my father assured me, "at the time of their numbering and I have eaten of their offspring."

This is what has been reported to us concerning some of his charismatic works (*karamat*). There are others, however, greater than all of this.

May God make His blessings (*barakat*) in this world and the next to accrue to us, and may He gather us together with Him in the assembly of our Prophet, our means of access (*wasila*), our intercessor (*shafi'*), and our beloved Muhammad. May god bless him and give him abundant peace as long as the sovereignty of God shall endure.

Chapter Two

— —

Correspondence with His Companions

Letter of Consolation to a Disciple in Qayrawan

He [al-Shadhili] wrote the following to my master the worthy Shaykh Abu Yahya Jamil al-Habibi. The latter was in al-Qayrawan and a dispute arose between him and his companions, whereupon they left him. As he took this to heart, the shaykh wrote him a letter from Alexandria to console him, as follows:

In the name of God the merciful and the compassionate, from God's servant 'Ali ibn 'Abd Allah al-Sharif al-Hasani, known as al-Shadhili, to the brother in God, the Shaykh Abu Yahya. Peace be upon you with God's mercy and blessings.

Now for twelve years, I come and go in whatever journeying of the spirit God has made feasible for me in visiting the soldier-saints of God ('asakir awliya' Allah).[1] Thus I have not passed by you without discovering in you an excellent spirit (ruh) whom men of intelligence understand, with whom souls (nufus) are accustomed to associate, by whom the heart is put at ease, to whom those in authority yield, with whom all the disunited unite, and of whom the understanding person is not ignorant and the ignorant person is not cognizant.

So I found the highest of them (that is, soldier-saints) in the position of the head and the lowest of them in the position of the feet. There is no head at all without feet, and no feet without a head, and all are one. God's setting them apart (takhsis) is obvious. When He purified them with the solvent fluid of His act of separation, they attained the stage of freedom from admixture (tamhis). The first act of purification (tahara), which is a necessary condition for following their Sufi way, is reversion from whatever is other than God. So, in the performance of ritual prayer, they turned the face toward God, and He communed with them with words delightful to the ear. He gave them to drink from the cups of love, and He intoxicated them with His drink. Then, He placed them in a position of excellence. When they became perfected, and when He sent them forth to mankind with those virtues in which they excelled, they became kings in guise of mendicants (*fuqara'*).[2]

The pillar of kings is arms and military defenders (*ansar*), while the pillar of the poor (*fuqara'*) is the finding of sufficiency with God and the patient bearing of the courses of His decrees.

Few are they who love them. Yet, much are they in significance. Many are they who hate them. Yet, little are they in significance. The sun is one, yet it is great in significance. The stars are numerous, but at the rising of the sun they are few. Indeed, "Few of My servants are grateful" (Q. 34:13), but this is the way (*sunna*) of God with His friends (*awliya'*). So it is that the evidence of the excellence of a friend (*wali*) of God lies in the great number of his foes and the fewness of his defenders (*ansar*). Therefore, he gives no heed to them. Rather, he incites them against himself and says, "Call your 'god-partners,' scheme [your worst] against me, and give me no respite, for my protector is God, Who revealed the Book, and He will choose and befriend the righteous" (Q. 7:195–196). And, "If ye help not, [it is no matter], for God did indeed help him" (Q. 9:40).

Therefore, my beloved friend (*habib*) Abu Yahya, have no care for anyone who antagonizes you, and rely not on anyone who becomes friendly toward you. It is only divine lordship that befriends servitude. God has said, "Thus have We placed leaders in every town, its wicked men, to plot and (burrow) therein" (Q. 6:123). The leaders are the wicked ones, and the righteous are its needy ones (*fuqara'*). And, "No change wilt thou find in the practice (approved) by God" (Q. 33:62), and, "Put thy trust in God, and enough is God as a disposer of affairs" (Q. 4:81).

Therefore, O my friend Abu Yahya, arise and sit up as one who is destitute of everything, and whom God console by His word: "All that is on earth will perish" (Q. 55:26), and by His saying, "Everything that exists will perish except His own face" (Q. 28:88). He is not a person of intelligence who does not strengthen himself by the strength of God. As for me, I have a great desire to meet you, and I hope for this from God, Peace to you.

That is the end of the letter. It is said that he went on pilgrimage, and the shaykh met him at the port of Alexandria.

Letter to Followers in Tunis

He also wrote to a company of his companions in the city of Tunis, may God defend it.

The letter reads: In the name of God the merciful and the compassionate, from the servant of God, 'Ali ibn 'Abd Allah al-Hasani, known as al-Shadhili, to the brethren in God, the best of men, the beloved the true friends, the God-fearing, the virtuous, the noble ones, the standard-bearers of the saints, the leaders of the noble God-fearing men: Abu al-Hasan 'Ali ibn Makhluf, and the most gracious master, the jurist, the sincere and honored friend Abu 'Abd Allah Muhammad ibn Muhammad ibn 'Umar, and the unique exemplar Abu Muhammad 'Abd Allah ibn Salama al-Habibi, and the most loving companion and the most upright emigrant (*muhajir*) Abu Muhammad 'Abd al-'Aziz al-Zaytuni, and the most sincere saint Abu al-'Abbas Ahmad al-Sabuni, and the most honest, excellent, and eminent jurist Abu 'Abd Allah ibn al-Rimah, and the brother in God Abu al-Hasan 'Ali ibn al-Hajj al-Iqlibi, and Abu Muhammad 'Abd Allah ibn al-Fahham, and al Hajj Zakariya, and Abu 'Abd Allah al-Bija'i al-Khayyat, and all other companions and friends—peace be upon you with the mercy and blessing of God.

To proceed, may God make real in you the realities of faith. May He station you among the people of excellence (*ihsan*).[3] May He provide you with a pure sense of servitude with consciousness of His presence (*shuhud*) and spiritual vision ('*iyan*).[4] May well-being accompany you in every hour and season. May He appoint you to be a mercy among His servants and a means of security in His land. May He send down rain by you, and by you provide sustenance in abundance. By you, may He repel evils and by your blessings (*barakat*) may He ward off misfortune. May He make you to be reciters, purifiers, learned men, and teachers. May He give you the Scripture, the wisdom, and the great dominion that He gave to the house of Ibrahim, in order that you may be, by His grace, perfect ones, perfecting [your deeds as] learned men and teachers by following the example of our Prophet Muhammad whom God appointed to be a reciter, a purifier, and a teacher. May He bestow upon you the most sublime proximity (*qurb*), and may He turn toward you the most exalted light. Certainly He is powerful over all things. May God illuminate your hearts by the light of His attributes and make real in you the realities of His essence.

Now, I am writing to you from the seaport [of Alexandria]. May God watch over it. As for us, we go about in the abundance of the favors of God, while He, through His bounty and love toward us, endears Himself to us. He has bestowed upon us and our friends His protection, and He has brought us near Him. And how gracious He is! We call upon Him, and He responds to us. With the gift before the request, He anticipates us. So to Him be praise in abundance as it becomes His noble dignity and His high majesty.

With regard to the household, the children, the relatives, and the friends, they go about in the fullness of the favor of God, and by His goodness, outwardly and inwardly, they are overwhelmed. We ask of God an abundant and general increase for you and for them, one and all, and that He take our place in thanking Him, as He is the most generous of the most generous. May He give you refuge and protect you. And so this blessed year we have resolved to go on the pilgrimage to the Sacred House of God and to visit the tomb of His Apostle, our master Muhammad. We have resolved to travel to Cairo shortly after the writing of this letter, if God wills, in order to consult with the Sultan concerning the matter of the caravan. If God prepares it, we shall tarry until the time for it; and if it be otherwise, we shall journey the beginning of the month of Rajab, God willing. If anyone of you has a like resolve, let him come promptly. We shall await your arrival among us. So, if anyone intends to come, let him come at once. And you, O Abu al-Hasan ibn Makhluf, long has been our expectation of you. Therefore, if you are so minded, hasten to come to us and to abide at our house, and do not tarry. And if it be feasible for anyone of you to come our way, let him come speedily. But if the decrees prevail for your staying, or for the staying of anyone of you, then write us immediately concerning your circumstances. God is the One solicited for your help. Upon Him place your trust (*tawakkul*), if you are believers. Know, may God watch over you, that true trust is the aversion of the heart from every thing other than God. Its real nature is the forgetting of every thing except Him. Its secret is the awareness of the Being (*wujud*) of the True One regardless of every thing you may encounter. The secret of its secret is the divine dominion and His bestowal of the dominion on others for the sake of whatever He cherishes and gives satisfaction (*rida*) to Him. Know, may God assist you by the light of His grace, that real satisfaction lies in the awareness of the Being of God beside the [human] self (*nafs*) and creature (*khalq*). It is like a parable that has been cited for the purpose of facilitating the understanding, as follows: I saw a company of men who had come together with me—kings, princes, and other people below them in rank. To each one of them clung his son. Not one would be satisfied to exchange his son for another; neither would he ask to have it otherwise. So it is said that the reality of satisfaction lies in the Being of God beside, not in replacement of, the self and creatures. So understand that and know.

An anecdote: There came to me one night a prayer of supplication in which I said, "O God, make Thy decree, the things that nurture my love to Thee, my meeting with Thee, Thine essence (*dhat*),[5] the essence of Thine Apostle, the secret of the essence of Thine Apostle, dearer to me than myself, my family, my son, my goods, and all humanbeings." I was reciting this prayer while in a state of ecstasy (*wajd*), and I found pleasure in it. The experience increased in intensity, and I said, "Something is befalling and something decree is happening."

While I was sitting thus, someone informed me, "A bull that you had has fallen into the well." I immediately exclaimed, "To God we belong, and to Him is our return" (Q. 2:156). Again I was told, "It was for this reason that the preceding came to you."

So I remained in that state until night, when I saw as if I had come to the gate of Paradise, where I was confronted by palaces and magnificent objects. Suddenly a bull appeared, followed by a great number of bulls. A person was saying to me, "They are seven hundred bulls, of which the length of each one is forty miles and the breadth twenty miles."

The person asked, "What is the wisdom of what is given the servant in Paradise? If that were given in the world, he would not profit by it although it were the abode of might and riches. That is, Paradise represents the wisdom of relationship and sovereignty, of the name and attribution of knowledge, of divine power and will, of remembrance and comprehending (*ihata*). Therefore, whatever may be the domain of which you are the locus and upholder, you will reach its uttermost part as you reach its nearest."

A spiritual truth (*haqiqa*): It has been said, "If you desire My token of esteem (*karama*), then cease not to comply with My orders and to avoid disobedience toward Me. And if you slip because of the overmastery of physical desire (*shahwa*) and My great poser, then know that I am near you, watching over you, surrounding you, powerful over you. Rescue yourself from Me and My great power and say, 'O Thou Who existed before every existing thing; Who art now existing as Thou ever wast; O Thou the First, the Last, the External, the Internal, my self (*nafs*) has become straightened within me and the earth has become too narrow for me, spacious as it may be. There is no shelter at all and no way of escape from Thee except toward Thee. So pardon me, have compassion on me and relent toward me,' 'For Thou art the Oft-Returning, most Merciful' (Q. 2:128)."

O Abu Muhammad ibn Salama, inform the people of al-Masruqin[6] that we intend to perform the pilgrimage, and, if anyone of them is so minded, let him hasten and not delay. Your letter has just been brought to us by al-Masruqi. We have understood its contents and we have rejoiced in what God has deposited in you. So I pray God never to extinguish for you any light (*nur*), by the virtue of our master Muhammad the chosen one. May God bless him, his household and his companions, and give him perfect peace. If you or anyone of you should be coming, and if you have some condiment, according to your well-known benevolence, please bring it to us.

O Abu al-Hasan ibn Makhluf, if it is decreed that you come to us, or any of the companions, then let the servant girl of whom we wrote to you accompany you, or al-Shatibi or anyone who is coming. Will you inform Abu Muhammad al-Shatibi that his household is well, praise be to God. May He unite us all with you soon in the best of circumstances, and may He Himself take the affairs of all of you upon Himself, for He is the most bountiful of the most bountiful. Amen. The most perfect peace be upon you all, with the mercy and blessings of God.

The scribe for this letter is your brother in God who is under obligation to you for your beneficence and deference, and who makes entreaties to God for you, Ahmad ibn Ahmad ibn Muhammad ibn 'Uthman al-Bija'i who greets you all and asks your prayers for himself and for his parents, his children, and his household. "Praise be to God, the Cherisher and Sustainers of the Worlds"

(Q. 1:2). It is written in the month of Rabi' the First, the fifteenth day, in the year A.H. 656.

A treasure: Whenever the *dhikr* becomes heavy on your tongue and meaningless words recur in your speech, when your members (*jawarih*) are given over to your physical desires (*shahawat*), and the door of reflection closes in the pursuit of your own interests (*masalih*), know that this is because of your grave faults or is due to hypocritical craving lurking in your heart, and there is no way open to you except repentance, making amends, seeking protection with God, and sincerity in the practice of the religion (*din*) of God.

Have you not heard the word of God? "Except for those who repent, mend (their life), hold fast to God, and purify their religion as in God's sight; if so they will be numbered with the believers" (Q. 4:146). But He did not say, "of the believers." So meditate on this saying, if you have understanding. Peace be to you.

Will you inform Abu Muhammad 'Abd Allah ibn Salama that we have written a letter to Abu 'Abd Allah ibn Abi al-Husayn with respect to 'Ali ibn Khasib relative to the matter that he had brought up, and that it is enclosed in this letter.

Exhortation to Certain Judges

Al-Shadhili wrote a message to certain judges as follows:

You, may God strengthen you, are most cognizant of the improbability of the common people to set up their defenses, to be quit of obligations imposed on them, to understand readily what is advantageous to them in obtaining their rights, to ward off the injustice of those who would thwart their rights or pounce upon them while taking them away. What is requested of your beneficence, may God be your helper, is the dealing with this kinsman mentioned above in a manner that is neither obligatory upon you nor contrary to your rights, showing him generous consideration and guiding him. Indeed, it pertains to the learned judges to possess a breadth of view and to execute the statutes by taking into account the facts and their causes (*asbab*), and their accessory and attendant circumstances, favorable or prejudicial. Your attention and care are adequate, making unnecessary any further insistence with regard to him.

Letter to 'Ali Ibn Makhluf

He wrote also to my master 'Ali ibn Makhluf of the city of Tunis, where he died and was buried in the Zallaj Cemetery.[7]

In the name of God the Merciful, the Compassionate, and praise be to God, Lord of the worlds, blessing be upon our master Muhammad, seal of the prophets.

This is from 'Ali ibn 'Abd Allah, known as al-Shadhili, to his goodly son, the blessed, the sincerely beloved, the righteous, freed from the way of ruination, 'Ali ibn Makhluf al-Siqilli, peace be upon you with the mercy and blessings of God.

Know—may God assist you by the light of spiritual vision (*basira*) and a purity of intention—that the Apostle was asked, "Who are the friends (*awliya'*) of God, O Apostle of God?" He answered, "They who, when they see, cause God to be brought to remembrance."

But understand the significance of his saying, "When they see," and turn away from the physical sight toward the ideational and conceptual sight, turning completely away from the common seeing of the eyes in which man has partnership with cattle which have no insight (*basira*); and be guided by the light of God deposited in hearts, by which light they have observed, pondered, studied, and attained unto the Truth. They are the ones of whom God has said, "Thou wilt see them looking at thee, but they see not (*la yubsirun*)" (Q. 7:197).

This truth is manifest with reference to the choicest of men and with the most perceptive of persons. By him [Muhammad], his light, and his goodness everything becomes good. It is an amazing thing regarding his preference for perfume (*tib*), according to the agreement of the learned, that his fragrance is the choicest of all perfumes. So understand and enter into the circle of his knowledge. Why is it that you do not say as someone has said, "By God, he did not eat except for us, he did not drink except for us, and he did not marry except for us"? In like manner, he did not perfume himself except for us.

So then, he is the source of every choice thing (*tib*) and the splendor of every mine (*ma'din*). He is the mine of mines. Therefore, seek to borrow from his light, dip up for yourself from his sea, drink of his mystical knowledge, and adorn yourself with his obedience. Then, things will be under your power.

God, bestow upon him divine knowledge (*'ilm laduni*),[8] good works, and easy sustenance. Put things under his power, and cause him to abstain from them even though he had dominion over them. Make him to be of the family of Ibrahim and of the family of Muhammad, for "We had already given the people of Ibrahim the Book and wisdom, and conferred upon them a great kingdom" (Q. 4:54).

Now, ponder this abstention (*zuhd*). Hide it from your self and conceal it from your fellow men except one who emulates you in what you do. Where do you find it after the manifestation of the lights of prophecy and the mine of veracity, unless it be with one who has been favored with His greatest name that is joined with [the creative command] "Be"? Or even one who has attained a view of the original decree and the decree attained a view of the original decree and the decree which embraces [all particular] decrees, and by which has come a satisfaction that cannot be gainsaid, and from which have ramified the particular and general decrees until [they reach] a place of division and contraries where the religious law exhorts in terms of what is liked and disliked?

If anyone does not know this and has false suppositions regarding it, I shall give him an illustration in the case of Adam, who was the first human being, embracing all mankind. Do you find in him anything dislikeful? Not at all. He it is who embraces every believer and disbeliever, obedient and disobedient, monotheist and polytheist, sincere believer and hypocrite. When the various classes of mankind branched off from him, the religious law exhorted in terms of love and hate, satisfaction and wrath. But the original state was only one in which the one satisfied was one beloved—that is, Adam and the descendants issuing from him as I have explained to you.

Such is the original decree in relation to the diverse particular decrees. The prophets, apostles, poles (*aqtab*), all of them clave closely to it, for they were conscious only of God and His decree. They made clear statements, explicated, commented, and prescribed religious laws to those who were beneath them in rank, until the command of God should come to that sincere and beloved friend chosen for Himself whom He willed for the purpose of revealing this science, along with the elementary science, the science of the spirit (*ruh*), the science of love, the science of the intermediate state (*barzakh*) before the beginning of existence (*wujud*), from which are derived the intermediate states in everything pertaining to contraries (*addad*), equals (*andad*), and similars (*amthal*).

Those who hold the opinion that this science—I mean the science of the Spirit and the others mentioned and not mentioned—was not comprehended by the eminent elect ones, the most illustrious "people of *bada*',"[9] have fallen into two great errors: they have imputed ignorance to the saints of God in that they have characterized them as falling short of grasping that, and they have supposed that their Lord has withheld that science from them.

But how is it permissible to bring imputation to bear upon an elect one when by so doing the denial of the knowledge of the Sufis leads to a denial of the divine power and the religious law, through the evidence of His saying with reference to the Jews or the Arabs, whatever contrary opinion may be implied. "They ask thee concerning the Spirit (of inspiration). Say: The Spirit (cometh) by command of my Lord" (Q. 17:85).

Now what indication have you from this of the ignorance of the veracious mystics (*siddiqin*) and of the eminent elect of God? The disclosure thereof is that a question is expressed by means of four particles: *hal*, *kayfa*, *lima*, and *min*. With *hal* occurs the question regarding a thing. Does it exist or does it not exist? With *kayfa* occurs the question regarding the state of a thing. With *lima* is raised the question regarding the cause. There is nothing of the foregoing in the verse quoted.

If, however, you say, "In it is the meaning of *hal* [is it?]," this question requiring the question "Is the Spirit existent or is it non-existent?", then surely they knew beforehand that it existed, for, if this were not so, He would not have said, "They ask thee concerning the Spirit" (Q. 17:85). So it is established that they already knew that it existed, and this argument is rendered of no account.

Also, it contains no question regarding the state of "How is it?", and no question regarding the cause, "why this or that?" If their question had referred to these two, they would not have been contented with His answer. "Say, the Spirit (cometh) by command of my Lord" (Q. 17:85), and they would have created a disturbance and departed, because that was their chief preoccupation, customary way, and desire. So it is established that the question refers only to the object itself—"Whence (*min*) is it?"—by the evidence of the reply and the clear and conclusive explanation in His statement, "Say, the Spirit (cometh) by command of my Lord" (Q. 17:85).

As the Apostle knew about what they asked, he answered for God with those words, as you say, "We ask you about Adam," and the one questioned understands your request and answers, "Adam is of (*min*) the dust." If the reply is satisfactory, one is contented, and the opponent does not withdraw save with a great understanding from the great truth that has no refutal. So how can one assert that it is not known and that it is not conceivable that it be known? For God has made it obligatory upon us to know Him Who has no likeness. If we were to forfeit this knowledge, we would be unbelievers or disobedient. So how is it with a created being whose likenesses are many? It is the essence of ignorance to say, "It is not possible to know one who has a likeness and a correspondent"— that is, the Spirit—while God makes obligatory the knowledge (*ma'rifa*) of one Who has no like or correspondent. What I profess is that, with God, there are secrets the delineation of which is not possible and the concealment of which is not befitting. They are not sketched in books for those who are spiritually blind or qualitatively inferior. Their concealment is not fitting because they are obvious and clearly manifest.

So pay no attention to them in spite of the multiplicity of their arguments. Be submissive to the True One (*Haqq*) and obey Him in respect of those things with which they are concerned. Shun them in those things of which they have no knowledge. God has commanded our Prophet Muhammad to follow after Ibrahim and the rest of the prophets. He is the most righteous, the like of whom no one can attain, and who says, "I have become their partners in prophecy, apostleship, guidance, and experiences coming over souls, bodies, minds, and spirits." So imitate them in those things in which sharing is possible, and those things that have been made our special property concern us and are for us.

In like manner, whoever understands the secret [of mysticism] yields to God, together with the common believers, with those of average rank, and with the more advanced. And outrank them with respect to whatever is the special property of the especially favored ones. So, if you are one of them, increase through your knowledge and religious practice your indigence before God and your humility toward His servants, and incline with compassion toward the common believers, even though they be evil-doers, except where God commands you to deal harshly with them, even while employing pious petitions and pleading on their behalf. So then, I have mentioned this—although you know that you have not realized what you must do before this—lest the soul be perturbed and call for what it does not possess.

Arise and sit by the door [of divine mercy] and you will obtain everything you may desire from the Lord of lords. Continue in the decorum pertaining to the Presence (hadra),[10] if you know it. If you do not know it, then understand from your "mother"[11] something that will please you. Now, he who has access to the Presence has four areas, all of which are focal centers of his secret (sirr): his spirit (ruh), his soul (nafs), his heart (qalb), and his intellect ('aql). These are brought to a state of tranquility by faith, unity (tawhid), divine illumination (nur), knowledge ('ilm), mystical knowledge (ma'rifa), intuitive certainty (yaqin), respect, awe, intimacy, and love. He speaks out clearly and says according to the rules of the focal centers: "God, I ask to look unceasingly on Thee, to be attentive before Thee, to repose in whatever comes to me from Thee. If Thou shouldst return me to Thy creatures, I request of Thee goodly decorum in turning toward those who turn toward Thee, and in turning away from those who turn away from Thee. And if to go back to Thy rights (huquq) over me is required by Thee, grant me the discipline of decorum of the Apostle sent from Thee, and cause me not by my knowledge to be veiled from Thee. And if Thou shouldest let me turn back to my own interests, I ask Thee for the enabling of Thy permission through compliance (muwafaqa) with Thine utterance and by the mystic sign (ishara) that comes from Thee. Make me one of those who accept that for Thy sake. Bring wisdom near to our mouths, make our tongues to utter it, with it fill our hearts, and with it engage every part of us, whether without or within. Aid us by a spirit from Thee that we harm not our selves by our desires, and that we follow not our Satan. Appoint us to be of Thy partisans, for Thy partisans are the conquerors."

Know that your letter has reached us. From it has radiated joy to our hearts, by it our breasts have been cheered. The expression of union (jam') with Him is given free course, while the expression of separation (farq)[12] from Him is restrained. But union with your companion is a thing of which it is not becoming to speak. Enfold it in your innermost being by the witness (shahid) of union (tawhid) of Thy Lord. This is according to what is preferable for you and for me, for I have said to someone before you—I speak as if you were the person addressed in place of him—"if you desire that which is without reproach, then manifest separation (farq) in your speech while you witness union (jam') in your inmost heart."

Be not deluded by your passing away from them [that is, the people] or by your keeping them company, and flee to God from both. Turn not back to any thing small or great except by His permission.

How should you be heedless of Him who has shown mercy to you in the person of your teacher, since he is with you as if he were standing over you in all your doings? Your insight (*basira*) sees him as if you were he. So what do you think of Him who is well aware of what every soul has acquired? The explanation of "permission from God" is His knowledge, according to His saying, "Behold! I taught thee the Book and Wisdom, the Law and the Gospel" (Q. 5:110). Then He said, "By My permission" (Q. 5:110), and by the permission of God, repeating the expression, that is, by the knowledge (*'ilm*) of God, and He enabled Jesus to possess this knowledge. So when the divine utterance was joined to the permission, it completed and made still more inclusive what was implied in the permissible (*mubah*) and the personal interests. As for the obligatory (*wajib*) and the commendable (*mandub*), they are comprehended in the divine command, but the permissible is outside of their sphere. So the saint at this point is in want of the permission. But do not confuse permission with command. If you do, you will fall into error, or you will render null and void one of the stipulations of the law, and thus you will revert to the category of the ignorant people.

The meaning of permission[13] in the case of a saint is a light that spreads over the heart, which light God creates therein and thereon. That light extends over the thing that he has in mind, and so it overtakes it, light with light, or darkness underneath light. That light advises you to take, if you wish, or leave, advance or turn back, grant or withhold, stand up or sit, journey or remain. This is the category of the allowable in which what is permitted is a matter of choice. When the divine utterance accompanies it, the allowable action is confirmed by what God has willed. If a valid intention of action accompanies it, it leaves the rule of the allowable and becomes commendable.

If the darkness appears underneath the light that spreads from the heart, inevitably a sign of restraint will manifest itself upon the darkness with a contraction of the heart. So be wary of it and shun it, for it is a thing to be feared, or almost. Do not decide that except by a clear proof from the Book of God, a text of tradition (*sunna*), a consensus (*ijma'*), or a variant opinion from a master whose opinion you have followed, like Malik or al-Shafi'i or, besides these two, one of the Rightly Guided Caliphs. So then, form a judgment according to a sound legal source.

If a darkness assumes the likeness of a mist with which the heart is not split asunder but with which the mind remains engrossed, move far away from it, for it is on the border of being a thing disliked (*makruh*).

Do not form a judgment by your intellect (*'aql*) or personal opinion (*ra'y*). In doing so, many people have gone astray. Do not pronounce a legal decision for anyone, even if you are requested to do so. Give to scrupulousness (*wara'*) its due. "And pursue not that of which thou hast no knowledge" (Q. 17:36). So if you observe in this respect the decorum [appropriate to the Divine Presence], before long your Lord will give you the clear proof with the witness from Him following it.

This is a large treatment of this matter. It was not my intention to set it down, but the tongue and the pen ran on as He willed.[14] So I ask of Him grace, pardon, and contemplation in the highest of the stages of the ranks of excellence (*ihsan*).

With regard to that which you have sent us, it has reached us and we have rejoiced in it. We have recalled the gracious assistance in former times and past days. If it were not that we desire eagerly to meet you, we would make you a gift as you have favored us. So we petition God for a reunion according to whatever He likes and is pleasing to Him. We are mindful of what you have mentioned concerning your journey. Although our hearts are in expectancy until the arrival of the ship of al-Mahdiya,[15] it is as though they had become dried and shriveled because of your failure to arrive.

Concerning al-Zaytuni, my heart had been anxious about his affair before the arrival of your letter, and our souls have grieved for him. Tell him to remain firm until God shall decree what He desires. Let thousands be against him, to the number of one hundred thousand or ten thousand, while he listens to things and observes things, and let friends despair and grieve, although we have not despaired. That predicament was a beneficent judgment. "Who, for a people whose faith is assured, can give a better judgement than God" (Q. 5:50)? May God bring a happy ending as if that had never been. So we beseech God that He arouse in us thankfulness for His grace and that He deliver our brother and friend from that abasement to the dignity of sufficiency and the consciousness of His munificence and beneficence.

The moment to get under way on your journey has arrived for you and for the brother, al-Hajj Zakariya, and al-Hajj Yahya, and al-Hajj 'Abd Allah, and al-Zaruti, and al-Warishi, and 'Abd Allah al-Fayturi, and the Murabit Muhammad. The lad Mas'ud has arrived. 'Ali, their cousin, has passed our way. We urged him to tarry, but he set forth on the pilgrimage without tarrying at all with us, notwithstanding our desire that he do so.

On the arrival of news of the breaking off of your journey, our hearts were broken. So also is al-Qabisi[16] with regard to what he intended to do. One of you seeks advice, one of you is silent, and one is overcome with anxiety. So, by God, than Whom there is no other, if my sight (*basar*) were strong enough to help me do it, I would venture forth over every land and sea to my companions until I should free them for our friendship which they cherish, by the will and help of God, for there is no strength and no power except with God, the High and Mighty.

Someone inquired about the journey, whether by land or by sea before autumn. So know that the ship of al-Mahdiya came to us in nineteen days, and we found Ahmad al-Sabuni eager to set out for the Sacred House of God. We decided to proceed before your arrival, even though I was expecting you. Were it not that seventy persons have made up their minds to journey with me this year and sold [their] things, even a hundred odd souls, of whom the seventy are leading personalities—among whom are jurists, excellent men, scholars—and, I don't know, a group of Khalifahs, stewards, chiefs, nobles, concealed substitutes (*abdal*), and choice men, whose native land, I have discovered, is Yemen, and some of whom I hope to meet—if it had not been for this group, I would have waited for you a year until you should come. But their impetus carried me away and my soul (*nafs*) yielded to the call of God, for "He doth guide whom He pleaseth to a Way that is straight" (Q. 10:26). So we, God willing, are on the point of departure with all of our people in the month of the date of this letter, or shortly afterward.

The cause of being detained ordinarily is some grain of ours that is to be thrashed and that has been cultivated for us in three places without toil and without fatigue, without owning property or receiving shares, but by a bounty of God at the hands of one of His servants whom He loves. There is no consciousness of the divine presence (*shuhud*) with annoyance, and no sincere supplication (*ibtihal*) with endeavor. May God bless the people of bounty.

We are proceeding to Cairo and then to Upper Egypt. Everyone desires to render us service. We wish to take a half year before halting (*wuquf*),[17] God willing, and after the year we shall talk about remaining there [in Mecca] or in Medina. I do not fear that anyone will cause me uneasiness, unless it be those who remain attached to me, and my opinion is that they will not leave me, for the reason that I have told you.

This is my desire. Of God I seek aid. He is my sufficiency, and "He is the best disposer of affairs" (Q. 3:173). My womenfolk also stay by their daughters, and they have taken to the port [of Alexandria] as their abode. I have no abode at all and look forward toward nothing except what His Will projects according to the expanse of His Power, as I look toward Him Himself. All is His, the command is His, the secret is His, and the authority and dominion are His. He giveth it to whomsoever He willeth, with compassionate regard for him, although He has no need of him, for "God is the Lord of bounties abounded" (Q. 3:174).

With regard to what you have mentioned concerning the journey by land or by sea, do not depend upon the land, for either one of two reasons: hunger and danger. The price of the measure [of grain] in Barqa[18] has reached an extraordinarily high and terrible sum. Rarely is food to be found. The inhabitants take from one entering the country, and seldom does he receive anything from them. But even though there were an abundance, do not venture upon that road except with sufficient resources and with the customary protection of some generous leader possessing high rank, or else with the assurance (*yaqin*) of an elect person who receives help and protection from the True One (*al-Haqq*), is motivated by sincerity (*sidq*), is oblivious of himself and of his own trusting (*tawakkul*), and has the True One as his guide, upon whose head the hand of

God rests. The divine power will provide for him, love will bear him up, and longing will animate him. The fire will say to him, "Pass, O believer, for your light has eclipsed my blaze." This assurance is seldom found in any except you.

But if anyone should find within himself this assurance while he is aloof from his fellows, because they have no rank at all in the dominion, then weep and weep with your very eyes over the absence of bearers for our burdens, of those who are slipping away [or perishing in death] from us, and of those who are aware of our circumstances. It is as if those [others] were virtually ignorant persons [traveling] with us and whom we reckon as part of us.

But God has not rendered the earth void of one or three or seven of those who are the elect ones (*khusus* or *khasah*) of this Muslim people in every particular time. However, our wretchedness, our pretensions, and our rebellion through the impurity of our actions have caused us necessarily to be veiled (from God).

But, "For [anyone] who fears God, He (ever) prepares a way out, and He provides for him from (sources) he could never imagine" (Q. 65:2–3). Sahl ibn 'Abd Allah[19] explained this fear to be fear of the might (*hawl*) and power [of God], and a turning away from that appearance of fear with which the imposters made show, nothwithstanding the impurity of its inner nature. And rightly so, in that any servant whose external appearance is one of disobedience and carnal desires, while he undertakes to perform various kinds of obedient acts, having filled the horizon with his pretentions and attributed the might and power of God to himself, is a servant who has overstepped the bounds and exalted his imposture and conceit. His good actions do not counterbalance his evil. Discerning persons (*muhaqqiqun*) impute dubious things to him and examine the motives and fruits. Whenever good fruits are lacking, it is known that his knowledge and religious works are corrupt (*madkhul*). Whenever valid motives are lacking at the roots, let people have no esteem for his works.

God has said, If anyone fears God, "He (ever) prepares a way out" (Q. 65:2). So, O you who claim to fear God, where is the way out? For if you were to see a way out, it would be because of God's promise and guarantee. But when you experience with your fear nothing but dismay, then who is the veracious and who the fallacious? "And whose word can be truer than God's?" (Q. 4:122). And if anyone places his trust in God, He will be his sufficiency. Trust is not sound except for one who fears, and fear is not perfected except for one who trusts. So examine minutely the motives, the roots, and the fruits, for "God loves those who are firm and steadfast" (Q. 3:146).

With regard to travel by sea, it is nearer, to me it is preferable, and it is less costly. In case anyone of you should find passage at al-Mahdiya, we have recommended you to the Shaykh Abu 'Ali al-Sammat. Let no one of you journey to us except with firm assurance, unless I be mistaken, lest his provisions be lost, along with vexation of soul and weariness of heart.

If the affair be such, then consider and reflect upon our journeying from the port of Alexandria, for we shall have already departed. One of you comes and finds no companion with whom to associate. So his heart is saddened and time becomes tedious for him, as he is traveling neither toward the Sacred House of God nor toward his own home, unless possibly he be one who has accustomed himself to find profit in whatever direction he may turn, and who is one of those of whom God has said, "Their limbs do foresake their beds of sleep, [the while they call their Lord]" (Q. 32:16). Do you believe that their sides are denied couches for sleep and that their hearts, at ease and tranquil, are given over to any other? No. Rather, their hearts are removed from everything and in their innermost beings (*asrar*) they recline beside nothing. So understand this meaning. Their sides shrink away from keeping company with others except God, and from showing displeasure with the divine decrees, and "they call on their Lord in Fear and Hope" (Q. 32:16). Fear of Him has cut them off from all others,[20] and with yearning for Him has He made them desirous of Him. "They spend (in charity) out of the sustenance which We have bestowed on them" (Q. 32:16).

If I were able to speak at length here, I would write you volumes; but God (*al-Haqq*) has subdued [the thoughts of] the heart with His power, enlivened them with His wisdom, and made them dispense with addressing His creatures by communion with Him.

With regard to the affair of al-Hajj Zakariya, he mentioned that he has been hindered from coming by a lack of fifteen dinars. But if he were to come with a loan of such-and-such a sum, the repayment of it would be a thing to be hoped of God. However, his letter requires a better reply than that, in view of its contents. But God is the Guide to the proper course.

Concerning the jurist Abu Yahya, I have learned of his resolve. Greet him and inform him that his cousin on his father's side performed the pilgrimage and is now at the port of Alexandria with the two sons of his paternal aunt, Ibrahim and Muhammad. Both of them are of superior worth in virtue and knowledge. The elder of them is devoted to the Sufi way, a man of probity, and esteemed for his religious practice, good deeds, and forbearance. Muhammad, who is far advanced in the science of the foundations [both the *Qur'an* and the *Sunna*], has begun to study the science of the derivatives ('*ilm al-furu'*).[21] He is married, but his brother is unmarried.

If one of you should come alone, direct him to the two illustrious jurists Abu 'Amr and his brother Jamal al-Din, and to the reliable Jurist Abu Muhammad 'Abd al-Wahhab, and to my kinsman Sharaf al-Din. If someone comes with his family, let him go to a house in which I used to live and ask for the Jurist Sadid and for his kinsman Abu Muhammad 'Abd al-Wahhab known as Ibn Kadusa, who will lodge them with them. We shall leave instructions with regard to that.

Concerning the book which you say has been purchased, if it be possible for you, let someone bring it. Consign it to some responsible person in order that he may give it to one of these excellent jurists, or al-Jamal, or my kinsman, or Sadid.

I urge you to greet on my behalf my companions both near and far, by word of mouth and indirectly, and by your correspondence so far as you are able. Peace be upon you, upon those mentioned and those not mentioned, and upon the people of the city and those of the countryside one and all, with the mercy and blessings of God. Dated, the fifteenth night of Muharram in the year A.H. 646.

Chapter Three

— —

Supplication, Devotional Recitations, and Prayers of Confrontations

In the name of God the Merciful, the Compassionate, prayers and peace be upon our master Muhammad, his family, and companions. God, we seek of Thee incontrovertible certainty (*yaqin*). We ask of Thee a unity (*tawhid*) that no association (*shirk*) contravenes, and an obedience that no insubordination can confront. We petition Thee for love neither of anything nor for anything, and for fear neither of anything nor for anything. We pray to Thee for detachment from neither want nor squalor, after having become detached from all wants and squalors. Grant us to declare Thy holiness (*taqdis*) unreservedly, perfection (*kamal*) unsurpassed, and insuperable knowledge ('*ilm*).

We ask of Thee the envelopment of secrets and their concealment from the best of men. O my "Lord! I have indeed wronged my soul" (Q. 27:44).

Pardon my sins.
Instill in me a godly devotion and make me one of those who love
    and fear Thee.
Prescribe for me a way out from all sin, anxiety (*hamm*), grief
    (*ghamm*), and anguish, from every carnal impulse, desire, alarm,
    involuntary thought, idea, will and act, and from every divine
    decree and command.
Thy knowledge encompasses everything.
Thy might overspreads all powers.
Thou art too majestic for any creaturely thing to concur in or be at
    variance with Thy divine will.
"God sufficieth me." (Q. 9:129)

God sufficieth me. God sufficieth me.
I truly am innocent of (Q.6:19) worshiping what is other than God.

God, "There is no god but He: On Him is my trust—He the Lord of the Throne (of Glory) Supreme." (Q. 9:129)

There is no god but He, Light of the throne.
God, there is no god but He, Light of the tablet of God.
There is no god but He, Light of the pen of God.
There is no god but He, Light of the Apostle of God.
No god is there except God, Light of the secret of the essence of the Apostle of God.
There is no god but He, and Adam is the vicegerent of God.
There is no god but He, and Noah is the confident (*naji'*) of God.
There is no god but He, and Ibrahim is the friend (*khalil*) of God.
There is no god but He, and Moses is the mouthpiece (*kalim*) of God.
There is no god but He, and Jesus ('*Isa*) is the spirit (*ruh*) of God.
There is no god but He, and Muhammad is the beloved (*habib*) of God.
There is no god but He, and the prophets are the choice (*khassa*) of God.
There is no god but He, and the saints are the helpers (*ansar*) of God.
There is no god but He, the Lord, Divinity, Sovereign, Clear Truth.
No god is there except God, the King, Kind, Provider, Strong, Mighty, Possessor of great power.
There is no god but He, the High, the Magnificent.
There is no god but He, the Clement, the Generous.
May God be extolled, Lord of the seven heavens and Lord of the great throne.
Praise be to God, Lord of the universe.
In the name of God, by God from God, toward God, and in God let the believers trust. (Q.14:13)

God sufficieth me. (Q. 9:129)

I believe in God.
My contentment is in God.
My trust is in God.
There is no power but with God. (Q.18:37)

I turn to Thee in repentance, by Thee, from Thee, unto Thee.
If Thou wert not, as Thou art, I would not repent to Thee.
So efface from my heart love for any other but Thee. Guard my members from violating Thy command.
By God, if Thou dost not watch over me with Thine eye and guard me by Thy power, I myself will surely perish, and I as a people (*umma*) of Thy creation will perish.

Such a loss cannot but revert to Thy servant.
I take refuge in Thy requital from Thy punishment.
I seek refuge in Thy good pleasure from Thine anger.
I flee for refuge in Thee from Thee.
I cannot reckon praise due to Thee; Thou art just as Thou hast
   praised Thyself.[1]
Indeed, Thou art too exalted to be praised.

These expressions of praise are but tokens indicative of Thy generosity which Thou hast granted us on the tongue of Thine Apostle that we may use them to serve Thee according to our abilities, not according to Thine ability [to praise Thyself]. Shall the reward for the first and perfect kindness (*ihsan*) be other than kindness from Thee?

O Thou by Whom, from Whom, and to Whom everything returns, I beseech Thee by the virtue of the Teacher (*ustadh*)—indeed by virtue of the Prophet, the Guide; and by the virtue of the two and the four; and by the virtue of the seventy and the eight; and by the virtue of their secrets from Thee to Muhammad Thine Apostle; and by the virtue of the sovereign of the verses of the *Qur'an* from Thy word (*kalam*), and by the virtue of the seven oft-repeated verses and the glorious recital from among Thy Scriptures; and by the virtue of Thy great name possessing which nothing on the earth or in the heavens does harm—for "He is the One who hears and knows all things (Q. 41:36), and by the virtue of [the Scripture which says],

Say, "He is God, the One and Only; God, the eternal, Absolute,
He begetteth not, nor is He begotten; and there is none like unto Him."
(Q. chapter 112)

O God, spare me every act of forgetfulness, passion, and disobedience whether of the past or the future. Spare me every one of Thy creatures who comes seeking of me, whether rightly or wrongly, [some boon] for this world or the next, for Thine is the conclusive proof (Q. 6:150), and Thou art powerful over all things. (Q. 2:19)

Spare me anxiety for sustenance and fear of people.

Make me travel the pathway of sincerity (*sidq*) and be my helper in truth.

Deliver us from every affliction from above us or from below our feet, whether it troubles us with discord or causes one of us to suffer the injury of another.

Spare us every anxiety, every terror outside of the Garden. Save us from whatever evil Thou dost know, whether of the present or the future, for over everything Thou art powerful.

Exalted be the King, the Creator.
Exalted be the Maker, the Provider.
Exalted be God above what they ascribe to Him, Knower of the unseen and the seen. Lifted up be He over what they associate [with Him]. (Q. 23:92).
Exalted be the Possessor of glory and might.
Exalted be the Owner of power and royalty.
Exalted be the One who gives life and death (Q. 2:260).
Exalted be the living who does not die.
Exalted be the King, the all Powerful.
Exalted be the Magnificent, the Victor Who is victorious over His servants, and who is the Wise, the Informed (Q. 6:18).
Say: My sufficiency is God, beside Whom there is no god, and in Him have I put my trust. (Q. 9:129)
So let the trustful put their trust in Him.

I take refuge with God from the severity of affliction, decreed misfortune, overtaking distress, and malice of enemies.

I take refuge with God, my Lord and the Lord of everything, from every haughty disbeliever in the day of reckoning.

O Thou, in Whose hand is the governance of all things, Who protects all—but is not protected (of any)? (Q. 23:88)—be my helper, through my fear of Thee and my trust in Thee, so that I fear no one but Thee, and rely on nothing save Thee.

O Thou, Creator of the seven heavens and of the seven earths likewise, and through which heavens the divine command descends, I bear witness that Thou art powerful over all things and that Thy knowledge encompasses all that is. I ask Thee, in the name of that command that is the source (*asl*) of all creation, to which belong the beginning and the end, and whose is the outmost of the outmost, that Thou render this sea (*bahr*) subservient to us, sea of the world with what it contains and who are in it, just as Thou didst make the sea subservient to Moses and the fire subservient to Ibrahim, and the mountains and iron subservient to David, and made the winds, Satans, and *jinn* subservient to Solomon.

In like manner, make subservient to me every sea of Thine, make subservient every mount, make subservient every iron, make subservient every wind, make subservient every Satan, of *jinn* or men, and make subservient to me my lower self (*nafs*), make all subservient, O Thou in Whose hand is the dominion over everything (Q. 23:89). Bear the burden of my affair with the certainty, and help me with the manifest victory. Thou art powerful over all things.

The Noble Litany and the Mighty Veil (Hijab), *or the Great Litany*

I take refuge with God from the stoned Satan. In the name of God the Merciful the Compassionate, prayers be upon our master Muhammad. God hath purchased of the believers their persons and their goods, for theirs [in return] is the Garden [of Paradise]. They fight in His Cause, and slay and are slain, a promise binding on Him in Truth, through the Law, the Gospel, and the *Qur'an*. And who is more faithful to his Covenant than God? Then rejoice in the bargain which ye have concluded. That is the achievement supreme.

Those that turn [to God] in repentance; that serve Him, and praise Him; that wander in devotion to the Cause of God; that bow down and prostrate themselves in prayer; that enjoin good and forbid evil; and observe the limits set by God. These do rejoice. So proclaim the glad tidings to the Believers (Q. 9:111–112).

Happy they, the believers,
Who in their worship are lowly,
Who vain talk avoid,
Who in almsgiving are diligent;
Those who withhold their passions—save from their wives or what
 their right hands possess, for thus they are blameless.
But they who desire beyond that, they are the transgressors
Who respect their trusts and pledge,
Who are mindful of their set prayers,
They are the ones who are the heirs,
Who will inherit Paradise,
Therein to abide eternally (Q. 23:1–11).
The resigned, men and women,
The believers, men and women,
The submissive, men and women,
The truthful, men and women,
The long-suffering, men and women,
The humble, men and women,
Those who give to charity, men and women,
Those who constantly remember God, men and women—God has
 prepared for them forgiveness And a generous recompense. (Q. 33:35)

Man was created restless,
Whenever evil touches him, he becomes uneasy.

But when some good passes his way, he is niggardly.
Except those who perform prayers,
Who unceasingly continue to pray,
Those of whose wealth is a rightful portion for the beggar and bereft,
Those who hold the judgment day a truth,
And of the punishment of their Lord are apprehensive,
For from their Lord's chastisement they are not secure,
Those who withold their passions—save from their wives or what
    their right hands possess, for thus they are blameless,
But they who desire beyond that, they are the transgressors
Who respect their trusts and pledge,
And hold to their testimonies,
Those who observe the set prayers—They in Gardens will be highly
    honored. (Q. 70:19,35).

God, we ask of Thee, to be accompanied by fear, to be overcome by longing, to be well grounded in knowledge, to continue long in reflection.

We ask of Thee, the secret of divine secrets which wards off harmful things; that, in sin and shame we may not abide. Choose and lead us to act according to these words that Thou didst utter for us upon the tongue of Thine Apostle, and by which Thou hast tried Ibrahim, Thy sincere friend. So he fulfilled them, and God said, "I will make thee an Imam to the Nations." Ibrahim asked, "Of my children also?" He replied, "My promise is not within the reach of evildoers" (Q. 2:124).

So appoint us to be among his well-doing children and among the children of Adam and Noah. Guide us to the path of the rightly guided leaders, for God beholds His servants, who pray,

Our Lord, we believe. So forgive us our sins, and
Spare us the torment of the fire:
The enduring, the truthful,
The obedient, the charitable,
The daybreak pardon-seekers. (Q. 3:16–17)

Those who remember God standing, sitting, and on their sides, and
    reflect on the creation of the heavens and the earth;
Our Lord, Thou hast not created this futilely.
Glory be to Thee.
So spare us the torment of the fires.
Our Lord, Thou, whomsoever Thou dost cause to enter the fire
Thou dost put to shame, and the wrong-doers have no helpers.
Our Lord, we have heard a herald bidding us to the faith, saying,
    "Believe in your Lord." So we believe.

Our Lord, give us what Thou hast promised us by Thy messengers and shame us not on the day of resurrection.
Thou wilt not fail to hold to Thy promise. (3:191–194)

Our Lord, give us good in this world, and good in the next, and spare us the agony of the fire. (Q. 2:201)

Our Lord, forgive us our sins and anything we may have done that transgressed our duty.
Establish our feet firmly, and help us against those that resist Faith. (Q. 3:147)

Our Lord, chastize us not if we forget or commit a fault.
Our Lord, do not impose on us a burden as Thou didst burden those who were before us.
Our Lord, do not burden us with what we are unable to bear.
Grant our pardon and forgive us.
Have mercy on us.
Thou art our Protector.
Render us victorious over the disbelieving people. (Q. 2:286)

Our Lord, cause not our hearts to err after Thou hast bestowed on us mercy from Thyself, for Thou art the Bestower. (Q. 3:8)

Our Lord, Thou art the Gatherer of men for a day of which there is no doubt.
God does not dishonor His compact. (Q. 3:9)

Our Lord, we believe in what Thou hast sent down and we follow the Apostle.
So inscribe us with those who bear witness. (Q. 3:53)

And why should we not believe in God and in the truth that has come to us, and desire that He let us in, O our Lord, with the righteous people? (5:84)

So God has requited them for their declaration with gardens through which flow rivers, there to abide forever.
That is the reward of those who do good. (5:85)

Moses said, "O my people, if you believe in God, put your trust in Him, if you are resigned [*muslimin*]."

"We trust in God," they replied. "Our Lord, make us not a temptation [*fitna*] for the unjust people, and deliver us by Thy mercy from the disbelieving people." (Q. 10:85–86)

Our Lord, grant us from Thyself a mercy and provide for us right conduct in our affair (Q. 18:10).

Our Lord, we have believed, so forgive us and be merciful to us. Thou art the best of the merciful (Q. 23:109).

Our Lord, turn away from us the torment of Hell. Its torment is a lasting affliction—evil it is as an abode and resting place (Q. 25:65–66).

Our Lord, grant us joy and comfort from our wives and children, and make us a leader for the God-fearing (Q. 25:74).

Our Lord, Thou dost encompass all things in mercy and knowledge. Forgive, therefore, those who have repented and followed Thy way, and spare them the torment of Blazing Fire. Our Lord, let them into the Gardens of Eden which Thou hast promised to them and to their fathers, spouses, and children who have lived rightly, for Thou art the Mighty, the Wise. And spare them [punishment for their] evil deeds, for if Thou spares anyone [punishment for] evil on that day, that person has been the object of Thy mercy, and that is the great victory (Q. 40:7–9).

Our Lord, lift from us [the sentence of] punishment. We are believers (Q. 44:12).[2]

Our Lord, forgive us and our brothers who have gone before us in the Faith. Put not into our hearts rancor toward those who believe. Our Lord, Thou art the All-Kind, the All-Merciful (Q. 59:10).

O our Lord, in Thee have we trusted, toward Thee have we turned, and to Thee shall we come in the end. O our Lord, subject us not for trial to the disbelievers, and pardon us, our Lord, for Thou art the Mighty, the wise (Q. 60:4–5).

Our Lord, make perfect for us our light, and pardon us, for Thou art the all-Powerful (Q. 66:8).

In the name of God the Merciful, the Compassionate, say: "He is one God, God the Eternal. He did not beget, Neither was He begotten. There was none meet for Him" (Q. chapter 112).

In the name of God the Merciful, the Compassionate, say: "I take refuge in the Lord of the dawn, from the evil of twilight when it deepens, and from the evil of the sorceresses who blow on knots, and from the evil of an envier when he envies" (Q. chapter 113).

In the name of God the Merciful, the Compassionate, say: "I take refuge in the Lord of men, from the evil of the stealthily withdrawing whisperer, who whispers in the hearts of men, both *jinn* and men" (Q. chapter 114).

In the name of God the Merciful, the Compassionate, praise be to God, Lord of the worlds, The Merciful, the Compassionate, King of the judgment day, Thee we worship. Thee we ask for aid. Guide us on the straight path, The path of those to whom Thou hast been gracious, not of those with whom Thou hast been angry, nor of those who go astray (Q. chapter 1).

Praise be to God Who created the heavens and the earth, and appointed [the periods of] darkness and light. Then those who disbelieved gave their Lord equals. He it is Who created you of clay; then decreed He a term, and a term with Him is fixed. Still you have doubts, even though He be God in the heavens and on the earth. He knows what you conceal and what you reveal. He knows what you are earning (Q. 6:1–3).

Praise be to God Who has guided us to this. We would not have been rightly guided if God had not guided us, for the Apostle of our Lord came with the truth (Q. 7:43).

Those who believe and perform righteous works, their Lord will guide them aright for their faith. At their feet rivers will flow in the Gardens of delight. Their cry therein will be "Glory be to Thee, O God." Their greeting there will be "Peace!" The end of their cry will be "Praise belongs to God, Lord of the worlds" (Q. 10:9–10).

Say "Praise be to God Who has not taken to Himself a son, Who had no partner in the Kingdom, nor had He a protector because of lowness. And repeatedly declare His greatness (Q. 17:111).

Praise be to God Who has sent down upon His servant the Scripture, and has not put into it any deviousness, but directness, to warn of a terrible woe from Him, and to bear good news to the believers who perform righteous deeds That they will have a goodly reward [a garden], in which they will remain forever (Q. 18:1–2).

Say "Praise belongs to God, and peace be on His servants whom He has chosen. Is God better, or [the gods] they associate [with Him]? (Q. 27:60)

Praise be to God, to Whom belongs what is in the heavens and on the earth. To Him be praise in the life to come. He is the Wise, the Informed. He knows what enters the earth and what leaves it, what descends from the sky and what arises to it. He is the Merciful, the Forgiver (Q. 34:1–2).

To God be praise, Maker of the heavens and the earth, Appointer of the angels as messengers, Having pairs of wings—two, three or four—Adding to creation whatever He wills. Over all things is God powerful (Q. 35:1).

Whatever mercy God grants to men, no one can withhold. Likewise, whatever He withholds, no one thenceforth can send forth. He is the Mighty, the Wise (Q. 35:2).

God has set forth a parable of a servant enslaved with power over nothing, and a person whom we have supplied of ourselves with a goodly supply from which he expends privately and publicly. Are they on the same level? [No], To God be praise, but most men know it not (Q. 16:76).

God has set forth the parable of a man with associates who quarrel among themselves, and another who is subservient to one man. Is the one just like the other? [No], To God be praise, but most men know it not (Q. 39:29).

Then say "God be praised. He has kept His promise to us and bequeathed to us the earth in which to settle down wherever we will. The reward of those who do [what is right], how agreeable it is." (Q. 39:74).

And thou shalt see the angels hovering around the throne and exclaiming the praises of their Lord. Among them will judgment be made with justice, and the declaration will be "Praise belongs to God, Lord of the universe" (Q. 39:75).

To God belongs praise, Lord of the heavens, Lord of the earth, and Lord of the universe; and to Him be the greatness in the heavens and on the earth, for He is the Mighty, the Wise (Q. 45:36–37).

God be exalted when you come to the evening and when you come to the morning. To Him be praise in the heavens and on the earth after the setting of the sun and when you are at midday, He brings the living out of the dead and the dead out of the living, and He gives life to the earth after its death. In like manner you will be brought forth (Q. 30:17–19).

Exalted be thy Lord, the Lord of glory, above what they ascribe [to Him], and peace be to Thy messengers, with praise to God, Lord of the universe (Q. 37:180–182).

Whenever those who believe in Our signs come to thee, say "Peace be upon you. Thy Lord has prescribed for Himself mercy. If anyone of you does evil in ignorance, and afterward repents and makes amends, He is the Forgiving, the Merciful (Q. 6:54).

Originator of the heavens and the earth—How should He have a son, when He had no consort? He created everything, and of everything He is cognizant. That is God your Lord. Beside Him there is no god. He is the Creator of everything. So worship Him, for He is over everything a Guardian. Eyes do not perceive Him, but He perceives the eyes. He is the Subtle One, the Informed (Q. 6:101–103).

Alif lam ra' ha' mim 'ayn sin qaf kaf ha' ya' 'ayn sad.[3] Say "My Lord, do Thou judge with the truth. And, our Lord is the Merciful. Whose aid is sought against what you attribute [to Him]" (Q. 21:112).

Ta' ha'. We have not sent down upon thee the recital to cause you distress. It is but a reminder to one who fears. It is a revelation from One who created the earth and the lofty skies. The Merciful mounted the throne. His is whatever is in the skies, on the earth, between them, and underneath the ground. Ahthough thou speak out openly, He knows the secret, even the well-concealed. God—no god is there but He—is Possessor of the Most Beautiful Names (Q. 20:1–7). [Repeat this thrice.]

My God, Thou knowest that I am recognized as an ignorant one, while Thou art described as One Who is knowing. Thou hast encompassed it in Thy knowledge, and pardon me, "For Thou has power over all things" (Q. 66:8).

O God, O Sovereign, O Bestower, bestow on us those favors that Thou knowest to have made us find satisfaction in Thee. Clothe us with a garment with which we may be guarded from being subject to temptation in all of Thy gifts, and with which we may be cleared of every attribute that renders unavoidable some deficiency that Thou alone dost know exclusively of any other.

O God,
O Mighty One,
O Exalted One,
O Great One.

We ask Thee to grant us deprivation of all but Thee, and such a sense of sufficiency with Thee that we may be conscious only of Thee; and such kindness toward us in both [conditions] that Thou knowest to be befitting for one who has become Thy friend. Clothe us with outer garments of majesty, which befit our souls and moments. And make us bondservants of Thine in all circumstances. Impart to us from Thy presence a knowledge that will render us perfect in life and in death.

Our God, Thou art the Praiseworthy, the Lord, the Glorious One, the Doer of what Thou desirest. Thou knowest our gladness—why it is and what occasions it. Likewise, Thou knowest our sadness. Indeed, Thou hast constrained to be what Thou hast willed for us and from us. We ask not a warding off of what Thou willest, but we plead for the strengthening of a spirit from Thee in whatever Thou willest, as Thou didst strengthen Thy prophets and messengers, and the elect of the utterly sincere of mankind, for powerful art Thou over all.

Our God.
Maker of the heavens and the earth,
Knower of the hidden and the visible,
Thou judgest between Thy servants. (Q. 39:46)

How pleasant—for one who knows Thee, and acquiesces in the decrees that come from Thee. But woe to him who has not known Thee. Nay, rather woe upon woe to him who affirms that there is no god but Thee, but finds no satisfaction in the judgments declared by Thee.

Our God! Thou hast sentenced the people to abasement until they become exalted, and Thou hast sentenced them to loss until they find. If any exaltation inhibits a state inferior to Thee, we ask in exchange for it abasement accompanied by the subtle influences of Thy mercy.

If any finding (*wajd*) veils us from Thee, we ask in place of it loss (*faqd*) accompanied by the illuminations of Thy love. Bliss has shone on him to whom Thou hast shown Thy love, but wretchedness has lowered over him whom Thou hast spurned. So bestow on us the tokens of the blissful, and protect us from the misfortunes that befall the wretched.

O God, we are powerless to thwart from ourselves the harm that comes from a source and in a manner we know. So how could we not be powerless to do it whence we know not? Commands and prohibitions Thou hast given us. Praise and dispraise Thou hast forced upon us. The man of virtue is he whom Thou hast rendered virtuous, and the man of corruption is he whom Thou hast caused to err.

The fortunate truly is he whom Thou hast relieved of asking of Thee, and the unfortunate truly is he whom Thou hast refused despite much petitioning to Thee. Therefore, relieve us, by Thy bounty, of our asking from Thee, and refuse us not Thy mercy, despite our much petitioning to Thee. Thou canst do all things.

O Thou of violent force.
O Compeller.
O Irresistible One.
O Wise One.
We take refuge in Thee from the evil that Thou hast created.
We take refuge in thee from the darkness that Thou hast originated.
We take refuge in Thee from the stratagems of people in things that Thou
  hast willed and designated.
We take refuge in Thee from the mischief of him who is envious of Thy
  biessings with which we have been ingratiated.

We ask of Thee high rank in this world and the next, as our master Muhammad, Thy servant and prophet, made request of Thee—high rank in this world through faith (*iman*) and divine knowledge (*ma'rifa*), and high rank in the Next World through meeting with and comtemplating Thee. Thou art One Who hears, Who is near, and Who responds.

O God, I present to Thee, with the occurrence of every breath, every look, every glance, every blink of the eyes of the inhabitants of the heavens and the earth, of everything that is now or has been within Thy knowledge—with all that I present to Thee [this declaration].

God, no god at all is there except Him, the living, the self-subsistent. Neither sleep nor slumber overtakes Him. His is whatever is in the heavens or the earth. Who is he who can intercede before Him except by His permission? He knows what is before them and behind them, but they have no comprehension of what He knows, save what He wills [that they know]. His throne is as wide as the heavens and the earth. Their preservation is no burden to Him. He is the High, the Mighty. (Q 2:255)

I have adjured Thee by the spreading of Thy two hands, the kindness of Thy face, the light of Thine eyes, and the perfection of the sight of Thine eyes to give us whatever good thing Thy will has executed, with which Thy power has been attached, and that has been comprised in Thy knowledge. Protect us from the evil of what is contrary to that. Perfect our religion and bring to fullness Thy favor upon us.

Bestow on us the Ultimate Wisdom (Q. 54:5) along with the good life and the pleasant death. Take in hand the seizure of our spirits with Thine own hand. With the light of Thine essence, Thy mighty power, and Thy goodly bounty, intervene between us and all other save Thyself in the interval (*barzakh*) along with all before it and after it. Thou art able to do all things.

O God,
O Exalted One,
O Great One,
O Kind One,
O Knower,
O Generous One,
O Hearer,
O Near One,
O Thou Who dost respond,
O Affectionate One, intervene between us and the enchantment
    (*fitna*) of the world, women, forgetfulness, lust, the wrong of men,
    and the evil of creatures; forgive us our sins; render satisfaction
    for the consequences of our misdeeds for us; remove from us the
    offense; deliver us from the affliction, and make for us a way out
    of it. Thou hast power to do all things.
O God,
O God,
O God.
O Kind One,
O Sustainer.
O Powerful One,
O Mighty One.
To Thee belong the keys of the heavens and the earth. Thou givest
    sustenance with open hand to whom Thou willest, or thou givest
    it by measure.

So open to us Thy hand with sustenance wherewith Thou wilt cause us to attain unto Thy mercy, with Thy mercy whereby Thou wilt bar us from suffering thy retribution, and with thy clemency wherewith we may receive Thy pardon. Make our end to be felicitous, as Thou hast so made the end of Thy friends. Make the best and happiest of our days to be the day on which we encounter Thee.

Tear us away, while in this world, from the fire of passion, and usher us, by Thy bounty, into the fields of mercy.

Clothe us, from Thy light, with garments of divine immunity.

Assign to us a helper for our intellects, a guardian for our spirits, and a constrainer for our souls, that we may abound in praise and commemoration of Thee. Thou dost truly see us.

Grant us the gift of contemplation accompanied by conversation. Open our hearing and seeing. Remember us whenever we are unmindful of Thee, just as Thou art so gracious as to remember us whenever we remember Thee.

Be merciful to us when we disobey Thee, just as Thou art plenteously merciful when we are obedient. Grant forgiveness for our sins, both the former and the latter. Be kind to us with kindness that veils us from all other while it veils us not from Thee, for Thou knowest all things.

God, we beseech Thee, grant us a tongue constantly employed in mentioning Thee, a heart delighted in thanking Thee, and a body object and yielding to perform Thy bidding. Impart to us, with all that, what eye has not seen, nor ear heard, nor entered into the heart of man, such as the message Thine Apostle imparted according to the knowledge Thou didst possess.

Satisfy our needs, even though we lack means of livelihood, and may we be a means of satisfying the needs of Thy friends (*awliya'*), and a barrier between them and Thine enemies, for all things are within Thy power.

> God,
> We beseech Thee for an unfailing faith.
> We beseech Thee for a humble heart.
> We beseech Thee for knowledge that avails.
> We beseech Thee for sincere and certain belief,
> We beseech Thee for the right religion.
> We beseech Thee for relief from all affliction.
> We beseech Thee for the utmost in well-being.
> We beseech Thee for unceasing well-being.
> We beseech Thee for thankfulness for well-being.
> And we beseech Thee for freedom from need of humanbeings.

God, we ask of Thee perfect repentence, general pardon, all-inclusive love, unalloyed affection, comprehensive knowledge, radiant illumination, constant intercession (*shafaʿa*),[4] the Decisive Proof (Q. 6:149), the exalted rank, and release of our bonds for disobedience and from our pledge [with God] of punishment through divinely bestowed favor.

God, we implore Thee to grant us repentance (*tawba*) without ceasing.

We take refuge with Thee from insubordination and the things that cause it. Remind us to fear Thee before the assault of involuntary thoughts to commit it. Give us the urge to escape from it and from reflection on its ways; and efface from our hearts the charm of whatever acts of insubordination we have committed, and replace it with a repugnance for it and a craving for its opposite.

Deluge us from the sea of Thy generosity, Thy bounty, Thy generosity, and Thy pardon, that we may leave this would in security from its affliction. Grant that, at the moment of death, we may be pronouncing the Word of Witness (*shahada*), knowing it, in its triple form. Be compassionate toward us, as a beloved would show compassion toward his loved one when affliction befalls. Restore us, with gladness and ease, from the cares and anxieties of the world to the Garden and its delights. God, we ask Thee that Thou be the first to turn relenting toward us, that we may consequently turn in repentance toward Thee. Grant us to be recipients from Thee, as Adam [upon him be peace] received from Thee certain words, that he might be, for his offspring, a pattern of repentance and righteous works.

Separate us from stubornness, persistence [in error] and imitation of Satan who is the chief of seducers.

O God, make our wrong deeds to be ones of those whom Thou dost love, and make not our good deeds to be ones of those whom Thou dost dislike; for doing good, with dislike from Thee, is not profitable, while doing wrong, with love from Thee, is not harmful.

Thou hast rendered the matter obscure for us that we might hope and fear. So render us secure from fear, fail not our hope, and grant our request. Thou hast granted us security before our asking Thee. Thou hast written, caused us to love, adorned, made us to dislike, and loosened our tongue to expound.

What an excellent Lord, Thou. So praise be to Thee for the favors Thou hast bestowed. Then forgive, and punish us not by taking away after Thou hast given, or for our ungratefulness and withholding of satisfaction. God, make us contented with Thy judgment. Make us persevering in obedience to Thee and restrain us from disobedience to Thee and with the appetitive desires which necessarily lead to falling short of reaching the goal and remoteness from Thee. Bestow on us the real faith in Thee so that we may have no fear but of Thee, and no hope but in Thee, and worship nothing save Thee. Prompt us to give thanks for Thy blessings. Cover us with the garment of Thy protection. Grant us the victory through sure faith (*yaqin*) and trust in Thee. Set our faces aglow with the light of Thine attributes. Make us laugh and rejoice on the day of resurrection among Thy friends (*awliya'*). May Thine open hand be placed upon us, our households, our children, and whoever is with us, with mercy.

Commit us not to our own save keeping for a twinkling of an eye, or even less than that.

O how gracious, Thou Who answerest.
O Thou Who art He, He, He in His exaltedness, near.
O Thou possessor of majesty and honor.
O Thou Who dost encompass nights and days.

I complain to Thee of the concealment of the veil, the evil of the reckoning, and the severity of the chastisement. That is, "The Doom [of thy Lord] will indeed come to pass; there none can avert it" (Q. 52:7-8), if Thou show me no mercy.

There is no god but Thou. Glory to Thee. I was indeed wrong (Q. 21:87). [Repeat this thrice.]

Jacob pleaded his grief to Thee, and Thou didst free him from his sorrow, restore his lost sight, and reunite him with his son.

Also of old, Noah called Thee, and Thou didst deliver him from his trouble. Later Job cried to Thee, and Thou didst take away his affliction.

Furthermore, Jonah called to Thee, and Thou didst save him from his distress.

Zacharia appealed to Thee, and thou didst bestow on him a son as his own offspring after his wife had given up hope and he himself was advanced in years.

Thou didst know what befell Ibrahim, and Thou didst deliver him from the fire of his enemy.

Lot thou didst rescue together with his family from the affliction falling on his people.

Here am I, Thy servant. If Thou dost punish me by every means that Thou dost know, I am deserving of it. Wert Thou to show mercy on me, as Thou didst to them—despite the enormity of my crimes—Thou hast all the more reason and the greater right [to do so].

In showing generosity to anyone, Thou dost not exercise it particularly toward one who obeys Thee or turns toward Thee. Indeed, generosity is offered in advance to whatever person Thou desirest, even though he disobey and turn away from Thee. It is not an act of generosity that Thou shouldst show beneficence only toward those who are beneficent toward Thee—Thou, the most Generous and Self-Sufficient. Rather, generosity consists in Thy showing beneficence toward those who are maleficent toward Thee—Thou the Merciful, the most hight—just as Thou didst command us to do good to those who do us evil. Thou art more worthy of that than we.

Our Lord, we have harmed ourselves, and if Thou hadst not pardoned and shown mercy to us, surely we would have been among the losers. (Q. 7:23).

O God!
O God!
O God!
O Merciful One!
O Self-Sufficient One!
O Thou who art He!
O He![5]
If we had not been worthy to receive Thy mercy—!
O Lord!
O Lord!

O Lord!
O Master!
O Helper of one who disobeys Him!
O Master!
O Helper of one who disobeys Him!
O Master!
O Helper of one who disobeys Him!
Help us! Help us!
Help us!
O Lord,
O Generous One!
And be Merciful to us!
O Lord, O Merciful One!
O Thou, whose throne is as wide as the heavens and the earth and
    the upholding of which fatigues Him not...For He is the
    Exalted, the Mighty. (Q. 2:255)

I ask Thee for faith in Thine upholding, a faith whereby my heart finds tranquility from care for sustenance and fear of men. Draw near with Thy power so close that Thou dost remove from before me every veil which Thou didst remove from before Ibrahim, Thy friend. He had no need of Gabriel, Thy messenger, nor of his asking of Thee, but Thou didst shield him on that account from the fire of Thine enemy. And how should not one, from whom Thou didst remove the benefits of friends, be shielded from the wrongs of enemies? Nay, I pray Thee that, by Thy nearness to me, Thou shouldst remove me [from benefits of friends] until I neither see nor feel the nearness or remoteness of anything. Certainly Thou art able to do all things (Q. 2:20).

Did you then think that We created you for no purpose and that you would not be returned unto Us? So may God be exalted, the King, the True One! No god is there save Him, Lord of the throne of honor! Whoever invokes along with God another divinity for which he has no proof will have to reckon but with his Lord. Assuredly the disbelievers shall not enjoy felicity.

And say "O Lord, pardon and have compassion, for Thou art the best of those who show compassion" (Q. 23:115–118).

He is the Living One. There is no god at all except Him. So call upon Him, purifying of all others, your worship to Him. Praise be to God, Lord of the worlds (Q. 40:65).

God and His angels bless the Prophet. O ye who believe, bless him, and wish him peace (Q. 33:56).

O God, bless our master Muhammad, and the family of our master Muhammad, and consummate the bliss of our master Muhammad, and of the family of our master Muhammad, as Thou didst bless. Have compassion on and consummate the bliss of our master Ibrahim and of the family of our master Ibrahim in the worlds. Verily, Thou art worthy of praise and glory. [Repeat this thrice.]

God! Be pleased with the eminent and rightly guided successors [of Muhammad] Abu Bakr, 'Umar, 'Uthman, and 'Ali, with al-Hasan and al-Hussayn and their mother,[6] and with all the companions of the Prophet, with the followers of the Prophet, and with the followers of the next generation, with beneficence to the day of judgment. There is no strength and no power except with God, the High, the Mighty.

Blessed Supplication Known as the Litany of the Sea

The worthy Shaykh Abu al-'Aza'im Madi ibn Sultan related to me in the city of Tunis, may God the Exalted watch over it, as did also the worthy and blessed Shaykh Sharaf al-Din, son of the Shaykh (al-Shadhili) in the city of Damanhur al-Wahsh of Egypt in the year A.H. 715 that shaykh was on the point of setting out from Cairo to perform the pilgrimage to Mecca a short time after the departure of the pilgrims.[7]

He said, "I have been divinely ordered to go on pilgrimage this year. So find for us a Nile vessel in which to make the journey by way of Upper Egypt."

They looked about for a vessel, but found only one belonging to Christians on which was an elderly Christian man with his sons.

He said, "Let us get on board."

We entered the vessel and set sail from Cairo and traveled for two or three days. Then the wind shifted so that we were sailing into it. So we tied up to the bank of the Nile at an uninhabited spot. We remained there about a week within sight of the hills of Cairo.

One of the pilgrims accompanying us asked, "How is it that the Shaykh says that he was ordered to perform the pilgrimage this year when the time for it has passed? And how long will this journey take?"

In the middle of the day the shaykh slept and awoke, and then offered this prayer [known as Litany of the Sea]. "Where is the captain of the vessel?" he inquired.

"Yes" he answered, "here I am."

"What is your name?" the shaykh asked.

"Mismar."

"O blessed Mismar, unfurl the sail," the shaykh ordered.

"O my master," the captain objected, "[If I do that], we shall come again to Cairo by sailing before the wind."

"We shall again become travelers," the shaykh replied, "if God wills."

Again the captain objected, "This wind will drive us back to Cairo before the end of this day, and, furthermore, with the wind as it is, to get the ship under sail will be absolutely impossible."

"Unfurl the sail," the shaykh ordered him, "with the blessing of God." So we unfurled the sail, and God [He is exalted] commanded the wind so that it shifted and filled the sail [so quickly that they] were unable to cast off the rope from the stake. They cut it and we departed under a gentle breeze.

The captain converted to Islam, both he and his brother.

Their father did not cease to lament and say, "I have lost my two sons on this journey."

"On the contrary," the shaykh said to him, "you have gained them."

That night the Christian had a vision in which the day of resurrection, as it were, had come, and he was beholding the Garden and the fire. He witnessed the shaykh (al-Shadhili) conducting to the Garden a large crowd of people. Among them were the Christian's sons. He wanted to follow them, but he was prevented. He was told, "You are not of them until you enter their religion."

The Christian related that to the shaykh, and he [the Christian] converted to Islam. Then the shaykh told him, "The people whom you saw with me are my companions to the day of resurrection."

We continued our journey easily and successfully with incidents the telling of which would consume a long time. They finished the pilgrimage that year.

My master, Madi, related, according to a report from the shaykh,

> The Christian became one of the great saints of God. Consequently, he sold his vessel and performed the pilgrimage with us, along with his sons. He had a *zawiya* (worship place) in Upper Egypt and was one of those who were endowed with charismatic powers. This blessed journey was an occasion for the manifestation of such a power. May God have mercy on him and be pleased with him.

The shaykh said,

> By God, I did not utter it [the Litany of the Sea] except as it came from the Prophet of God, from whose instruction I learned it. "Guard it," he said to me, "for it contains the greatest name of God."

It is not recited in any place without security reigning there. If it had been with the inhabitants of Baghdad, the Tatars would not have taken the city.

> In the name of God, the Merciful, the Compassionate. Blessings of God and peace be upon our master Muhammad and his family.
> O God,
> O Exalted One,
> O Gentle One,

O All-Knowing One,
Thou art my Lord, and Thy knowledge is sufficient for me.
What an excellent lord is my Lord!
What a wonderful sufficiency is my sufficiency!
Thou plea to Thee is for protection, in movements and moments of
   rest, in words, desires, and passing thoughts, from doubts,
   suppositions and fancies—veilings, they, over hearts, occluding
   sight of the unseen.
The faithful were tried;
They were severely shaken.
Then the hypocrites would say, with those of disease-ridden hearts,
   "God and His Messenger promised us only delusion. (Q. 33:11–12)

Even so, make us firm, aid us, and subject to us this sea, as Thou didst subject
the sea to Moses, and the fire to Ibrahim, and the mountains and iron to David,
and the wind, the Satans, and the *jinn* to Solomon.

Put in subjection to us every sea of thine in earth and heaven, in this domain
and the celestial, the sea of this world and the sea of the next. Render subservient
to us every thing, "O Thou, whose hand holds sovereignty over every thing"
(Q. 23:88).

Kaf ha' ya' 'ayn sad
Kaf ha' ya' 'ayn sad
Kaf ha' ya' 'ayn sad[8]
Help us, for Thou art the best of helpers.
Open to us the hand of mercy, for Thou art the best of openers.
Pardon us, for Thou art the best of pardoners.
Be compassionate toward us, for Thou art the best of those who
   show compassion.
Sustain us, for Thou art the best of sustainers.
Guide us and rescue us from the unjust people.

Send us a gentle breeze, as Thou dost know how to do, and let it blow on
us from the storehouses of Thy mercy. Let it bear us along as it by miraculous
intervention, with security and well-being, in religion, worldly affairs, and the
hereafter.

Thou art powerful over all things.

God, facilitate for us our affairs, with ease of mind and body, with security
and well-being in religious and worldly matters. Be a companion for us on our
journey, and a substitute for our households.

Blot out the countenances of our enemies, and transform them where they
stand, disabling them from leaving or coming to us. If We willed, We would blot
out their eyes. Yet, they would race forward to the path. But how would they

see? If We willed, We should transform them where they stand. Thus, they would be unable to leave or return (Q. 36:66–67).

Ya' sin!
By the Wise Qur'an!
Surely thou art one of those sent on a straight path!

A revelation sent down by the Mighty, the Merciful, that thou mightest warn a people whose fathers had not been warned. Yet, they do not take heed.

The declaration has been confirmed against the greater part of them. Yet they do not believe. We have circled their necks with chains up to the chin, but they hold their heads high. Before them have We placed a barrier, and behind them a barrier, and We have obscured their vision; so they see not (Q. 36:1–8).

May their faces be deformed!
May their faces be deformed!
May their faces be deformed!
Let their faces be submissive before the Living, the Self-Subsistent,
    For he who is laden with wrong has already met frustration.
Ta' sin, ha' mim, 'ayn sin qaf. (Q. 27:1)

He has released the two seas that meet; Yet between them is a
    barrier [barzakh] that they do not overpass.... (Q. 55:19–20)

Ha' mim, ha' mim, ha' mim, ha' mim, ha' mim, ha' mim, ha' mim!
    (Q. 40:1)
The affair has been decreed. The triumph has come. Over us they
    shall not triumph.
Ha' mim!
[It is] the sending down of the Scripture from God,
The Mighty, the All-Knowing,
Forgiver of sin,
Receiver of penitence,
Severe in punishing,
Forbearing.
No god is there except Him.
To Him is the returning. (Q. 40:1–3)

In the name of God (bismillah) is our door.
May [God] bless our walls.
Ya' sin (Q. 36:1) is our ceiling.
Kaf ha' ya' 'ayn sad (Q. 19:1) is our sufficiency.
Ha' mim 'ayn sin qaf (Q. 42:1) is our shelter.

So God is sufficient for thee against them, for He hears all, knows all.

[Repeat this thrice]

The veil of the throne has been dropped over us, and the eye of God is gazing at us. God is behind them, round about.

Indeed, it is a glorious recital [Qur'an], inscribed on a guarded tablet [lawh mahfuz] (Q. 85:20–21).

[Repeat this thrice]

My Protector is God, Who revealed the Book (from time to time), and He will choose and befriend the righteous. (Q. 7:196)

[Repeat this thrice]

My sufficiency is God.

No god is there except Him.

In Him have I put my trust,

For He is Lord of the majestic throne (Q. 9:129).

[Repeat this thrice]

In the name of God, with whose Name nothing in the earth or sky can do harm, for He is the All-Hearer, All-Knower.

[Repeat this thrice]

There is no force and no power except with God, the High, the Mighty.

Litany of Light

Quoted from our master the worthy teacher, the saint and mystic Abu al-'Abbas Ahmad al-Mursi, and recited to his companions is the "Litany of Light." The worthy teacher and saint Abu Khadhar Mas'udi al-Kurdi related to me that it was transmitted to him by al-Mursi in Cairo in A.H. 710.

It is as follows:

I take refuge with God from Satan the Rejected One (Q. 16:98).

In the name of God the Merciful, the Compassionate. Blessings of God and peace be upon our master Muhammad, his family and companions.

Say "He is one God, God the Eternal. He has not begotten; neither was He begotten, and there was none meet for Him." (Q. chapter 112)

Say, "I take refuge in the Lord of the dawn, from the evil of what He created, and from the evil of twilight when it deepens, and from the evil of sorceresses who blow on knots, and from the evil of an envier when he envies." (Q. chapter 113)

Say, "I take refuge with the Lord of men, King of men, God of men, from the evil of the stealthily withdrawing whisperer, who whispers in the hearts of men, both *jinn* and men." (Q. chapter 114)

Praise be to God, Lord of the worlds, the Merciful, the Compassionate, King of the judgement day! Thee we worship. Thee we ask for aid. Guide us on the straight path, the path of those to whom Thou hast been gracious, not of those against whom Thou hast been angry, nor of those who go astray. (Q. chapter 1)

Alif lam mim!

That Scripture, no doubt is there in it, a guidance for the God-fearing who believe in the unseen, and perform the worship, and of what We have provided for them expend; who believe in what has been sent down to thee, and in what was sent down before thee, and have sure faith in the life to come. They are under their Lord's guidance. They are the ones who will enjoy felicity. (Q. 2:1–4)

Your god is one God. There is no divinity except Him, the Merciful, the Compassionate. (Q. 2:163)

God!
There is no divinity except Him,
The Living, the Self-Subsistent.
Neither sleep nor slumber overtakes Him.
His.
Whatever is in the heavens or the earth.
Who is he who can intercede before Him,
Except by His permission?
He knows what is before them and behind them,
But they have no comprehension of what He knows,
Save what He wills them to know.
His throne is as wide as the heavens and the earth.
Their preservation is no burden to Him.
He is the High, the Mighty. (Q. 2:255)

No compulsion in religion!
Right guidance has been distinguished from misguidance.
He who rejects belief in idols [*al-taghut*] and accepts belief in God
    has grasped the most solid handle, without crack, and God is
    All-Hearing, All-Knowing. (Q. 2:256)

God is the Protector of those who believe.
He brings them out of the dark shades into the light.

Those who have rejected belief in God have as protectors the idols
who bring them out of the light into the dark shades.
They are the people given over to the fire,
Therein to abide forever. (Q. 2:257)

To God belongeth
Whatever is in the heavens or on the earth!
Reveal what is within you, or conceal it,
God will call you to account for it.
He pardons whom He will,
And He punishes whom He will,
For God is Omnipotent. (Q. 2:284)

The Apostle believes in what was sent down to him from his Lord, as also
do the believers. All believe in God, His angels, His Scriptures, and His
messengers. We make no distinction among any one of His messengers and others.
They said,

We hear and obey.
Thy pardon, our Lord, and to Thee is the returning. (Q. 2:285)

God charges a soul only to its capacity.
In its favor is what it has earned; against it is what it has merited.
Our Lord, censure us not if we forget or commit a fault.
Our Lord, burden us not with a load like that with which Thou
didst burden those who were before us.
Our Lord, place not on us a burden beyond our strength to bear
it. Pardon us, and forgive us, and be merciful to us. Thou art our
Master. So help us against the unbelieving people. (Q. 2:286)

Alif lam mim.
God!
No divinity is there except Him, the Living, the Self-Subsistent!
He sent down upon thee the Scripture with the truth, confirmatory
of what was before it, for beforehand He had sent down the
Torah and the *Injil*[9] as guidance to men, and He sent down the
Furqan. (Q. 3:1–2)

O thou!
Enwrapped in thy mantle,
Arise and warn!
Thy Lord, magnify Him!
Thy garments, purify them!
Defilement, flee it!

Give not, begrudging it!
Toward thy Lord, be patient! (Q. 74:1-7)

Recite!
In the name of thy Lord who has created, created man of bloodclots!
Recite!
And thy Lord, the most Generous,
Who taught the use of the pen,
Taught man what he knew not! (Q. 96:1-5)

The Merciful!
He taught the *Qur'an.*
Created man.
Taught him speech.
The sun and the moon (He moves) with calculation.
Sprouts and trees prostrate themselves.
The sky, He set it on high, and placed the balance, that in the
    balance you should not deal fraudulently. (Q. 5:1-7)

Blessed be the name of the Lord, the Majestic, worthy of honor!
    (Q. 55:1-7)

Blessed be the name of the Lord, the Majestic, worthy of honor!
    (Q. 55:78) [Repeat this thrice]

All that is in the heavens and the earth praises God, the Mighty,
    the Wise.
His, the sovereignty of the heavens and the earth. He gives life and
    causes death, and over everything He has power.
He is the First and the Last, the Outer and the Inner, and of every
    thing He has knowledge.

He it is who created the heavens and the earth in six days, then settled Himself on the throne. He knows what goes into the earth and comes out of it, what descends from the sky and ascends into it. He is with you wherever you may be. Whatever you do, God sees it. His is the sovereignty of the heavens and the earth. Unto God, all things are returning. He runs the night into the day, and the day into the night. He knows the secret thoughts of the breast (Q. 57:1-6).

He is God, except Whom there is no god,
Knower of the invisible and the visible,
He, the Merciful, the Compassionate.

He is God, except Whom there is no god, the Sovereign, the Holy, the All-Peaceful, the All-Faithful, the Preserver, the Mighty, the Compeller, the Imperious. God be exalted above what they associate with Him. He is God, the Creator, the Maker, the Fashioner. His, the Most Beautiful Names. Whatever is in the heavens and the earth glorifies Him. He is the Mighty, the Wise (Q. 59:22–24).

Say, "He is God, One, God the Eternal. He has not begotten, neither was He begotten, and there was none meet for Him" (Q. chapter 112).

I take refuge with the Lord of men, King of men, God of men, from the evil of the stealthily withdrawing whisperer, who whispers in the hearts of men, both *jinn* and men (Q. chapter 114).

God, O Thou Who art thus, and true to the attributes ascribed to Thee by the sincere servants of God from among the prophets, the veracious, the martyrs, the learned men possessing sure knowledge, and saints who have attained proximity to Thee, from among the inhabitants of His heavens and His earth, and the rest of God's creatures altogether—

I petition Thee,
By virtue of these attributes;
By the verses of Scripture cited;
By all of the Beautiful Names;
By the greatest Name from among them;
By the "mother" (*umm*) and the sovereign (verse);[10]
By the final verses (*khawatim*) of *Surat al-Baqara*;
By the beginnings and the endings;
By the utterance of "Amen" in confirmation;
By the letter *ha* of "*al-Rahma*," *mim* of "*al-Mulk*," and *dal* of "*al-Dawam*."

Muhammad, Apostle of God. Those who are with him are strong against the disbelievers, compassionate among themselves. You see them inclining in worship, prostrating themselves, ardently seeking a boon from God and His good pleasure. On their faces is their distinguishing mark, the trace of prostration. That is the parable of them in the Torah, and the parable of them likewise in the *Injil*. They are like a grain of seed which, planted in the ground, sends up its blade, then strengthens it. It thickens and stands straight, pleasing the sower. This was told that, through them, He might vex the disbelievers. To those among them who believe and perform good works, God has promised pardon and a generous recompense (Q. 48:29).

Alif ha' waw nun, qaf Adam, ha' mim, ha', Amin, kaf ha' ya' 'ayn sad!
Pardon me, and show me the compassion that Thou didst show to
   Thy prophets and messengers.
Give me not by my supplication, Lord, to suffer misfortune.

I feared. And I fear that I may have fear, and thus may not be guided on the road of Thee.

So guide me to Thee, and render me, with Thee, secure from every fear and object of fear in the religious life, the life of this world, and the hereafter. Thou hast power over all things.

O God!

O Maker of the heavens and the earth! (Q. 2:117)

O Upholder of the two dwellings!

O Upholder of everything!

O Living One, O Self-Subsistent One!

O our God!

There is no god except Thee.

Be for us a Protector and Helper.

Make us secure, with Thee, from everything, so that we fear only Thee. Assign to us a place of proximity to Thee.

Shield us with that with which Thou didst shield Thy friends.

Thou dost see, but none of Thy creatures sees Thee.

Pour forth on us the most perfect and most beautiful of what is good.

Avert from us the smallest and greatest of what is evil.

Ta' sin, ha' mim, 'ayn sin qaf.

He has released the two seas that meet; yet between them is a barrier which they do not overpass. (Q. 55:19–20)

O God!

We ask of Thee,

Fear of Thee,

Hope of Thee,

Love for Thee,

Longing toward Thee,

Intimacy with Thee,

Satisfaction in Thee,

Obedience to the command from Thee,

On the carpet of contemplation of Thee,

Looking from Thee toward Thee,

Making utterance of Thee from Thee—

There is no god beside Thee!

Be Thou exalted!

O God, "We have wronged ourselves." (Q. 2:23)

But we have repented to Thee verbally and resolutely;

So relent toward us liberally and affectionately. We have performed deeds with which Thou art pleased.

So make restoration to us in our descendants. We have repented to
Thee, and we are Muslims.
O Thou the Forgiver!
O Thou the Loving One!
O Thou the Beneficent One!
O Thou the Merciful One!
Forgive us our sins. Draw us close to Thee through Thy love.
Confer on us Thy unity. Show mercy to us because of our
obedience to Thee.
Punish us not for our slackness, or delaying with something besides Thee.
Urge us forward on the right way.
Protect us from one who deviates from it.
Thou art powerful over all things.
Our God!

"O Thou who dost bring men together for a day of which there is no doubt"
(Q. 3:9), bring us together with the virtues of veracity, right intention, sincerity,
submissiveness, awe, reverence, watchfulness, light, certainty, knowledge, gnosis
(*ma'rifa*), safekeeping, divine immunity, zeal, strength, remission, pardon fluency
in utterance, clarity in exposition, and understanding of the *Qur'an*.

Endow us particularly with love, purification, attainment to the grade of the
elect, and Thy befriending.

Be for us hearing, seeing, tongue, heart, mind, hand and strengthener.

Bestow on us divine knowledge (*'ilm laduni*), righteous works, and wholesome
sustenance through which there is no veiling (*hijab*) from Thee in this present
life and no reckoning, questioning or punishment in the life to come on the
basis of the science of oneness (*'ilm al-tawhid*), and jurisprudence, free from the
defects of passion, appetitive desire, and natural disposition.

Usher us through the entrance door of veracity (*sidq*). Lead us through the
exit door of veracity, and grant us from Thy presence a power that assures victory.

O Exalted One!
O Great One!
O Gentle One!
O Knowing One!
O Hearing One!
O Seeing One!
O Willing One!
O Powerful One!
O Living One!
O Self-Subsisting One!
O Merciful One!
O Compassionate One!

O Thou who art He, He!
O He!
I make request of Thee,
By Thy greatness inherent in the supports of Thy throne,
By Thy power that Thou hast exercised over Thy creatures,
By Thy mercy that embraces everything,
By Thy knowledge that englobes everything,
By Thy will that is challenged by nothing,
By Thy hearing and seeing nearer than any thing,
O Thou Who art nearer to me than anything,
Scant is my shame! Much is my imposture.
Remote is the object of my desires; imminent is my distress.
Seer art Thou of my tribulation, perplexity, low desire, and iniquity.
Knower art Thou of my erring, my folly, my indigence, and my
    repulsive qualities.
I believe in Thee, Thy names, Thine attributes, and Muhammad,
    Thine Apostle.
Who, then, save Thee,
Will have mercy on me?
Who, then, except Thee,
Will gladden me?
So be merciful to me.
Show me the right way,
And guide me on the pathway [access to Paradise] to it.
Show me the way of error,
And keep me away from the pathway to it.
Grant me to be accompanied by the truth, light, discernment, ability
    to distinguish between the true and the false, and clarity from Thee.
Safeguard me by Thy light, O God, O Light, O True One, O Clarifier.
My God! How I have come to loathe evil!
May God be exalted!
Praise be to God!
There is no force and no strength except with God. (Q. 18:39)

So guide me by Thy light to Thy light, in whatever befalls me from
    Thee, in whatever proceeds from me to Thee, and in whatever
    occurs between Thy creatures and myself.
Hold me tightly close to Thee.
Shelter me with the shelter of Thy strength, and the strength of
    Thy shelter.
Be Thou my shield, so that nothing befalls me unless it falls upon Thee.
Put within my power the commanding of this sustenance.

Protect me from avidity and from toil in seeking it, from preoccupation of the heart and anxious attachment to it, from humiliation before men on account of it, from thinking and planning in the acquisition of it, from niggardliness and greed after acquiring it, from what occurs to the soul as a consequence of that and from the distress of dependence on Thy creatures for filling needs, a distress that Thou dost create by Thy power according to Thy knowledge and will.

Make it [as in seeking sustenance] a means to the fulfillment of the duties of servantship (*'ubudiya*)[11] and to a witnessing of the rules of divine lordship (*rububiya*).

Grant me a secret from Thy storehouse of secrets, a ray of light from Thine illuminations, recollection from Thy recollection of all things, obedience from the deeds of obedience of Thy prophets, and companionship of Thine angels.

Do Thou Thyself take charge of my affairs, and entrust me not to myself for a blink of the eye or even less.

Make me a benefaction to others from Thy many benefactions, and a mercy (*rahma*) among Thy servants through which "Thou guidest whom Thou wilt to a straight path, the path of God to Whom belongs all in the heavens and on earth. Is it not to God that all things tend?" (Q 42:52–53)

> My God!
> To Thy light guide me.
> Of Thy bounty grant me.
> From every enemy of Thine guard me.
> From all that distracts me from Thee restrain me.
> Endow me with a tongue unceasing in making mention of Thee,
> With a heart hearkening to the truth from Thee,
> With a spirit reverential in looking toward Thee,
> With an inner being possessing the spiritual realities of Thy proximity,
> With a mind stilled before Thy greatness in sublimity.
> Adorn the visible and invisible parts of me with various kinds of
>   obedience to Thee,
> O Thou the All-Hearing,
> All-Knowing,
> All-Mighty,
> All-Wise.
> My God!
> As Thou didst create me, so guide me!
> As Thou wilt have caused me to die, so life grant me!
> As Thou didst nourish them, so nourish me and with drink satisfy
>   me!
> My illness is not hidden from Thee, so heal me!
> My faults have enveloped me, so forgive me!

Bestow upon me knowledge that is in harmony with Thy knowledge, and judgment (*hukm*) that concurs with Thy wisdom.

Grant me truthfulness in speech among Thy servants, and a place among the inheritors of Thy Garden.

Deliver me from the Fire and usher me into the Garden directly and, in the end, by Thy mercy.

Show me the face of Muhammad, Thy Prophet, and lift the veil from between Thee and me.

Assign my place with Thee to be continually before Thee, gazing from Thee toward Thee.

Let fall from me the distance (*bayn*), so that, between Thee and me, there will be no separation.

Afford me such a disclosure of the inner reality (*haqiqa*) of the matter that thenceforth I shall not make inquiry for Thy servant, along with the increase [of bliss] assured through Thy generous promise.

Thou art able to do all things. (Q. 2:20)
O God,
O Mighty One,
O Wise One!

Thou hast aided whomsoever Thou wilt, with whatever Thou wilt, as Thou wilt, against whatever Thou wilt. So aid us with Thy help for the service of Thy friends, and open wide our breasts to receive Thy knowledge (*ma'rifa*) on encountering Thine enemies.

Bring to us for our service one with whom Thou art pleased so that we yield to him and humble ourselves, even as Thou didst bring help to Muhammad, Thine Apostle. And turn away from us the stratagem of him with whom Thou art displeased as Thou didst turn it away from Ibrahim, Thy friend.

Send us our recompense in this world with security from the causes of the Fire's torment, from the injustice of every despotic tyrant, and, with regard to all others, heart contentment.

Make loathsome to us this World, endear to us the Next, and grant that, therein, we may be among the righteous. Certainly Thou art able to do all things.

O God, the All-Great!
O the All-Hearing, the All-Knowing!
O the All-Beneficent, the Merciful!
Thy servant—his faults have enveloped him;
But Thou art the All-Great.
My calling is as if it were not heard;
But Thou art the All-Hearing.
I have been powerless to govern my own soul;

But Thou art the All-Knowing.
So as for me—it is for me to show mercy on it;
But Thou art the All-Beneficent, All-Merciful.
How can my sin be great,
when Thou art the All-Great?

Or how canst Thou respond to one who has not asked of Thee, or refrain from responding to one who has asked of Thee?

Or how can I govern my own soul with beneficence, when my weakness does not escape Thee? Or how can I show mercy on it in any way, while the storehouses of mercy are in Thy hand?

My God!

Thy greatness filled the hearts of Thy friends, and everything became small in their presence. So fill my heart with Thy greatness, until nothing becomes small or great in its presence.

Harken to my cry with kindness that only Thou dost possess, for Thou dost harken to everything.

My God!

My standing with Thee is hidden from me, so that I disobey Thee while I am in Thy grasp and commit outrages. So how can I plead excuses to Thee?

My God!

Disobedience to Thee has evoked my obedience, and obedience to Thee has evoked my disobedience. So, for which of the two shall I fear Thee, and for which of the two shall I find hope in Thee?

If Thou sayest disobedience, Thou wilt repay me with Thy bounty, and thus Thou wilt not have ceased to be just toward me.

If Thou sayest obedience, Thou wilt repay me with Thine equity, and thus Thou wilt not have ceased to afford me hope.

Would that I knew how I should consider my beneficence in view of Thy beneficence, or how I should ignore Thy bounty in view of my disobedience to Thee.

Qaf[12] and *jim* are two secrets from Thy secret, both of which denote other than Thou. So, with the all-comprehensive secret that denotes Thee, leave me not to any other. Thou art the All Powerful.

O God,
O Opener (*Fattah*)!
O Pardoner,
O Gracious One (*Mun'im*)!
O Guide,
O Helper,
O Mighty One!

Bestow on me such illumination of Thy names that will enable me to know for a certainty the spiritual realities of Thine essence (*dhat*).

Open to me, pardon me, be graciously disposed toward me, guide me, help me, and uplift me.

O Thou, the Uplifter!

O Thou, the Abaser!

Abase me not by allowing me to govern (*tadbir*) what is Thine to govern, and allow me not to cease to be occupied with Thee through what is Thine [with which to be occupied], for all is entirely Thine. The command is Thy command, the secret is Thy secret, my nonbeing (*'adam*) is my being (*wujud*), and my being is my nonbeing. So the truth is Thy truth, the appointing is Thine appointing, there is no divinity besides Thee. Thou art "the Plain Truth" (Q. 24:25), O Knower of the secret, and the yet more hidden.

O Thou who art ever generous and gracious to respond, Thou dost know all about Thy servant. He was distressed with petitioning Thee. So how can distress be avoided by one petition to another?

Thou hast shown such kindness to me that I know my asking of Thee to be folly, and my asking of any other to be infidelity.

So shelter me from my folly, and protect me from infidelity.

O Thou who art near, Thou the Near, though I be far removed, Thy nearness has taken away my hope in any other, and my remoteness from Thee has driven me back to petitioning Thee.

So be so bountiful to me that my petitioning becomes nought but petitioning Thee alone.

O Powerful One!

O Mighty One!

Thou art Omnipotent!

Our God!

Chastise us not for our act of willing and for the love of our desiring, for we are preoccupied with, or conceal, or find joy in having what we want. Or we are sad, or displeased, or hypocritically resigned in face of deprivation, and Thou knowest well our hearts.

So mercifully grant us the greatest felicity, the most bountiful increase, and the most perfect light. Conceal us from the world, and hide everything from us. Do Thou cause us to bear witness to Thee with the witnesses, and help us in this present life and on the day when the witnesses will stand up.

O God, O the All-Powerful,

O Willer, O the All-Great,

O Wise, O the All-Praiseworthy!

We beseech Thee, by the greatest power, by the supreme will, by the verses of Scripture and all the divine names, and by this greatest name of all of them, to subject to us this sea and every sea of Thine in earth and heaven, in this domain and the heavenly, as Thou didst subject the sea To Moses, the fire to Ibrahim, the mountains and iron to David, and the wind to the Satans, and the *jinn* to Solomon. Render subservient to us everything, "O Thou in whose hands lies the sovereignty over all, who protects others, but needs no protection" (Q. 23:88).

O God, O Exalted One, O Great One, O Kind One, O Knowing One!

Alif ha' waw nun qaf Adam ha' mim ha' amin!

God and His angels bless the Prophet. O ye who believe, bless him and wish him peace (Q. 33:56).

My God, bless our master Muhammad and the family of our master Muhammad, as Thou didst bless our master Ibrahim; and consummate the bliss of our master Muhammad and of the family of our master Muhammad, as Thou didst consummate the bliss of our master Ibrahim and of the family of our master Ibrahim in the worlds. Thou art worthy of praise and glory.

Our God! Be pleased with our masters Abu Bakr, 'Umar, 'Uthman and 'Ali, and with al-Hasan and al-Husayn, and with all the companions of the Prophet and the followers of the next generation, with beneficence to the day of judgement.

There is no strength and no power except with God, the High, the Mighty.

Thy Lord, Lord of might, is exalted above what they ascribe to Him. Peace be upon the messengers, Praise be to God, Lord of the worlds (Q. 37:180–82).

> My God! I entreat Thee by Thyself.
> God! I adjure Thee by Thyself.
> My God! As Thou wast my guide to Thyself, be my intercessor
>   before Thyself.
> My God! My good deeds are of Thy giving, and my evil deeds are
>   of Thy decreeing.

So be generous, my God, in what Thou givest according to the measure of what Thou hast decreed, so that the latter becomes canceled by the former.

He who obeys Thee in anything is not to be praised, and he who disobeys Thee in anything is not to be excused, for Thou didst declare, and Thy word is truth, "He will not be asked about what He does, but they will be asked (Q. 21:23).

Our God! Were it not for Thy gift of good deeds, we would be of those who perish, and were it not for Thy decreeing of evil, we would be of those who attain bliss. But Thou art too exalted, too great, too mighty, and too generous to be obeyed except by Thy permission and good pleasure, or to be disobeyed except by Thy sentence and decree.

My God! I did not obey Thee until Thou wert pleased that I do so. Nor did I disobey Thee until Thou didst decree that I do so. I obeyed Thee through Thy willing and the bestowal [of good deeds] by Thee upon me, and I disobeyed Thee through Thine allotment and Thine argument against me.

Therefore because Thine argument is unassailable and mine is breached, nothing remains except that Thou have mercy on me.

And since I stand in need of Thee while Thou hast no need of me, nothing is left except that Thou be my sufficiency, O Thou most merciful of the merciful.

My God! I have not committed offenses while emboldened against Thee or esteeming lightly Thy right over me.

But Thy pen (*qalam*)[13] ran on writing that, Thy sentence executed it, and Thy knowledge comprehended it. There is no strength and no power except with Thee. Acceptance of excuses is Thine. Thou art the most merciful of those who show mercy.

O God! My hearing, my seeing, my tongue, my heart, and my mind are all within Thy power. Thou didst not give me to exercise control over any of these. So whenever Thou dost decree anything, be Thou my protector (*wali*), and guide me to the straightest path.

O Thou, the Best of those to whom petition is made!
O Thou, the Most Generous of those who give!
O Thou, the Merciful of this world and the next,
Show mercy to a servant who possesses no control over this world
    or the next.
Thou art able to do all things.

An Anecdote

He said, "Passing a certain night in great mental distress, I was inspired to say"—

Thou hast bestowed on me faith, love, obedience, and union, and Thou hast received from me forgetfulness, appetitive desire, and disobedience.

My soul has flung me into the murky depths of the sea. They are black, and Thy servant is saddened, distressed, duped.

The fish of passion swallowed him, and he called to Thee with the cry of the beloved, the one divinely protected, Thy prophet and servant, Yunus ibn Matta, saying, "There is no god besides Thee. Thou art exalted. I have been one of the offenders" (Q. 21:87).

Answer my prayer, therefore, as Thou didst answer his prayer, and cast me forth on the barren shore of love in a spot isolated and lonely, and cause to rise up over me trees of kindness and tenderness.

Thou art God, the King, the Munificent. None is for me but Thee alone. Thou hast no associate. Thou art not one to break Thy promise for one who believes in Thee, since Thou didst declare, and Thy word is truth. "We responded to his petition and rescued him from distress, for thus we rescue the faithful" (Q. 21:88).

O God, O Exalted One, O the Eminent in Kindness, show kindness to me as Thou didst show kindness to Thy friends, and help me with the casting of intense fear over Thine enemies. Thou art over all things powerful.

A Devotional Recitiation (Dhikr)

O God, O Opener, O Knower!
O Thou the One without need, O Generous One!
Open my heart with light from Thee.
Be merciful to me for my obedience to Thee.
Shield me from disobedience to Thee.
Bestow upon me knowledge from Thee.
Render me free, through Thy power, from need of my power;
Through Thy knowledge, from need of my knowledge;
Through Thy willing, from need of my willing;
Through Thy life, from need of my life;
Through Thine attributes, from need of mine attributes;
Through Thy being, from need of my being;
Through Thy proximity, from need of my proximity;
Through Thy love, from need of my love;
Through Thy sincerety, from need of my sincerity;
Through Thy guarding, from need of my guarding;
Through Thy management, from need of my management;
Through Thy choosing, from need of my choosing;
Through Thy strength and force, from need of my strength and force;
Through Thy liberality, generosity, bounty, and mercy, from need of
    mine own knowledge and action.
Thou art able to do all things.

A Devotional Recitation:
Prayer for Happiness

O God!
O Thou the Knower of all!
O Thou the Willer of all!
O Thou the Powerful over all!

Thou hast girded the whole universe with Thy knowledge, and, by Thy willing, Thou hast made each part of it distinctive. The wretched man, in truth, is he who thinks that beneficence (*ihsan*) is from some source besides Thee, despite his lengthy supplications. But all lies within Thy grasp.

So make my life real, through Thine attributes, that I may be as one who has not undergone the process of creation (*takwin*), just as I was in Thy knowledge [before creation], and by an act of Thy will make me distinct from one who has his existence through a process of origination (*huduth*),[14] because Thou art not One to be described as having been originated in time (*hadith*).

Grant me sufficient light of Thy power to still my heart, as was the case with Abraham Thy friend.

Thou, Thou, my God, by Thee I am.

So I beg of Thee happiness wherewith I shall not suffer the wretchedness of looking to any other. Thou art the Omnipotent.

A Devotional Recitation:
The Veiling

O Hearer!
O Knower!
O Near!
O Answerer!
O Comprehender (*Muhit*)!
O Everlasting One (*Da'im*)!
Thou art God Who caused me to hear Thy pleasant discourse,
Who made Thyself known to me through the lifting of Thy veil,
And Who didst Thyself respond to me in a manner conformable
      with Thy will.

I found Thee comprehending, everlasting, but what was comprehended came to naught because of Thine everlastingness. If I direct my gaze toward myself, my sight fails to observe Thee. If I fix my gaze upon Thee, I have no constancy (*qarar*) despite Thy constancy. My reasoning powers ('*aql*) remove all human attributes from my idea of Thee. My heart (*qalb*) lends credence to Thee. My soul (*nafs*) is servile to Thee. My spirit (*ruh*) loves Thee, and my inner being (*sirr*) is conscious of Thy presence.

My God! Nearer to me art Thou than the discriminating power of my reasoning, the credence of my heart, the servility of my soul, the love of my spirit, or the consiousness of Thee in my inmost being. So I take refuge with Thee from my being veiled by Thine attributes.

My God! I long to be near Thee, such Thou art. So veil me not away from Thee, such as I am. There is no god besides Thee.

Thou strengthenest whom Thou desirest, for whatever purpose Thou desirest, with whatever Thou desirest. Thou art powerful over all.

A Devotional Recitation: Divine Grace

God the Gatherer and Nourisher
O Thou Resuscitator!
O Thou Inheritor!
O Thou Gatherer!
O Thou Equitable!

Thou art He who gathereth the good for whom Thou wilt and as Thou wilt, for Thou art the Gatherer, the Equitable.

Therefore, every desirable thing that is mine and not Thine, turn it away from me so that I may have nothing that is not Thine.

Nourish me with subtle graces (*lata'if*) from Thee as Thou didst nourish Muhammad, Thy Prophet. Certainly Thou art able to do all things.

A Devotional Recitation: God's Love All-Sufficient

O Thou the All-Sufficient (*Ghani*)!
O Thou the Strong!
O Thou the Potent!
O Thou the Exalted!
Whom has the needy but the All-Sufficient?
Whom has the weak but the Strong?
Whom has the impotent but the Potent?
Whom has the lowly but the Exalted?
So cause me to sit upon the carpet of sincerity (*sidq*).
Clothe me with the raiment of piety (*taqwa*),
Which is better, and one of Thy signs.
Seclude me by Thy greatness from everything of Thine.
Fill my heart with Thy love until there be room for no other.
Thou art powerful over all things.

A Devotional Recitation: Contemptibility and Respectability

How contemptible, O God, is the life of this world!
Contemptible, all that is in it!

How respectable is the life of the next world!
Respectable, all that is in it!

Thou art He who hast made the contemptible to be contemptible, and the respectable to be respectable.

It seems to me, however, that the respectable person is he who is in pursuit of other than Thou. If it were otherwise, how would he, who prefers for the sake of the life of his present world the pursuit of other than Thou, be divinely guided?

So grant me such an understanding of the real through the inner realities (*haqa'iq*) of renunciation (*zuhd*) that, with Thee, I may dispense with the pursuit of any other beside Thee.

Qaf and *jim* are two screts from Thy secret, both of which denote other than Thou. So, with the all-comprehensive secret that denotes Thee, Thou wilt not leave me to any other. Thou art the Omnipotent.

A Devotional Recitation:
On Hearing the Call to Prayer

Our God! Thou hast not made us witnesses to the creation [of our universe] nor to the creation of ourselves; and Thou hast not taken as supporters any one of those who lead others astray.

Thou didst have no associate in the Kingdom, and Thou didst have no protector because of low estate. Thou didst magnify Thyself before worshippers intent on magnifying Thee did so; and Thou didst exalt Thy being before those exalting Thee did so.

So we implore Thee by that exaltation, that implied no relationship to another and was expressed without physical means, to grant us high estate, not low estate, thereby; sufficiency, not poverty, along with it; intimacy, not annoyance, by engaging therein; and security, not fear, after it.

Aid us in our response to the affirmation of Thy unity when we seek to perform this prayerful act of obedience to Thee, as we were on the day of the original pact in Thy grasp. Thou art able to do all things.

A Devotional Recitation:
The Worship

There is no god except God, the Hearing, the Near, the Answerer.

Thou answerest the petitioner's petition, respondest to the prayer of the destitute, removest (the burden of his) ill, and appointest whom Thou desirest to be a successor.

My Lord is one who hearkens to supplication.
My Lord! Make me and my children devoted to the worship.
Our Lord! Wilt Thou accept my supplication?
"Our Lord! Pardon me and my parents and the believers on the day when the account will be taken" (Q. 14:41–42).

I ask Thee, with Thy blessing on our master Muhammad, Thy servant and Apostle, for a blessing whereby Thou wilt bring me out of the shadows of darkness into the light. Account me one of the believers, for Thou art toward the believers kind, merciful.

God! Make this worship (*salat*) a bond of union (*silah*) between Thee and me. Make it not an occasion of separartion of myself from Thee.

Make it to be a worship which restrains from the obscene and the disapproved, and remember me in it as a grace from Thee with the "greatest remembrance."

Make me to see the embodiment of the *dhikr* in my soul and in my performance. Let it accompany me as a divine gift to the end of my appointed time. Verily, Thou art pwerful over all.

A Dhikr *to Dispel Depression*

The Shaykh used to teach his companions [to recite the following *dhikr*] when in a depressed state, and they would experience joy and comfort:

O Thou, the All-Comprehensive, All-Knowing!
O Thou, Possessor of great bounty!
Thou art my Lord, and Thy knowledge is sufficient for me.
If Thou afflict me with harm, no one have I to remove it but Thee.
If Thou dost will for me some good, there is no one to repel Thy
    bounty.
Thou dost cause it to fall to the lot of whomsoever of Thy servants
    Thou willest.
Thou art the Forgiving, the Merciful.

A Devotional Recitation:
God the Living and Sole Provider

O Thou, the Living, the Self-Subsisting, there is no god but Thee!
Be for me with Thy life as Thou wast for Thy beloved ones; and be Thou the cause of my death to myself through the envelopment of Thine attributes (*sifat*), as Thou didst do for Thy sincere friends (*asfiya'*).

Render me, thereby, subsistent through immunity from others than Thou, as Thou didst for Muhammad, Thine Apostle. Thou art powerful over all things.

My God! Whenever I seek nourishment from Thee, it is because I have already sought it from others besides Thee; and if I ask of Thee that of which Thou hast assured me, it is because I have already suspected Thee.

If my heart relies on anyone save Thee, I have already committed association with Thee.

Exalted are Thine attributes above origination. So how can I be with Thee? Thou art far removed from defects. So how can I be near Thee?

Thou hast elevated Thyself above others. So how can my subsistence be in any save Thee?

My God! I ask of Thee such an understanding of divine unity that I shall not desire its contrary, and such sure faith that I shall not be carried away by uncertainty.

A Devotional Recitation:
Thanksgiving for Benefaction

O Thou whose gracious beneficence exceeds the beneficence of all benefactors, and whose thanks the thanksgiving of all thankful people is unable to express, Thou hast put to the test other than Thou who were hoping to receive something from me and from other than I who were asking of Thee. So then, everyone repairing to other than Thou is turned down, or turning to another besides Thee goes wanting and destitute.

O Thou through Whom and to Whom I have supplicated, upon Whom I have relied, and in Whom I have trusted in prosperity and adversity, my need is directed to Thee and my hopes are placed on Thee. So whatever good Thou dost judge fitting for me to assume and do, Thou art He who guides to it, who designates me for it, and who supplies me with the means to attain it.

O Thou Generous One Whom demands do not oppress! O Lord, in Whom everyone traveling the road to Thee takes refuge, unceasingly have I been surrounded by graces from Thee and the object of the customary gestures of beneficence and generosity.

O Thou Who didst give long-suffering to help bear Thine affliction, Who didst provide the giving of thanks as a means of further increase of Thy blessings, I beseech Thee to grant befitting long-suffering when trials befall, and divine assistance for thanksgiving when blessings fall.

Thy mercies are too sublime for me to thank Thee for them, and too great for one to comprehend the least of them. Therefore be graciously disposed to pardon my avowal of incapacity. Thou, for that, art more capable than I. Thy kindness is more befitting than mine, and, to show such, Thou art the more able. If, for my sin, there be no excuse acceptable to Thee, consider it to be a sin that Thou wilt forgive and a fault that Thou wilt conceal, O Thou most Merciful of those who show mercy.

In Praise of the Maker

God! To Thee belong all praise and glory! Praise without end or bounds! Uncomprehended by "before" and "after"! I am unable to praise Thee as Thou deservest. Neither tongue nor mind of any can achieve true praise of Thee.

So I praise Thee according to my ability and understanding, since I am incapable of what is fit for Thee and Thy right.

Praise is due to God, Lord of the universe (Q. 1:1), with thankful praise, the inner reality of which lies deeper than all expository formulations, and the least expressions of which surpass profuse remarks about it.

Relapse affects not His honor. Particularization of His attributes limits not His real essence.

No similitude or utterance or conjecture, whether repressed or expressed, is allowable with regard to Him. One does not enclose Him with the mind or line, or with directions left or right.

A quantity used to reckon Him does not summarize Him. An eternity is not vast enough to embrace Him. A span of time come to fulfillment does not apply to Him.

Whenever the leading expressions of praise go forth, the succeeding utterances follow closely after. I thank Thee for Thine innumerable graces, with an expression of thanks that invokes and urges an increase thereof, even though I am powerless to thank Thee, or discharge my duty in remembering Thee. For, if I formulate the idea of giving thanks, it is with the mind that has been given me; and if I speak, it is with utterance that has been proveded me; and if I devote myself to Thy service,it is with the force that has been entrusted to me. So where is the thanksgiving that I attribute to myself? All of that is Thine and from Thee.

If I were to possess in my heart the faculty of formulating an idea of giving praise without guidance from Thee, and of expressing this praise on my tongue without Thine assistance, all that would be insufficient for the urge of praise to arouse a remembrance of the least bit of the graces that I have received from Thee or the afflictions from Thee that I have disregarded.

If I should spend my whole life in devotion to Thee, so that I should never breathe except in worship of Thee, what is the attainment of that in comparison with Thy rightfully due majestic exaltation?

If some day, Thou shouldst cut off my material sustenance, I would be able to observe none of Thy commands.

Wert Thou not to preserve me from all harm, the weakest of Thy crawling creatures would distract me from the accomplishment of Thine injunctions.

Rather, divine grace (*ni'ma*) is one of the bounties of Thy generosity, and the worshiper is one of Thy weak servants (*'ibad*). If any thanksgiving is possible, it is through Thine assistance and enabling.

I ask Thee to bless our master Muhammad, whom Thou didst appoint to be the light of the right way, the guide of men to the day of the return (*mi'ad*), with a blessing that multiplies to eternity, that include an increase and prolongation, that announces to him mercy and benedictions, and bears to him my wishes for salutations and peace until the day of the gathering of all created beings.

May Thy blessing also be bestowed on his family, his companions, his wives, and the noble people of his household, and grant them abundant peace as long as the dominion of God endures. There is no force and no power except with God the Exalted, the Mighty.

A Prayer before the Prophet's Tomb

When he [al-Shadhili] approached Medina—may God ennoble and exalt it increasingly—he stood before the door of the sacred precinct from early morning until noon, bareheaded, and barefooted requesting permission of the Apostle of God to enter.

Asked why he did so, he replied, "That he might give me permission, for God says, 'O you who believe, enter not the Prophet's houses until permission be granted you' (Q. 33:53)."

Then, he heard the voice of one calling from within the Noble Garden, like that of the one dwelling there, saying "Blessing and peace in abundance, O 'Ali! Enter!"

So he stood before the Noble Garden and said, "Peace be upon thee, O Prophet, with the mercy and benediction of God! The blessing of God be upon thee, O Apostle of God!"

The most excellent, the purest, the most sublime, and loftiest prayer that he offered on behalf of any one of His prophets and chosen ones is this:

> I bear witness that thou, O Apostle of God, hast conveyed that with which thou wast sent, and hast admonished thy people, and served thy Lord until the certainty (*yaqin*) came to thee, and that thou wast as God described thee in Scripture: "An Apostle from among yourselves has come to you, for whom your adversity is hard to bear, who watches over you, and who is compassionate and merciful toward the believers." (Q. 9:128)

May the prayers of God, His angels, His prophets, His apostles, and all His creatures of the inhabitants of His heavens and His earth be upon thee, O our master, O Apostle of God.

Peace be upon both of you, O ye two companions of the Apostle of God, O Abu Bakr and 'Umar, with His mercy and blessings. So may God requite you two on behalf of Islam and its people with the most excellent reward that He has ever bestowed during his life, and for the excellence of your successorship to him over his community after his death. For, verily, you two were for Muhammad faithful ministers during his life, and you succeeded him with equity and beneficence among the people of his community after his death. May God reward both of you for that with his companionship in the Garden of Paradise, and us together with you, by His mercy. He is the most merciful of those who show mercy.

My God! I call upon Thee to bear witness, upon Thine Apostle, upon Abu Bakr and 'Umar, upon the angels who descend to visit this Noble Garden and who abide here devotedly, that I testify that there is no god at all save God alone. No associate has He.

I testify that Muhammad is His servant and Apostle, the seal of the prophets, and the leader (*imam*) of the apostles.

I testify that every command, prohibition, and information regarding the past and future that he brought is true, containing no uncertainty or doubt.

I acknowledge to Thee my crime and disobedience in thought, reflexion, will, and negligence.

Whatever Thou hast preferred for me, whether something for which Thou dost punish, if Thou wilt, or something for which Thou dost pardon, if Thou wilt, or anything that is comprised in unbelief, hypocrisy, heresy and error, or transgression or misconduct toward Thee, Thine Apostle, Thy prophets, or the angels, men and jinn who are near Thee, or whatever thing of Thy dominion that Thou hast especially allotted, in all of which I have wronged myself, bestow upon me what Thou didst bestow upon those near to Thee, for Thou art God, the King, the Generous Bestower, the Compassionate Forgiver.

A Prayer for Forgiveness

Al-Shadhili said:

> For a long time, I had been reciting the Throne verse (Q. 2:255), the last parts of the chapter of the cow from His saying, "The Apostle believes in what was sent down to him from his Lord, as do also the believers. All believe God, His angels, His Scriptures, and His messengers. We make no distinction among any one of His messengers and others." They

said, "We hear and obey. Thy pardon, our Lord, and to Thee is the returning" (Q. 2:285).

And

God charges a soul only to its capacity. In its favor is what it has earned; against it is what it has merited. Our Lord, censure us not if we forget or commit a fault. Our Lord, burden us not with a load like that with which Thou didst burden those who were before us. Our Lord, do not place on us a burden beyondour strength to bear it. Pardon us and forgive us, and be merciful to us. Thou art our Master. So help us against the unbelieving people. (Q. 2:286)

Then I recited,

"*Alif lam mim!* God! No divinity is there except Him, the Living, the Self-Subsistent!

"He sent down upon thee the Scripture with the truth, confirmatory of what was before it, for beforehand, He had sent down the Torah and the *Injil* as guidance to men, and He sent down the *Furqan*.

"Those who disbelieve the signs of God, to them a harsh punishment, for God is mighty, One Who avenges.

"God! Nothing in the earth or heavens is hidden from Him. It is He who fashions you in the womb as He wills. No god is there except Him the Mighty, Wise." (Q. 3:1-4)

I continued with the two verses:

Say, "O God, Possessor of the dominion, Thou givest the dominion
  to whom Thou wilt, and Thou takest it away from whom Thou
  wilt.
Thou dost exalt whom Thou wilt, and whom Thou wilt, Thou
  dost debase. In Thy hand is all good. Over all things Thou hast
  power.
Thou dost cause the night to run into day, and the day into night.
Thou dost bring the living out of the dead, and the dead out of the living.
Thou dost provision whom Thou wilt without calculation." (3:26-27)

My God! I ask of Thee
To be accompanied by fear (*khawf*)
To be overcome by longing (*shawq*),
To be well grounded in knowledge (*'ilm*),
To continue long in reflection (*fikr*).

We ask of Thee the secret of divine secrets which wards off harmful things, that in sin and shame we may not abide. Choose and lead us to act according to these words that Thou hast uttered to us upon the tongue of Thine Apostle, and by which Thou hast tried Ibrahim Thy sincere friend.

So he fulfilled them, and God said, "I am appointing you a leader for men." He asked, "Of my children also?"

God replied, "My promise does not apply to the evil-doers" (Q. 2:124).

So appoint us to be among his well-doing children and among the children of Adam and Noah. Make us to walk the path of the leaders of the God-fearing, for God beholds His servants.

God, I have sinned greatly against mine own soul, and only Thou dost forgive sins. So forgive me, be merciful to me, and relent toward me. "There is no god at all but Thee. Thou art exalted. I have been one of the wrong-doers" (Q. 21:87).

This prayer for forgiveness possesses effectiveness and power of precious illumination. If you offer it, you will behold wonders. Then, I would say,

O God, O Exalted One, O Mighty One,
O Clement One, O Knowing One, O Hearing One,
O Seeing One, O Willing One, O Powerful One,
O Living One, O Self-Subsisting One, O Merciful One,
O Compassionate One, O He Who is He,
O He, O First, O Last, O Outer, O Inner!
May the name of thy Lord be blessed, of Him Who is endowed with majesty and honor. (Q. 55:78)

An Invocation:
The Great Name

My God! Grant me Thy great name, having which nothing on earth or in heaven will cause harm. Bestow on me one of its secrets, having which sins will cause no harm. Assign to me from it a means whereby the needs of the heart, mind, spirit, inner soul, inward self, and body will be filled. Subsume my names below Thy names, mine attributes below Thine attributes, mine actions below Thine actions, in order that I may enjoy in inscribing of security to my account, the annulling of blame (*malama*), the descent of divine grace (*karama*), and the manifestation of Thy faithfulness.

Be for me a helper and protector in that with which Thou didst test the leaders of the guidance by Thy command. Grant me a sufficiency that, through me, Thou mightst render others sufficient, and [continuously] revive me so that, through me, Thou mightst revive whatever and whichever of Thy servants Thou desirest. Appoint me to the guardianship of the forty and to be of the pure quality of the God-fearing. Pardon me, for Thy promise does not include the evil-doers.

Ta' sin (Q. 27:1), *ha' mim 'ayn sin qaf* (Q. 42:1).

He released the two seas which meet. Yet between them is a barrier which they do not overpass (Q. 55:19–20).

Praise be to God, Lord of the worlds.
The Merciful, the Compassionate, King of the judgment day!
Thee we worship.
Thee we ask for aid.
Guide us on the straight path,
The path of those to whom Thou hast been gracious,
Not of those against whom Thou hast been angry,
Nor of those who go astray. (Q. chapter 1)

Say, "He is one God, God the Eternal. He has not begotten, Neither was He begotten, and there was none meet for Him" (Q. chapter 112).
Repeat this thrice.

A Devotional Recitation:
Inner Sight and Providence

O God!
O Light!
O Truth!
O Clarifier!
Infuse my heart with Thy light.
Grant me knowledge from Thy knowledge.
Guard me by Thy guarding.
Cause me to listen to Thee.
Give me understanding from Thee.
Provide for me a livelihood out of Thy bounty wherewith Thou
    wilt relieve me from poverty and raise me from abasement.
Dispose fittingly for me this world and the next, and enable me to attain
    to the vision of Thy face in the Garden of *Firdaus* (paradise).
Over all things Thou art powerful. (Q. 2:20)

O how excellent is the Master, and how wonderful the Helper (Q. 8:40)

A Devotional Recitation:
Granting of Requests

If you wish your requests to be granted more rapidly than in the glance of an eye, you must fulfill five conditions. They are: (1) following what has been commanded; (2) turning aside from what has been prohibited; (3) purifying the inner life (*sirr*); (4) concentration of the mind; and (5) necessity.

Take that from His saying, "Who is He Who grants the request of the necessitous whenever he calls to Him. . .?" (Q. 27:62). If you are incapable of these five, and He has not shown you an alternative, then you must isolate yourself from people, recall whatever shameful deeds and actions God wills that you recall, examine all your works, and bring before Him all the commendable actions you know which He had condoned for you, and say,

O God!
O Bestower, O Generous One!
O Thou Possessor of great abundance!

Whom has this disobedient servant besides Thee? For powerless is he to attain to acceptance by Thee, and desires have intercepted his admission to a place of obedience to Thee. There remains to me only Thy unity on which to hold. But how dare one estranged from Thee petition Thee? Yet, how can one needful of Thee fail to petition Thee, and made it sufficient for me to hope in Thee?

So reject me not, dejected, mercilessly from Thee. O Generous One! Thou hast put inviolability (*hurma*) into Thy names. Therefore, one who invokes Thee by them does not associate with Thee a thing that Thou hast granted. So by the inviolability of Thy names, O God, O King!

O Holy One, O Peace!
O Faithful, O Protector!
O Mighty One, O Almighty!
O Proud One, O Creator!
O Maker, O Fashioner!

Shield me from anxiety and grief, from debility and indolence, from cowardice and niggardliness, from doubt and wrong opinion, from the unbearable burden of debt and the coercion of men.

This I pray, for to Thee belong the most beautiful names, and all in the heavens and the earth extol Thee, the Mighty, the Wise.

My God! I beseech Thee to grant the good things of this world (*dunya*) and the good things of the religious life (*din*)—the good things of this world through security, friendliness, health, and well-being; and the good things of the religious life through obedience to Thee, trust in Thee, contentment with Thy decree, and thankfulness for Thy blessings and graces. Thou art powerful over all. (Q. 2:20)

A Devotional Recitation: Compassion

O God!
O Praiseworthy, O Glorious One, O Just One,
O Compassionate One!
O God!
O Powerful One, O Steadfast One!

Bestow upon me by Thy mercy the words wherewith to praise Thee. Thus I shall be one of the real believers. Provide me with the inner subtleties of power that will make me strong, steadfast, a bearer, and one borne in the worlds. Grant me from Thy generosity a gift whereby I shall be one of the just and God-fearing devout.

O Campassionate One, O Kind One, be kind toward me with a kindness that the imagination of no one can comprehend.

My God, I have found Thee compassionate beyond my hope in Thee. How should I not find Thee a helper when my hope is in Thee?

Whom have I if Thou sever me, and whom have I if Thou have not compassion on me?

So grant me help according to my need whence Thou knowest, while I know not, for Thou art powerful over all things (Q. 2:20).

Chapter Four

— —

His Opinions, Injunctions, Doctrine on Sufism, and Other Sciences

$\mathbf{H}$e said

A Sufi has four qualities: being characterized by the characteristics (*akhlaq*)[1] of God, abiding closely by the commands of God, relinquishment of attempting to defend one's self out of shame before God, and holding fast to the practice of spiritual converse (*bisat*) by truly passing away (*fana'*) with God.

He said

Proof (*dalil*) is divided into three classes: the way of the intellect (*'aql*), the way of the divine gift (*karama*), and the way of the inner soul (*sirr*). This third belongs to the prophets and to certain of the utterly sincere (*siddiqun*). Proof of the divine gift belongs to the saints (*awliya'*) of God who have been drawn near to Him. Proof of the intellect belongs to the learned (*'ulama*).

Some philosopher has said

Mystical knowledge (*ma'rifa*) from God comes in two ways: one, the path of "the Source of generosity" (*'ayn al-jud*); and second, the path of "the great endeavor" (*badhl al-majhud*).

The Shaykh said

"The Source of Generosity" refers to those people with whom God began with His divine gift, and who, by His divine gift, have attained to obedience to Him. The great endeavor refers to those people who, by obedience to Him, have attained to His divine gift.

He said

Certainty (*yaqin*) is a noun pertaining to the apprehension of divine realities (*haqa'iq*) without doubt and without an intervening veil (*hijab*).[2]

Mystical knowledge (*ma'rifa*)[3] is a disclosure of the sciences along with the veil. When the veil is removed, we call it certainty. He who has access to the divine realities is drawn away in rapture. He who has mystical knowledge is carried away (*maslub*) from himself. The mystical sciences are garnered treasures, and the illuminations (*anwar*) are spiritual insights (*basa'ir*). Mystical knowledge is divine amplitude (*si'a*); unity (*tawhid*) is sincerity (*sidq*); wisdom is instruction (*ta'lim*); and light is clarification (*bayan*).

The object of knowledge is of two kinds: one derived from divine bestowals (*mawahib*), and one from acquisitions (*makasib*). Acquisitons are of two kinds: one coming by way of instruction, and the other by speculation (*nazar*).

He said

The *qutb* (Sufi pole) has fifteen divine graces. If anyone should lay claim to them or some portion of them, let him manifest that he has been divinely provided with the help of mercy (*rahma*), protection from sin ('*isma*), turning to God (*inaba*), vicegerency (*niyaba*), and the help of the bearers of the [divine] Throne. He should have disclosed to him the real nature of the divine essence (*dhat*), and the envelopment (*ihata*) of the divine attributes (*sifat*). He should be endowed with the divine gift of discernment (*hukm*) and the ability to distinguish (*fasl*) among existing things, and to understand the separation of the first from the First, and what separated from it in turn, and of what has been scattered abroad in it. He should be able to discern the past and the future, as well as what was neither before nor will be. He should possess knowledge of the beginning (*bad'*), which is the science that embraces every science and every known thing that started from the first secret (*al-sirr al-awwal*) and continues to its final end and then returns to its origin.

He said

Real knowledge (*al-'ilm al-haqiqi*) is the kind that contrary propositions (*addad*) and texts serving as evidentiary examples for the disproof of similars (*amthal*) and equals (*andad*) do not challenge. Rather, it is like the knowledge of an apostle, of one utterly sincere (*siddiq*) or a saint (*wali*). He who enters this arena is like one engulfed in the sea whose waves break over him. In this situation, what partisans of the use of contrary propositions can vie with him, or find him, or hear him, or see him? He who has not entered this arena has need only of the saying of God, "There is nothing like unto Him." (Q. 42:11)

He said

The Sufi Way is the holding of one's course toward God by four things. He who accomplishes them is one of the veritable mystics well-versed in the science of reality (*siddiqin muhaqqiqin*). He who accomplishes three of them is one of the friends (*wali*) of God who have been drawn near to Him. He who accomplishes two of them is one of the firmly believing martyrs (*shuhada'*). He who accomplishes one of them is one of the upright servants of God.

The first of these four is remembrance (*dhikr*), the basis of which is righteous works, and the fruit of which is illumination. The second is meditation (*tafakkur*), the basis of which is perseverance, and the fruit of which is knowledge (*'ilm*). The third is poverty (*faqr*) the basis of which is thankfulness, and the fruit of which is an increase of it. The fourth is love (*hubb*), the basis of which is dislike of the world and its people, and the fruit of which is union with the beloved.

Rule of the Religious Retreat ('Uzla)

Know, may God help you, that if you desire to attain union (*wusul*) with God, ask God's aid, sit upon the carpet of sincerity (*sidq*), contemplating and remembering Him by the *dhikr* in truth. Bind your heart to the practice of pure servantship (*'ubudiya*) to obtain mystical knowledge (*ma'rifa*). Continue in thanksgiving, watchfulness (*muraqaba*),[4] repentance to God, and asking pardon.

I shall enlarge upon this summary to you in order that no mistake may occur in connection with it in your attainment of union (*wusla*) with God. That is, you say, "God, God," for example; or whatever *dhikr* God may will, watching over your heart with holy fear (*taqwa*) while ceasing to avert evil from or procure some good for yourself. You will find that in two verses of The Book of God where He says, "Nay, who is there that can help you, (even as) an army, besides God Most Merciful?" (Q. 67:20). This verse is one of averting evil. With regard to procuring some good, He has said, "Who is there that can provide you with sustenance if he were to withhold His provisions?" (Q. 67:21).

The characteristic of the *dhikr* is that you invoke with your tongue while you watch over your heart. If any good comes upon you from God, you accept it; and if the contrary comes upon you, you disapprove it, having recourse to God with respect to averting and procuring, as I have described to you. Beware lest you avert from or procure for yourself anything except by God. If any fault, or defect, or consideration of a right religious act or pleasing religious experience pervades your inner soul (sirr), hasten to repentance (tawba) and seek pardon from all these.

Concerning seeking pardon for the fault or the defect, it is obligatory according to the religious law. With regard to seeking pardon for a right act or pleasing religious experience, it is for some defect ('illa) contained therein. Consider the Prophet's seeking pardon after the good news and the certainty of "forgiveness of his earlier and later faults" (Q. 48:2). This was by a man under divine immunity from error who had committed no sin at all. So then, what do you think of one who is not without fault or defect at any time?

Concerning sitting upon the carpet of sincerity, make real in yourselves your attributes of poverty, weakness, impotence, and lowliness. Persevere in them, looking unto His attributes of sufficiency, power, force, and exaltedness. The former are some of the attributes of servantship ('ubudiya), whereas the latter are attributes of lordship (rububiya). With all sincerity, persist in your attributes, and do not remove from them what does not pertain to you, lest you be numbered among those who are thoroughly frustrated because of the inversion of the truths of the matter. So say

O Sufficient One!
O Strong One!
O Potent One!
O Exalted One!
Whom has the needy but the All-Sufficient?
Whom has the weak but the Strong?
Whom has the impotent but the Potent?
Whom has the lowly but the Exalted?

So cause me to sit upon the carpet of sincerity. Clothe me with the raiment of piety (taqwa), which is righteous and one of Thy signs.

Seclude me by Thy greatness from everything of Thine. Fill my heart with Thy love until there be room for no other. "Thou art powerful over all things" (Q. 2:20). May God bless our master Muhammad, his family, his companions, and give them peace.

Help-Procuring Sayings on Entering the Religious Retreat

Hold fast to these sayings and be not hasty with regard to any of your affairs. Say,

In the name of God,
By God,
From God,
Toward God,
And "in God let the trustful trust." (Q. 14:12)

The following are formulas of contentment and of enlarging of the chest (*sadr*) for whatever distress may come upon you in the religious retreat

My sufficiency is God;
I believe in God;
My contentment is in God;
My trust is in God;
There is no force at all except with God.

Say in some of your spiritual converse (*munajat*) and petitioning,

O Thou whose throne extendeth over the heavens and the earth, and the upholding of both of which burdeneth Him not, the High, the Great (Q. 2:255), I ask Thee for such a faith in Thine upholding that my heart will remain undisturbed and free from anxiety for sustenance and from fear of men. Draw near to me with Thy power, so close that Thou dost remove from before me every veil which Thou didst remove from before Ibrahim, Thy friend. He had no need of Gabriel, Thy messenger, nor of his asking of Thee, and Thou didst shield him on that account from the fire of his enemy. And how should not one, whom Thou didst remove from the benefits of friends, be shielded from the wrongs of enemies? Nay, I pray Thee that, by Thy nearness to me, Thou shouldst remove me from benefits of friends until I neither see nor feel the nearness or remoteness of a single thing. "Thou art powerful over all things." (Q. 2:20)

Section on Overcoming Satan

If anyone desires that Satan should not have power over him, let him strengten his faith (*iman*), his trust (*tawakkul*), and his servantship before God by expressions of neediness, of seeking refuge with God, and of soliciting his protection.
God has said

He [Satan] has no power over those who believe and who put their trust in their Lord. (Q. 16:99)
For thou hast no power over My servants. (Q. 15:42)
Whenever incitement from Satan arouses you, seek refuge with God. (Q. 7:200)

Faith is strengthened by thanksgiving for graces, endurance under trial, and contentment with the divine decree. Trust is strengthened by parting company with the lower self (*hijran al-nafs*), forgetting men, depending on the Sovereign or the True One, and persistence in invoking God in the *dhikr*. God has said,

"O you who believe, when you encounter a body of soldiers, stand firm, make frequent mention of God that you may be successful" (Q. 8:45).

Servantship (*'ubudiya*) is strengthened by persisting in neediness, impotence, weakness, and lowliness before God. The opposites of these are the attributes of lordship, and what have you to do with them? So hold fast to your attributes while depending on the attributes of God. Then say, as an expression of genuine neediness, "O Sufficient One, whom has the needy but Thee?" As an expression of weakness, say, "O Powerful One, whom has the weak but Thee?"

On the carpet of lowliness, you should say, "O Exalted One, whom has the lowly but Thee?" You will obtain the favorable response as if it were subservient to your authority. Ask God to help you and practise endurance, for God is with those who endure.

For one who is a chronic sufferer from the gnawing of physical appetite (*shahwa*), who is subservient to his passion (*hawa*), whose self (*nafs*) is not conducive to his finding release, and who is defeated beyond possibility of becoming free, servantship consists in two things.

One is the acknowledgement of the favors from God in the religious faith and the divine unity that He has bestowed on him, as He has endeared these to him and made them objects of beauty in his heart, and has rendered reprehensible to him those things that are the contrary, such as disbelief and acts of perversion and disobedience. So you should say,

> My Lord, Thou hast bestowed these upon me and Thou hast called me *rashid* (walking in the right way). So how can I despair of Thee when Thou dost provide for me by Thy grace, even though I be one who lags behind? I entreat Thee to receive me, even though I go astray.

The second thing is seeking refuge in God and standing in need of Him continually. You should say, "Save, save, deliver me, and rescue me."

There is absolutely no other way for one whom the decrees have overpowered and severed from servantship directed uniquely to God, except these two things. If he fails in the practice of both of these, wretchedness will result and estrangement [from God] will be inevitable. From this, let us take refuge with God.

Perils of the Religious Retreat

Know that the perils of the religious retreat for novices (*'awamm*) who are directing themselves toward God by the path of mystical knowledge (*ma'rifa*) and by rectitude (*istiqama*) in walking the way of knowledge (*'ilm*) to God are four: the attachment of the lower self (*nafs*) to worldly ties (*asbab*); the heart's (*qalb*) inclination toward a particular direction for acquisition (*iktisab*); the intellect's (*'aql*) contentment with whatever approximation [to knowledge] may come to it; and the Adversary's prompting of the fancies of the mind that deter you from attaining your objective.

Know that its perils likewise for the elect Sufis (*khawass*) are four: seeking to be familiar with the Whisperer (*waswas*); talking about returning to the society of men; setting limits to time, which is one of the signs of spiritual bankruptcy; and harkening to the mysterious voices (*hawatif*) of *jinn* upon the assumption of His (*being heard*) by the customary physical sense.

For each peril, there is a means to struggle against it—that is, by referring [everything] to the principle of divine unity (*tawhid*) and to mystical perception, and by undertaking to follow the way of [spiritual] rectitude. Whenever the idea of being attached to means of earning a livelihood (*asbab*) should cross your mind, or if you are inclined in a particular direction for acquisition (*iktisab*), turn [your lower self] back to the source of the knowledge of the preeternal decrees (*sawabiq*) with regard to what He has apportioned and caused to be fulfilled for it. Then, say to it, "Make in the presence of God a covenant that you will never receive sustenance except by this means and from this source." Constrain it with mystical perception, submerge it in the sea of Unity, and say, "Whatever God has willed is, and what He has not willed is not." Similarly, someone has said, "Submerge the world in the sea of Unity before it submerges you."

If you should suffer the suggestion to have a mind (*'aql*) contented with whatever [religious] knowledge (*'ilm*), (*religious*) works, light, guidance or secret communication (*najwa*) may accrue to it, be not heedless of the preeternal decree and ultimate fulfillment, nor of the action of the Free One Who does what He wills and shows regard neither for the good deeds of him who advances nor for the evil deeds of him who turns his back.

If suggestions from the Adversary should occur to you to dissuade you from your objective—suggestions that come in three ways, whether by way of the interests of this world, the hereafter; or by way of favors, stations, and states in the grades of ascent that deter you from your objective, the objective being sheer servantship and the awareness of the Being of the True One without any creatural support—then God requires of you that you be to Him a servant, and you on your part want Him to be as Lord to you. When you are a servant to Him, He is a Lord to you. When He is a Lord to you, because you do what is pleasing to Him, you are a servant to Him. As He allows you no other way to the divine realities, so how much less could He with the desires of the mind? Know this matter and be very certain of it. Seek God's aid and persevere, for God is with the persevering.

If you are one of those in the grade of the elect (*khawass*) who are directing themselves to God, and if, in your retreat, you are beset by the whisperings with regard to something resembling knowledge (*'ilm*) that has come presumably by way of inspiration (*ilham*) and unveiling (*kashf*), whereas it is the product of the imagination (*tawahhum*), be not receptive but return to the decisive truth from

Scripture or *Sunna*. Know that, if what beset you were a self-evident truth, and if you referred it to a truth in His Scripture or the *Sunna* of His Apostle, then, in that matter, you would be without reproof.

For you say, "God has warranted to me immunity from error with respect to the Scripture and the *Sunna*, but He has not warranted it to me with respect to the unveiling (*kashf*),[5] inspiration (*ilham*), and vision (*mushahada*)."

How is it that you have accepted that supposed knowledge by way of inspiration while you have not accepted it except by referring to the Scripture and *Sunna*? So, if you have not accepted it except by these two, what is your idea in having friendly communication with whisperings that excite the imagination? So bear this matter in mind that you may rest upon a clear proof (*bayyina*) from your Lord, and the witness will follow that. With the clear proof there is neither error nor obscurity. Praise belongs to God.

Whenever, in the religious retreat, you are prompted to contemplate returning to society to display to the people what you have attained, then you are still with them and you have in no sense left them. Be not deceived by the withdrawal of your body while your heart is with them. So flee to God. If anyone flees to God, He will provide for him a refuge. Fleeing to Him is characterized by aversion from them and love toward God (*al-Haqq*) while seeking refuge and divine protection. "If anyone seeks protection with God, he is led to a straight path" (Q. 3:101).

Whenever you are beset by the thought of setting limits to time, struggle against it with all known possible opposing forces that you can bring to bear against it, in so far as it be allowable to do so. Direct your spiritual stamina (*himma*) toward God with holy fear, that He may make for you a way out from that situation and provide for you whence you do not reckon.

If the voices (*hawatif*) of God, the True One, attract you, their perils lie in adducing the sensations (*mahsusat*) as evidence of the unseen realities. Do not relate the one to the other. If you do that, you will be one of the ignorant ones. Enter into no consideration of that with your reasoning ('*aql*). Be at their coming as you were before their occurrence, until God Himself assumes the responsibility for their explanation and elucidation, for "He assumes responsibility for the righteous" (Q. 7:196).

Fruits of the Religious Retreat

The fruit of the religious retreat is the obtainment of divinely bestowed favors. They are four: the removal of the veil (*kashf al-ghita'*), the descent of mercy, experiencing true love, and veracity (*sidq*) in speech. God has said, "And when he (that is, Ibrahim) separated himself from them and that which they worshiped beside God, we bestowed on him Isaac and Jacob as a farther gift, and we made each of them righteous" (Q. 9:49).

Watchfulness

So then, O thou traveler on the road of the Hereafter, it is incumbent upon you to accomplish what you have been commanded concerning your outward conduct (*zahir*). When you have done that, sit upon the carpet of watchfulness (*muraqaba*) and undertake the purification (*takhlis*) of your inner life (*batin*) until there remains therein nothing that He has forbidden you. Give to the legal prescription (*hadd*) its due. Diminish your attention to your outer self if you desire the opening of your inner self to the secrets of the kingdom of your Lord.

Whatever involuntary thoughts (*khatarat*) come over you to hinder you from the object of your desire, be cognizant, in the first place, of your Lord's nearness to you. Knowing this, your heart rejoices when you constantly consider how He has procured for you the things that are beneficial to you and averted the things that cause you harm.

Consider this: "Is there a creator other than God who nourishes you from heaven and earth?" (Q. 35:3). Of the earth is your lower self (*nafs*), but of heaven is your heart (*qalb*). Whenever, then, anything descends from heaven to earth, who is he who will turn it away from you except God? "He knows what goes into the earth and what comes forth from it, what descends from heaven and what ascends to it, and He is with you wherever you may be" (Q. 57:4).

Therefore, give to watchfulness its due by continuing in servantship with respect to His statutes, and abstain from contending with lordship with respect to His actions. For if anyone contends with Him, he will suffer defeat, because "He is victorious over His servants. He is the Wise, the All-knowing" (Q. 6:18). How excellent is the True One!

What I am saying to you is that there is not one breath of your breathing that God does not control, whether you be one yielded or a contender.[6] For you desire to yield at one time, but God refuses everything at that time except contending; and you desire contending at another time, but God refuses everything except yielding.

This watchfulness points to His lordship in all His actions, especially with one who is occupied with tending his heart for the attainment of His realities. If the matter is as described, give due respect to proper conduct with regard to whatever may come over you, in that you will not consider that anything pertaining to you is first, save by testifying to His firstness; or last, save by testifying to His being last; or outward, save by testifying to His outwardness; or inward, save by testifying to His inwardness. For, if you imagine youself to have the attribute of firstness of the First, you have in view what is first in respect of whatever He causes to be first.

If there comes over you some involuntary thought (*khatir*) of something desirable and congenial to the self (*nafs*), or of something reprehensible and in disharmony with it from among those things that the divine law has not forbidden, then consider what God creates in you through the effect of what occurs to your mind as a stray thought. If you discover some admonition, it is for you to verify its reality, for that is the proper thing for you to do that time. You do not have recourse to anything else. However, if you cannot verify its reality, then wait before Him, for that is the proper thing for you to do at that time. Whenever you turn to someone else, you miss your way. If you are not able to do that, then you must trust, be contented, and be submissive. If you do not find the way to do that, you must make supplication to God for a procuring of benefits and an averting of harms, on condition of yielding and committing yourself to God. I caution you against choosing for yourself, for it is an evil with the people of insight.

So there are four rules of conduct: the rule of verification, the rule of waiting, the rule of trust, and the rule of supplication. He who verifies the admonition is preserved from it. He who waits before Him has need of no other. He who puts trust in Him dispenses with making his own choices through the choosing of his Lord. He who makes supplication to Him, on condition of drawing near with love, will be given a favorable response—only if God wills and according to what is for his welfare—or deny him, if He wills, that which is not for his welfare. Each rule has its application.

The first is the application of verification (*tahqiq*). Whenever a passing thought (*khatir*) comes to you from some source other than God, and it discloses to you His attributes, then sit down there brooding within you inner soul, for you are forbidden to witness any other.

The second is the application of waiting. Whenever a passing thought comes to you from a source other than God, and it discloses to you His actions, wait there with your inmost thought. It is forbidden that you witness other than His attributes, as an internal witness and in the visionary consciousness. First there is the passing away (*fana'*) of the witness, and then the continuance of the visionary consciousness.

The third is the application of trust (*tawakkul*). Whenever a passing thought comes to you from a source other than God—I mean whatever desirable or undesirable thing mentioned previously—and it discloses to you its defects, then you should sit upon the carpet of His love, trusting in Him, contented with whatever effects of His action may come to you in the illumination of His veils.

The fourth is the application of supplications (*du'a*). Whenever a passing thought comes to you from a source other than God, and it discloses to you your need (*faqr*) of Him, it is an indication to you of His sufficiency. Assume for yourself the carpet of neediness, and beware lest you descend below this stage to some other, thereby incurring the plotting of God whence you are unaware. The least that you can expect, if you descend therefrom, is that you will return to your lower self, looking after its interests and making choices for yourself.

Now look to your inner states (*ahwal*). You have no religious state at all if you incite the self to exertion and struggling, whether in respect of your external acts or your inner life, out of desire to avert evil thereby from your lower self. How evil is your state whenever you strive to avert from it what God desires to avert? So, how would it be if you vied with Him in averting from yourself what He desires not to avert? The least thing in this matter is the allegations of association (*shirk*), for you say that you are the one who has conquered. But you have not conquered. For, if you are a conqueror, then, be as you will, you will never be as you will. Your striving (*ijtihad*) is a proof of your extreme ignorance of the actions of God. How ugly is an ignorant worker or a corrupt learned man (*'alim*)? For I know not with what words to describe you, whether with ignorance or with corruptness or with both together.

We take refuge with God from the self's being divested of acts of self-mortification and the heart's being devoid of acts of contemplation, because divesting (*ta'til*)[7] nullifies the divine law, and voiding the heart of contemplation nullifies oneness (*tawhid*), and the Judge of the divine law brought the two together. If you relinquish vying with your Lord, you will be a believer. If you act according to the pillars of the divine law, you will be a follower of the *sunna*. If you bring the two together in true union, you will be one who has attained the Reality. "Has it not sufficed that your Lord is witness of all things?" (Q. 41:53). So then if there also comes to you in your state of watchfulness a passing thought of something disapproved or undesirable according to the divine law, with regard to something of your past, consider what it calls to mind and be admonished. If it calls God to mind, then the proper thing for you is to declare His unity on the plane of devotion to Him alone.

If you have not been in that situation, the rules of decorum require that you catch a vision of His bountifulness manifested in the gifts of His mercy with which He has surrounded you, and in your obedience to Him with which He has adorned you by making you the special object of His love (*mahabba*) in the display of His friendship (*mawadda*).

If you have descended below this stage, and have not been in that situation, the rules of decorum require that you see His bountifulness in that He has covered you, in whatever act of disobedience toward Him you have committed, without disclosing your shame to any of His creatures.

If you have been turned away from this and are reminded of your disobedience without remembering the three preceding rules of decorum, then observe the rule of supplication, repenting of the act of disobedience, or of a similar act, and seeking forgiveness for it, just as a confused guilty culprit would seek it. This is relative to the thing legally disapproved. However, whenever there comes to you a passing thought in consequence of a previous act of obedience, and you recall Who has granted it to you as a benefit, be elated not over it, but by its Author, for if you are elated by any other, you have already fallen from the grade of mystical realization (*tahqiq*).

If you were not of this station (*manzila*) of recalling the Author of the act of obedience, then be in the one below it—that of being conscious of the great bountifulness of God toward you, because He has made you to belong to the people of this lower station, the heritage of which is being provided with good from it. This good is even one of the tokens that point to the validity of that lower station.

If you are not made to lodge there, but to lodge in a place below it, then the rule of decorum for you is to examine minutely this act of obedience and ask, is it really an act of obedience for which you are secure from being called to account? Or is it the opposite of that for which you are held punishable? We take refuge with God from good deeds that become evil deeds through misreckoning, for, as Scripture says, "there appeared to them from God things upon which they had not reckoned" (Q. 39:48).

If you descend from this grade to some other, then the proper thing for you is to seek to escape from it with its good and its evil. Flee more often from your benefactions than from your malefactions, if you desire to be one of the righteous.

On Sainthood

Know that, if you wish to have some share in what the saints (*awliya'*) possess, you must cast off humans altogether, except those who direct you to God with a trustworthy sign and (*unquestionable*) solid works (*a'mal thabita*) that neither Scripture nor Sunna will render invalid. Shun the world entirely, and be not of those who shun it in order to receive something on that account. Rather, do it as a servant of God who has ordered you to cast off His enemy.

So whenever you come to the religious retreat with these two good habits of mind, shunning the world and renouncing the company of human beings, practice devotion to God with watchfulness, and continue in repentance to God with spiritual mindfulness, in seeking pardon with contrition (*inaba*),[8] and in submitting to the divine statutes with rectitude (*istiqama*).

The explanation of these four things is that you remain a servant of God in whatever you do or refrain from doing, while you watch over your heart lest you see in God's kingdom anything belonging to any one except Him. If you come with this (that is, something belonging to another), the voices (*hawatif*) of God will call out to you from the illuminations of splendor, saying "You have strayed from the right path."

How can it be that the practice of devotion to God with watchfulness is your doing, since you hear Him saying, "God watches over all things" (Q 33:52)? In this case you should be overcome by such shame that you are driven to repentance

— 118 —

for what you considered nearness to God by your own watching. So, persist in repentance with spiritual mindfulness lest you view that experience to be in any way your own doing and therefore return to your previous state. If this repentance is genuine on your part, the voices will call out to you again on behalf of God, saying "Repentance is not of yourself. Indeed, contrition is from Him, and your being occupied with one of your own attributes is a hindrance to the object of your desire."

In that case, you are considering your own attributes, but you should seek refuge with God from them and begin to implore pardon with contrition. For imploring pardon is seeking concealment from your attributes by having recourse to His attributes. If you are in this condition—I mean seeking pardon with contrition—He will soon proclaim to you

> Yield to My statutes, desist from contending with Me, and comply closely with My will by putting aside your will. It is only lordship that has been invested with power over servitude. Be a slave in bondage, having power over nothing, for when have I seen you in possession of any power over nothing, for when have I seen you in possession of any power which I have entrusted to you, for I am cognizant of all things.

If you are well grounded in this matter, and if you adhere to it, you have, thereby, a view over secrets that are hardly heard from any one in the universe.

Contraction (Qabd) and Expansion (Bast)

Seldom is the servant free from these two states that come on us alternately as the succession of night and day, and God requires of you an attitude of servitude with respect to both.

Anyone whose soul experiences a time of contraction either knows the cause for it or does not know it. There are three causes of contraction: some sin which you have committed; or some worldly goods that you have lost or that are lacking; or an evil-doer who injures you or your honor, or imputes to you irreligion or something else.

When contraction comes from one of these causes, servantship consists in returning to knowledge of the faith, dealing with it as the religious law has commanded you—in respect to the sin, with repentance, contrition, and seeking cancellation (*iqala*); in respect to some worldly goods that you have lost or that you lack, with resignation, acquiescence, and reckoning a recompense from God; and in respect to injury done you by an evil-doer, with patience and forbearance. Take care not to harm yourself, lest two harms unite to injure you—the harm of others toward you, and your harming of yourself.

If you exercise the requisite patience and forbearance, He will recompense you with ease of heart so that you pardon and forgive. Perhaps He will provide you with such light of contentment that you will be able to have compassion on him who has wronged you, or so that you will supplicate for him and your supplication will be answered in his favor. How excellent is your condition whenever God shows mercy on your account toward someone who has wronged you! This is the grade of the veritable mystics (*siddiqin*) and the merciful. So trust in God, for God loves the trustful.

Whenever there comes over you a feeling of contraction for which you do not know a cause, know that time is in two periods—night and day. Contraction is an experience most resembling the night, while expansion resembles the day. So, when contraction comes from no cause known to you, your duty is to remain quiet. Quietness refers to three things: utterances, desires, and movements. If you do that, the night will soon depart from you with the rising of your day, or a star will appear to guide you, or a moon will appear to provide illumination.

The stars are the stars of knowledge of the faith. The moon is the moon of Unity (*tawhid*). The sun is the sun of intuitive knowledge (*ma'rifa*). If you move about in the darkness of your night, you will hardly be saved from destruction. Ponder this saying of God: "Out of His mercy He has appointed for you the night and the day that you may be at rest and seek earnestly after His bounty, and perchance you will give thanks" (Q. 28:73). This is the rule of servantship in relation to contraction as a whole.

With regard to him whose time (*waqt*) is expansion, inevitably he either knows or does not know a cause for it. There are three causes. The first is an increase of spiritual blessings through obedience, or the receiving of something from the One obeyed, such as faith knowledge, and intuitional knowledge. The second cause is an increase of earthly goods by acquisition, miraculous supply, gift, or present. The third cause is praise and commendation of men by their flocking to you, asking of you an invocation, and kissing you hand.

Whenever expansion comes upon you for one of these causes, servantship (*'ubudiya*) requires that you consider the grace and favor upon you to be from God. Take care lest you hold any part of them to be from yourself, and beware of them lest fear take hold of you—fear of being bereft of what He has bestowed upon you, so that you become as one despised. This is relative to the act of obedience and the favor from God.

The increase of worldly goods is a grace also like the preceding. However, be cautious of their hidden perils. In respect to men's praising and commending you, servantship requires thanksgiving for His favor in covering your faults. Also, servantship requires fear, lest He bring to light an atom of any hidden part of you so that men nearest you loathe you. These are, on the whole, the rules of conduct for contraction and expansion in respect of servantship. Our help is with God.

With regard to expansion for which you do not know a cause, servantship demands that you refrain from questioning, acting affectedly, and rushing upon women and men. Only say, "Lord, save, save, until death." So this is the matter, if you understand. Peace to you.

Loss and Gain

Know that loss (*faqd*) and gain (*wajd*)[9] come over us alternately as the succession of night and day. The matter revolves about four points: being thankful for the blessings of God when you are in a state of gain; being acquiescent toward God when you are in a state of loss; being generous of your abundance when you have been supplied; and commiting your way to God in everything you purpose. And, "If they dispute with you, then say, 'I have committed my way to God, as have those who follow me;' and say to those to whom the Scriptures have come and to those who have no Scripture, 'Have you resigned yourselves?' If they resigned themselves, they are rightly guided; but if they turn away, your duty is only to convey the message, for God beholds His servants" (Q. 3:20).

Be not a contentious servant, nor an obstinate ascetic, nor an inordinate rebel, nor a contentious slanderer. If you attain the foregoing four states, you will enter into the praise of God through His word, "grateful for His blessings. God chose him and guided him to a straight path" (Q. 16:121).

He [al-Shadhili] said,

> The saint (*wali*) is kept secure from involuntary thoughts (*khawatir*) and evil whisperings (*wasawis*) in four situations. These are: during the worship, during supplication and seeking refuge with God, when difficulties befall, and when they are removed. In these situations nothing occurs or clings to their hearts save God. Their hearts are guarded and kept secure from all except four kinds of things: from thoughts of the hereafter and its opposite; from the remembrance of the saints and their opposites; from the remembrance of acts of obedience and their opposites; and from the remembrance of the real truths of the faith and their opposites. They are kept secure from all involuntary thoughts, from all except these four, on account of the advantages they contain for the accomplishment of servantship free from thoughts rising up from the opposite source (for example, the whisperings). How could that not be, since the messages of our Lord upon the tongue of our Prophet Muhammad are replete with every mention of God? So do not argue this matter at all. Observe proper conduct (*adab*) in whatever occurs in your heart. Seek protection with God and place your trust in Him, for God loves those who place their trust in Him.

You should exercise holy fear (*taqwa*) in three areas—fear in making resolutions ('*aza'im*), fear in requiring yourself to do what you resolve, and fear in the changing (*tahwil*) of states and places. Trust (*tawakkul*) is the apex of religious works, and renunciation (*zuhd*) is their foundation. Holy fear in resolutions means resolving, with reference to good, to perform it, and with reference to evil, not to perform it.

Then, you require of yourself at another time, with a renewal of holy fear, to act as you have resolved and to refrain from acting as you have resolved. Then, in your outer and inner states you experience changes of states, such as outwardly, with dignity and abasement, sufficiency and neediness, good health and illness, adversity and good fortune, and others; and inwardly, with contraction and expansion, fear and hope, and others. Among them also are pride and humility, fear of poverty, sense of security, and the remainder of contrasts. So you should give to holy fear its due portion in the various states and attributes in changing from city to city and from locality to locality, and so on.

Consider His sayings, "Whoever fears God, to him will He grant a prosperous issue" (Q. 65:4), "Whoever fears God, for him will He make his affair easy" (Q. 65:2), and "Whoever fears God, his evil deeds will He forgive and his reward will He increase" (Q. 65:5). So act with understanding and put all holy fear in its proper place. You will see marvels and the mysteries of God. "If anyone puts his trust in God, to him will He be all-sufficient" (Q. 65:3). If anyone practices renunciation with regard to the things of this world, he is beloved of God. If anyone is beloved of God, God protects him, God guards him, and God puts him in His shelter and place of security, in His safekeeping, and in His place of refuge. If anyone turns away from the warning of the Merciful for one breath or two, one moment or two, or one hour or two, "We will cause a Satan to take hold of him, and he shall be for him a companion. They will bar them from the path, while they reckon themselves to be rightly guided" (Q. 43:37).

He [al-Shadhili] said,

If anyone desires that some sin should not do him harm, let him say, "I seek refuge with Thee from Thy punishment on the day when Thou wilt raise Thy servants,"
And,
"I seek refuge with Thee from speedy punishment and from the evil reckoning, for Thou art quick to retaliate and Thou art the forgiving, the merciful. My Lord, I have wronged myself exceedingly. So forgive me and relent toward me. There is no god at all save Thee. Praise be to Thee. I have been one of the wrong-doers."

He said,

If you desire that your heart should not become tarnished, that no care or anxiety should afflict you, and that no sin should remain against you, say often,
"May God be extolled! May God the Greatest be extolled! There is no god at all save God!"
And,
God, establish the knowledge of these sayings in my heart. Pardon my sin. Pardon the believers, both men and women."
And say,
"Praise be to God and peace be upon His servants whom He has chosen."

He said,

If you desire to vanquish all evil, to overtake all good, and to be outstripped by none of the foremost, do what he may, then say,
"O Thou to Whom belongeth all command, I ask of Thee all good. I seek refuge in Thee from all evil, for Thou art God. No god at all is there but Thee, the Self-Sufficient, the Forgiving, the Compassionate. I pray Thee, through the guide Muhammad, who guides to 'a straight path, the path of God to Whom belong all things in heaven and earth, is it not to God that all things shall return?' (Q. 42:52–53)—for forgiveness by which Thou dost comfort my breast, remove my burden, arouse my remembrance, make easy my course, free my mind, and remove my decree. Certainly 'Thou art powerful over all things.'" (Q. 2:20)

He said once during his spiritual communings (*munajat*),

O God, O Friend, O Defender, O Self-Sufficient One, O Praiseworthy, I seek refuge with Thee from a world in which there is no portion pertaining to Thyself, and from an action for the sake of a hereafter in which there is a portion of any other. I seek refuge with Thee from every movement divested of imitation of the practice of Thine Apostle, or from any necessary act that does not lead to true knowledge of Thee. Keep my heart in Thy presence and cause me to dispense with my guarding of it by Thy guarding, for Thou art powerful over all things.

He said,

Measure and weigh your self by the worship, by men coming to you and turning away from you, and by your loss (*faqd*) and gain (*wajd*) in outer and inner states. If there should occur to your mind anything that puts you at ease, gives you joy, makes you sad, upon which or an account of which your mind is laden with care, that is a defect which will cause you to fall from the greatest sainthood and the magnificent stage of utter sincerity, and it may be that you will obtain the lesser sainthood in the ranks of religious faith and abundance of religious works.

In this lesser sainthood there are never lacking the whispering and passing thoughts, for you are far from the lowest heaven and near to Satan and your passion which listen stealthily, make suggestions, and give false reports. But if you are aided by the stars of knowledge of the faith, the planets of certainty (*yaqin*), and the constancy of the divine upholding, then your sainthood in this matter is achieved. But if not, then you are a poet (*sha'ir*). At one time, the matter is in your favor, and at another time against you, in accordance with that degree of sainthood which you possess, and you will have the recompense of the witness upon the path of God.

The Will

He said,

> The will (*irada*), according to the tenets of Sufis who have attained reality, has four principles: sincerity (*sidq*) in servantship, forsaking of personal volition (*ikhtiyar*) with recognition of God's lordship, adhering to knowledge in everything, and loving God in preference to everything. Sincerity is built on four principles: divine exaltation (*ta'zim*), love, shame, and reverent awe.
>
> Forsaking of personal volition is built on four principles: sensing the presence of God at the moment of death, experiencing real union, credence, and confidence in the guarantee and promise of God.
>
> The receiving of knowledge is based on four principles: the method of mystical allusion (*ishara*) the method of personal encounter (*muwajaha*), the method of the understanding (*fahm*), and the method of instruction.
>
> Loving God by preference is founded on four principles: preference for His being (*wujud*) over every existing thing (*mawjud*); preference for His attributes with recognition of His goodly creation of the whole universe; preference for His actions with contentment in face of every deprivation; and preference for the things that foster love for Him over the things that cause you to love yourself. This is for one who has made good spiritual progress. As for one who has not progressed so far, let him be with the teacher who has excelled in his progress toward God to this degree. Peace be to you.

Sincerity

He said,

> Sincerity is a light from the light of God that He has deposited in the heart of His believing servant and by which He cuts him off from all others. That is sincerity that no angel looks upon to record it, no Satan to corrupt it, and no evil inclination to cause it to deviate.
>
> From it emerge four wills: the will for sincerity in performing religious acts to honor God; the will for sincerity in honoring the command of God; the will for sincerity in seeking recompense and reward; and the will for sincerity in freeing religious practice from blemishes, in which regard is shown to nothing but that practice.
>
> With all of these wills has He subjugated us. If anyone holds fast to one of them, he is sincere. With God, there are various grades, and God beholds whatever they do. It is to this that His saying alluded, in that which Gabriel reported as from Him to the Apostle of God. "Sincerity is one of my secrets that I have planted in the heart of whomsoever I love of my servants."

He said, "Hypocrisy is turning the heart in a religious act to other than God in a way that God has not permitted."

He said,

> I saw as if I were circumambulating the *Ka'ba*, asking of myself the meaning of sincerity, while I was examining my inner soul to find it. Then a voice called to me, saying, "How long you go about mumbling with those who mumble, while I am the All-Hearing, the Near, the All-Knowing, the Informed! My teaching will make you dispense with knowledge of the ancients and moderns altogether, save the knowledge of the Apostle and that of the prophets."

Sincerity has only four aspects: what sincerity is; who the sincere person is; in what he is sincere; and toward whom he is sincere. It is of two kinds: sincerity of the faithful ones (*sadiqin*), and sincerity of the utterly faithful (*siddiqin*). The sincerity of the faithful ones is for the purpose of seeking remuneration and reward, while the sincerity of the utterly sincere mystics is to gain the consciousness of the Being of the True One, having him as the goal and nothing else. If anyone has that implanted in his heart, he is the one excepted in the saying of His enemy who said, "Certainly I will beguile all of them except those servants of Thine from among them who are sincere (Q. 38:82–83).

Religious Science

He said,

These [religious] sciences are shields, and a clear exposition of the involuntary thoughts that intrude to remain in souls, or of their transitory thoughts (*khawatir*), or of their cunning, or their acts of the will. They are a means of severing the hearts of man from observing, acquiescing, or placing confidence in other than God after the fashion of theology and religious law, through the radiance of love and sincerity in religious practice with loyalty to the *Sunna*. They possess, furthermore, additional virtues in respect of the stages of certainty (*yaqin*), such as abstinence, patient endurance, thankfulness, hope, fear, trust, contentment, and so on. This is the path of those who have God as their goal as they travel the road of social relationships.

The Elect

With regard to the people of God and His elect (*khassa*), they are a people whom He has drawn away from evil-doing and its roots, and employed for well-doing and its branches. He made them love the places of solitude (*khalawat*) and opened before them the path of spiritual communion (*munaja*). He made Himself known to them, and they came to know Him. He showed His love to them, and they loved Him. He guided them to the path that leads to Him, and they followed it. So they are with Him, they are His, and He does not give them over to any other. They are not veiled from Him; rather they are veiled with Him from others. They know only Him, and love none but Him. "They are the ones whom He has guided, and they are the ones who have understanding" (Q. 39:18).

The Way

He said,

This way (*tariq*) is neither one of monasticism (*rahbaniya*), nor of eating barley and bran, nor one of the other skills. It is only a matter of patient endurance and firm belief (*yaqin*) under divine guidance. "We appointed them leaders to guide according to Our command after they had endured with patience and firmly believed in Our signs. Your Lord is the One Who will decide among them on the day of resurrection as to that in which they differed" (Q. 32:24–25). This frontier is a noble one in which there are five virtues: patient endurance, holy fear, scrupulousness, firm belief, and mystical knowledge.

Patient endurance is applied whenever one suffers injury. Holy fear implies that one causes no injury. Scrupulousness has to do with what goes out and enters here—and he pointed to his mouth—and with the heart, that there should enter it nothing except what God and His Apostle love. Firm belief concerns daily sustenance.

Mystical knowledge is of the Truth, which no one who possesses it is belittled by divulging it to any creature. "Be patient, for the final issue is for the God-fearing, and grieve not for them, and be not distressed with what they plot, for God is with those who fear Him and do what is good" (Q. 16:127–128).

Understanding

He said,

> The understanding man is one who understands what God wills for him and from him, according to the religious precepts. God wills for a servant (*'abd*) four things: either fortune or misfortune, obedience or disobedience. Now, when you are in a state of fortune, God requires of you thankfulness according to the religious precepts. When God wills for you some act of obedience, He requires you to view the favor and see the help to perform it as from Him, according to the religious precepts. Whenever God wills for you some act of disobedience, then He requires that you repent and turn to Him with contrition, according to the religious precepts.

He who has an understanding from God of these four things, and is with reference to them as God wills him to be according to the religious precepts, is a servant in reality by the proof of the Prophet's saying, "If anyone is given, and gives thanks; if anyone is tried, and endures patiently; if anyone acts wrongfully, and asks pardon; if anyone is wronged, and pardons"—upon which he was silent.

Then they asked, "What has he for this, O Apostle of God?" He replied, "These have security, and are rightly led" (Q. 6:82).

In reply to a comment of one of them, he said, "That will never be easy except for a servant who loves but God uniquely or loves what God has enjoined in the divine law for his religious practice. Peace be to you."

Obedience

He said,

> The following has come down in one of the traditions. 'If anyone obeys Me in everything by his forsaking of everything, I will comply with him

in everything in that I will manifest Myself to him in everything until he sees Me as if I were everything.' This obedience and this seeing are within the sphere of the common righteous people.

As for the elect (*khawass*) of the utterly sincere (*siddiqin*), their obedience consists, with their people, in approaching everything for the sake of their Master's good will in respect of everything. It is as if He were saying, "If anyone obeys Me in everything by his approaching of everything on account of My good will in respect of everything, I will comply with him in everything in that I will manifest Myself to him with everything until he sees Me as if I were nearer to him than everything."

Recitation and a Prayer

He said,

For a long time I had been reciting the "Throne" verse (Q. 2:255) and the last parts of the chapter of the Cow from His saying, "The Apostle believed" (Q. 2:285) to the end of the chapter, and the beginning of the chapter of the Family of 'Imran to His saying, "The Mighty, the Wise" (Q. 3:6), along with the two verses of His saying, "Say, O God, the Possessor of the dominion" (Q. 3:26), to His saying, "Without reckoning" (Q. 3:27). Then I prayed.

God, I beseech Thee to be accompanied by fear, to be overcome by longing (*shawq*), to be well grounded in knowledge ['*ilm*], to continue long in reflection (*fikr*).

We ask of Thee the secret of divine secrets, which wards off harms (*adrar*), that in sin and shame we may have no abode (*qarar*). Choose and lead us to act according to these words that Thou hast uttered to us upon the tongue of Thine Apostle, and by which Thou hast tried Ibrahim, Thy sincere friend. "So he fulfilled them, and God said, "I am appointing you a leader for men." He asked, "Of my children also?" He replied, "My promise does not apply to the evil-doers" (Q. 2:125).

So appoint us to be among his well-doing children and among the children of Adam and Noah. Make us to walk the path of the God-fearing leaders, for God beholds His servants.

God, I have sinned greatly against mine own soul, and only Thou dost forgive sins. So forgive me, be merciful to me, and relent toward me. "There is no god at all but Thee. Thine be the praise. Verily I have been one of the wrong-doers" (Q. 21:87).

This prayer for forgiveness possesses great effectiveness and power of precious illumination. If you offer it, you will behold wonders.

Then I would say,

"O God, O Exalted One, O Mighty One, O Clement One, O Knowing One, O Hearing One, O Seeing One, O Willing One, O Powerful One, O Compassionate One, O He Who is He, O He, O First, O Last, O Outer, O Inner—"May the name of thy Lord be blessed, of Him who is endowed with majesty and honor." (Q. 55:78)

"God, grant me Thy great name, having which nothing on earth or in heaven will cause harm.

"Bestow on me one of its secrets, having which sins will cause no harm.

"Assign to me from it a means, on the one hand, whereby Thou wilt supply the needs (*hawa'ij*) of the heart, mind, spirit, inner soul, lower self, and body, and, on the other, whereby Thou wilt repel the wants from the heart, mind, lower self, and body.

"Inscribe my name below Thy name, mine attributes below Thine attributes, mine actions below Thine actions that I may enjoy the inscribing of security to my account, the annulling of blame, the descent of divine grace (*karama*), and the manifestation of faithfulness (*amana*).

"Be for me a helper and protector in that with which Thou didst test the leaders of the Guidance by Thy command.

"Provide for me a sufficiency that, through me, Thou mightest make others sufficient, and quicken me that, through me, Thou mightest quicken what and whichever of Thy servants Thou desirest. Appoint me to the guardianship of the forty and to be of the pure quality of the God fearing ones. Pardon me, for Thy promise does not include the evildoers."

Ta' sin, ha' mim, 'ayn sin qaf. "He released the two seas that meet; yet between them is a barrier that they do not overpass" (Q. 55:19–20). "Praise be to God, Lord of the worlds" (Q. 1:1).

Say, "It is that God is one, God the eternal. He did not beget; neither was He begotten; and there is none like unto Him" (Q. chapter 112).

Miscellaneous Instructions

He said, "The heart (*qalb*) has four defenses against evil: binding the heart to God; renouncing what is other than God; looking not with your eyes upon what God has forbidden; and moving not your feet where you do not expect God's reward."

He said, quoting from his teacher, "There are two evils, having which, an abundance of good works is seldom profitable: discontent with God's decree and wronging God's servants. There are two good works, doing which, an abundance of evil actions is seldom harmful: being content with God's decree and pardoning God's servants."

He said,

> Do not take as a companion one who prefers himself to you, for he is vile. Neither take one who prefers you to himself, for he will not last long. Hold companionship with him who, when he remembers, remembers God, for God will take his place when he is absent, and bring enrichment through him when he is present. Remembrance of Him is the light of the heart, and His presence is the key to the invisible. May God be your aim and death your desire with every step, and indulge not in a long future hope. Hold not companionship with anyone of such a description, neither rely on him. Dismiss him without delay. Treat him with kindness as long as he is in your company.

He said, quoting from his teacher, "There are three classes of human beings: the person with whom the bargain has not been made, because of his freedom; the person with whom the bargain has been made, because of his nobility; and the person without distinction, having neither freedom nor nobility."

He said, "If anyone does not experience intimacy (*uns*) with God, when anyone who may benefit or harm turns away from him with greater enjoyment than when people turn toward him, then he has no intimacy with God, neither little nor great, even though among the most excellent of good works are the extending of invitations and discharge of social obligations."

He said, quoting from his teacher, "The most excellent of religious works are four plus four. They are love toward God, acquiescence in God's decree, asceticism in life, reliance upon God, performance of God's ordinances (*fara'id*), avoidance of what God has forbidden, enduring what has no significance, and caution with regard to every thing that distracts."

He said,

> Whenever the lower self (*nafs*) is dominant and the spirit (*ruh*) subordinate, then occur drought and sterility, the whole order is overturned, and every evil befalls. So heed the guiding Scripture of God and the healing word of His Apostle, for you will never cease to enjoy the good as long as you give preference to these two. But evil has already befallen him who turns away from them. The people of the Truth, "upon hearing vain talk, turn away from it" (Q. 28:55), and upon hearing the truth, welcome it. "Whoever commits a good deed, for him will We increase it with goodness." (Q. 42:23)

He said, "Blindness of spiritual insights is manifest in three things: in giving rein to the members (*jawarih*) to perform acts of disobedience toward God, in pretending obedience to God, and in covetousness toward the creatures of God.

Anyone who claims spiritual insight while manifesting one of these has a mind that is near to wrong opinions of himself and to the whisperings of Satan."

He said, "If you desire to be safe from the Deceiver, then perform your religious works unto God alone upon the stipulation of faith, and do not be self-satisfied in anything."

He said, "Faith means that you consider your attribute being first through His firstness, your being last through His lastness, your outwardness through His outwardness, and your inwardness through His inwardness."

He said, "The exalted man (*'aziz*) is he who is rooted in the science of reverence (*hayba*), who conducts himself according to the will (*mashi'a*), and not by passion, appetitive desire, or natural disposition."

He said, "Real asceticism (*zuhd*) is emptying the heart of whatever is other than the Lord."

He said, "Real truthfulness (*sidq*) and piety (*taqwa*) are experiencing with the Master what you desire. God has said, 'He who comes with the truth and believes it to be the truth—they are the pious. They have with their Lord what they desire' " (Q. 39:33–34).

He said, "Real knowledge of what is good implies dwelling in it, and real knowledge of evil implies departure from it."

He said, "Real intention means the absence of everything save the act intended upon undertaking it; and its perfection is in holding fast to that until its completion."

He said, "Real prostration (*sujud*) is the yielding of the heart to the ordinance (*ahkam*) of the Lord."

He said, "Real vanishing of passion (*hawa*) from the heart implies fondness for meeting with God in every breath without man's choosing a certain situation in which to be."

He said, "Real forsaking (*hijran*) is forgetting the thing forsaken."

He said, "Real love (*mahabba*) is beholding the beloved face to face, and its consummation is your destitution (*fiqdan*) in every time and season."

He said, "Real spiritual aspiration (*himma*) is the attachment of the heart to the things to which one aspires, and its perfection is the union of the heart with God while separating itself from all except Him."

He said, "Real nearness (*qurb*) to God means unawareness (*ghayba*), through nearness, of the nearness by reason of the great nearness."

He said, "Real abundance is the loss of the sense of abundance through the greatness of the abundance."

He said, "The real power of God is revealed in the fact that His despair for anyone He loves is greater than His despair for anyone He dislikes."

He said, "I saw the Apostle of God, and I asked, 'O Apostle of God, what is the true meaning of being a follower?' He replied, 'It is seeing the one followed on the occasion of everything, and in everything.' "

He said, "The (*Sufi*) shaykh is one who directs you to your ease, not one who directs you to your toil."

He said, "Any shaykh from whom there have not come to you the benefits (*fawa'id*)[10] that are behind a veil is not a teacher."

He said, "The perfect man (*al-rajul al-kamil*) is not he from whom personal fear has subsided. The perfect man is only he through whom fear has subsided from someone else. God has said, 'Are they not the saints of God, those upon whom there is no fear and who do not grieve?' (Q. 10:62). The perfect man is not one who lives in himself. The perfect man is only one through whom others live."

He said, "Sufism (*tasawwuf*) is training the self in servantship and restoring it to the rules of lordship."

He said, "The Sufi is one who does not turn his attention to mankind (*khalq*), and who has relied on nothing except the promises of the True One (*Haqq*)."

He said, "The Sufi has four qualities: being characterized by the characteristics of God, abiding closely by the commands of God, relinquishing the defense of one's self from shame before God, and holding to the practice of spiritual converse by truly abiding with God."

He said, "The Sufi, in respect of mankind, within his innermost soul is like scattered dust particles (*haba'*)[11] in the atmosphere, neither existent beings (*mawjudin*) nor nonexistent beings (*ma'dumin*), just as they are known by God. So the accidents that pass over the soul are only for the purpose of defining or confirming, that the Sufi may know, in this way, the reality of the divine unity (*tawhid*)."

He said,

> Sitting in assembly with the elders is characterized by four things: first, avoidance of opposing them and dealing with them with partiality, friendship and favoritism; second, giving ear in audience before them while relinquishing what you desire for the sake of what they desire; third, showing deference to what they say and do while holding back from their convictions; and fourth, a concern for those things with which they are concerned on condition of conforming to them in their actions.

He said,

> There are four proprieties (*adab*). If a poor devotee (*faqir*) who has stripped himself of all means of substinence is devoid of them, put him on the same level with dirt. Those properties are: compassion for those of low estate, respect for those of high estate, requiring of one's self to act with equity toward others, and abstaining from the same for one's self.
>
> If the poor devotee who is occupied with his means of livelihood does not observe the following four proprieties, heed him not, even though he be one of the most learned of men: avoiding oppressors, preferring

the people of the other world, relieving the poor, and assiduity in the five prayers with the congregation.

Avoiding oppressors indicates fear (*khawf*). Preferring the people of the other world indicates love (*mahabba*). Relieving the poor indicates hope (*raja'*), and assiduity in the five prayers with the congregation indicates longing (*shawq*).

He said, "The vilest of men in rank is one who is niggardly of worldly possessions toward one deserving them."

He said, "The most miserable of men in rank is one who opposes his Master, who reverts to his former state through his managing of his worldly affairs, and who forgets the beginning, the end, and religious works in view of his future life."

He said, "Anyone whose divine illumination (*nur*) takes precedence over his reason ('*aql*) is blessed indeed, but anyone whose reason takes precedence over his illumination is impoverished."

He said, "Take piety (*taqwa*) as your abode, and praise of yourself will not harm you, so long as you have not persisted in sin, nor become complacent with what is not persisted in sin, nor become complacent with what is shameful, nor cast away your dread of the Unseen (*ghayb*)."

He said, "Unity (*tawhid*) is a light (*nur*) which makes you nonexistent to others and makes others nonexistent to you."

He said, "Implied in commenting on the words, 'In the name of God the Merciful, the Compassionate,' is an invalidation of what is firmly established."

He said,

> The self (*nafs*) has four focal centers: center for the evil desire (*shahwa*) in misdemeanors; center for the evil desire in obedient acts; center for the evil desire in the attainment to the mystical stages; and a center for the evil desire in the inability to fulfill the divine obligations. Therefore, "kill the infidels wherever you find them, seize them, besiege them, and lie in wait for them at every post." (Q. 9:5)

He said, "The head of the self is the human will (*irada*). Its two hands are its knowledge and reason ('*aql*), and its two feet are its self-management (*tadbir*) and its own choosing (*ikhtiyar*)."

He said,

> If you desire to struggle against the lower self (*jihad al-nafs*), condemn it to impotence in every movement, smite it with fear (*khawf*) at every evil suggestion, confine it to the grasp (*qabda*) of God wherever you are heedless, for it is this (*nafs*) over which you have no power; but God knows all about it. So if it subjected for you in the divine grasp, it is fitting for you to remember the goodness of God and say, "Praise be

to Him who has subjected this for us, for we were not able to do it of ourselves, and, as for us, to our Lord shall we return." (Q. 43:13–14)

He said, "The death of the lower self (*mawt al-nafs*) is through religious knowledge (*'ilm*), mystical knowledge (*ma'rifa*), and following the Scripture and the *Sunna*.

He said, "You are forbidden to be united with the Beloved while in the universe you still have any companion."

He said, "Piety (*taqwa*) is being clothed with His illuminations (*anwar*), being conscious of the envelopment of His attributes, and constant devotion to Him Himself. 'That is good indeed; it is one of the signs of God' (Q. 7:26)."

He said,

> The one who is cheated in this world and the next is he who allows the misfortunes of gains to accompany the misfortunes of ruin, and pursues those things that cause displeasure to God. Being pleased with God has as its reward the pleasure of God for, if you are pleased with God, He will be pleased with you. If you are displeased with God's decree, He will be displeased with you. "They disliked what God sent down; therefore He thwarted their works." (Q. 47:28) "That is because they were a people who did not know." (Q. 9:6)

He said, "With us there is no great sin greater than these two: love of the world by preference over other objects of love, and remaining in a state of ignorance with contentment. Love of the world is the apex of all iniquity, and remaining in ignorance is the root of every act of disobedience."

He said, "The ranks of the saints (*awliya'*) are four in number: rank in respect of nearness to God, rank in the dominion, rank in respect of the fulfillment of divine obligations, and rank in respect of election."

He said, "Proper conduct in the presence of God includes three things: looking toward Him continually, giving ear to Him, and being disposed to receive whatever bits of divine wisdom may arrive."

He said, "Cast yourself before the door of divine satisfaction and be detached from your resolves and your will, even from your repentance because of His relenting. God has said, 'Then He relented toward them that they might repent, for God is the Relenting, the Compassionate' (Q. 9:118)."

He said, "Any affliction for which a hope for reward is entertained and a punishment is feared is not an affliction. An affliction for which a reward is not hoped and a punishment is feared—that only is an affliction."

He said, "Whenever the Whisperer besets you insistently, say, 'Praise be to the King, the Creator. If He willed, He could drive you away and bring forth a new creation, and that would not be difficult for Him' (Q. 35:15–8)."

He said, "The wise man (*hakim*) is he who knows the beginning and the end and who forms an opinion on matters of the unseen (*ghayb*) according as God has given him wisdom to do so."

He said, "Seldom is a servant secure from duplicity (*nifaq*) when he becomes party to an agreement."

He said, "The ultimate in discontent (*sakhat*) toward God is to will what God has not willed by His judgment."

He said,

> While occupied with devotions on a certain mountain a thought occurred to my mind that he, in whose heart dwells the fear of poverty, rarely has a religious work accredited to him. That was very distressing to me, and I pondered over it for a year. Then, in a dream I saw the Prophet who was saying to me, "O blessed one, O blessed one, you have tormented yourself unduly. Distinguish between dwelling and occurring. In the heart of the believer there is an occurring but not a dwelling of fear of poverty." With that word my difficulty subsided.

He said,

> In al-Qayrawan I was ill, and I saw in a dream the Prophet who said, "Cleanse your raiment of defilement and you will obtain the help of God with every breath (*nafas*)." I asked, "What is my raiment, O Apostle of God?" He replied, "God has clothed you with the vestment (*hulla*) of mystical knowledge, then with the vestment of love, then with the vestment of belief in the divine unity (*tawhid*), then with the vestment of faith (*iman*), and then with the vestment of submission (*islam*). If anyone knows God, everything becomes of little importance for him. If anyone loves God, everything becomes contemptible for him. If anyone asserts the unity of God, he associates nothing with Him. If anyone has faith in God, he is safe from everything. If anyone is resigned to God, rarely does he disobey Him. If he does disobey Him, he begs of Him to be excused. If he begs of Him to be excused, his excuse is accepted." With these words I understood the meaning of His saying, "And thy garments keep from stain." (Q. 74:4)

He said, "The saint attains unto such a consummate degree of sanctity that he is told, 'We have made you to be accompanied by security (*salama*) from evils and faults, and we have withdrawn from you blame (*malama*), so do what you wish.'"

He said, "If anyone has faith in the divine apportionment (*qisma*), he should not dispute the divine wisdom (*hikma*)."

He said, "Let not your portion from supplication be the joy of the fulfillment of your wants without the joy of your communings (*munajat*) with your beloved, for then you would be one of the veiled (*mahjubin*)."

He said,

> I went out to a garden with certain of my companions of the city of
> Tunis and then returned to the city. We were riding on donkeys. When
> we arrived near the city, they dismounted. It was a muddy place.
>   They said to me, "O our master, dismount here."
>   I asked, "Why?"
>   They replied, "This is the city and we are ashamed to enter it mounted
> on a donkey."
>   So, desiring to do as they did, I doubled up my leg to dismount, when
> a voice called to me. "God does not inflict punishment for ease
> accompanied by humility, but He does inflict punishment for toil
> accompanied by pride."

He said, "I have given up all hope of being of any benefit to myself, so how
should I not give up hope of my being of benefit to others? Likewise I have hoped
in God for others, so how should I not hope in Him for myself?

He said,

> Your tracing of the origin of the secret of His very proximity (*qurb*) to
> you is like its extension to the farthest limit of His remoteness (*bu'd*)
> from you. These two—proximity and remoteness—are only two aspects
> of the same soul, corresponding to the aspects of passing away (*fana'*)
> and of continuance (*baqa'*). If you are in the state of passing away, there
> is neither proximity nor remoteness, as there is neither union nor
> separation. If you are in the state of continuance, you have learned what
> the tradition says. "By Me he hears, and by Me he sees," and so forth.

He said, "Any servant who knows the truth (*haqq*) and is humble toward its
people bears the mark of felicity. But any servant who knows the truth and is
haughty toward its people bears the mark of misery, whatever works he may
perform."

He said, "Love (*mahabbah*) is a fundamental principle for enabling one to
understand. So, if anyone loves God, he has from Him an understanding of
everything."

He said, "There are two virtues that facilitate the way to God: mystical
knowledge and love. Your love for material things renders you blind and deaf."

He said, "If you desire to defeat the Adversary, then you must have faith, trust,
and sincere servantship, and seek refuge with God from his incitements. God
has said, 'He has no power over those who have faith and who put their trust
in their Lord' (Q. 16:99). God also said, "For thou hast no power over my servants"
(Q. 15:42); and He said, 'Whenever incitement from Satan arouses you, seek refuge
with God' (Q. 7:200)."

He said, "Take God as your Friend and Satan as your enemy, and you will be at ease."

He said, "The strongest of strongholds is the seeking pardon of which I tell you and the central truth of which is that, with God, you have consolation (*qarar*). God has said, 'God is not one to punish them while they seek pardon' (Q. 8:33)."

He said, "Religious works revolve around four things: love, sincerity, shame, and faith. Love is through fear. Sincerity is through religious knowledge. Shame is through respect for God's ordinances. Faith is through truthfulness."

He said, "Mystical knowledge is that which has severed you from everything except God and brought you back to Him."

He said, "Whenever He hinders you from attaining what you desire and makes you resort to what He desires, it is a sign of His love for you."

He said, "My teacher admonished me, saying, 'Flee from the good of humans more often than you flee from their evil, for their evil afflicts your body while their good afflicts your heart, and that you should be afflicted in you body is better than that you should be afflicted in your heart.' "

He said,

> The continual occupations (*awrad*)[12] of the faithful (*sadiqin*) are fasting, prescribed prayer, recitation of the *dhikr*, recital of the *Qur'an*, guarding the bodily members, turning the lower self away from the appetitive desires (*shahawat*), enjoing what is approved, and prohibiting what is disapproved. These are based on the following four principles: abstinence in respect of worldly things, trust in God, acquiescence in what God decrees, and patient endurance of God's testing (*bala'*).
>
> Also included is sincere love built upon four foundations: faith, unity (*tawhid*), sincere intentions, and a high spiritual urge. If anyone does not have within him the following four virtues, do not expect him to enjoy felicity: religious knowledge, scrupulousness, awe before God, and humility toward the servants of God.

He said, quoting from his teacher,

> The religious worship (*'ibada*) of the utterly sincere mystics (*siddiqin*) consists in twenty things: "Eat and drink" (Q. 7:31), clothe yourselves, travel, marry, and settle down. Put yourselves to everything "as God has commanded you" (Q. 2:222), and "do not go to excesses" (Q. 7:31). "Serve God and associate no others with Him" (Q. 4:36), and "be thankful" (Q. 2:167) to Him. It is incumbent upon you to desist from injury and to expend liberally. These compose one half of the constraining order. The second half consists in performance of the prescribed duties, avoidance of the unlawful, and contentment with the divine decree. Serving God consists in reflecting upon God's command and studying thoroughly the religion of God.

The foundation of service is asceticism (*zuhd*) with regard to the world, the apex of which is trust (*tawakkul*) in God. This is the service (*'ibada*) of the ablest of the believers. If you are weak, seek a remedy, listen carefully to the learned *'ulama*, and choose from among them the pious, the true guides, the trustful in God.

He said, "I inquired of my teacher concerning the constant occupation (*wird*) of those who have attained reality (*muhaqqiqin*) and he replied, 'It is incumbent upon you to have done with passion (*hawa*) and to love the Master. The sign of love is the lover's being occupied with nothing save his Beloved.'"
He said,

> While in the Maghrib, a certain person came to see me and said, "I have heard that you possess a knowledge of alchemy; so teach me."
>
> "I will teach it to you," I replied, "without omitting for you a particle, if you are able to receive it."
>
> "By God," he said, "I am able to receive it."
>
> So I said to him, "Eliminate the creatures from your heart, and stop desiring that your Lord give you other than what He has previously ordained for you."
>
> "I am not able to do that," he replied.
>
> So I remarked, "Did I not tell you that you would not be able to receive it?"
>
> Then he left me.

He said, "If anyone is completely satisfied with his possessions, he is poor. If anyone is completely satisfied with his high repute, he is despicable. If anyone is wholly satisfied with his kinsmen, he is contemptible. If anyone is entirely satisfied with his good works, he is bankrupt. But if anyone is completely satisfied with God, he has the true satisfaction."
He said that he heard his teacher reply to a man who had asked permission to fight against his lower self (*nafs*), answering with His saying: "They who believe in God and the Last Day will not ask permission of thee to fight with their goods and their persons" (Q. 9:44).
He said, "The sign of commitment (*tafwid*) to God is the lack of distress when distasteful things befall."
He said, "I had a companion who very often came to me to discuss the subject of mystical unity (*tawhid*). While asleep, I saw as if I were saying to him, 'O 'Abd Allah, if you desire that which is without reproach, then let separation (*farq*) on your tongue be expressed (*mawjud*) while union (*jam'*) in your inner soul is experienced (*mashhud*).'"
He said,

I was in a cave, and I prayed. "My God, when shall I become for Thee a thankful servant?" Then I heard a voice say from the interior of the cave, "Whenever you come to see that in everything that exists you have no Benefactor except Him, then you will be a thankful servant."

Then I replied, "The prophets are more bountiful than I and the kings of the earth are more beneficent than I."

"If it were not for the prophets," the voice said, "you would not have learned of Us and you would not have been guided to Us. And if it were not for the kings, living would not be easy for you. So everything is a benefaction bestowed by Us upon you."

He said,

There came in to me a certain high personage of the government while in the Maghrib. He remarked, "I do not observe that you perform any great religious works. So tell me how it is that you have attained such a place of eminence among the people that they esteem you highly."

I replied, "I have a single good work that God has prescribed to His Prophet and to which I have adhered."

"What is that?" he asked.

I replied, "Withdrawal from you and your world. God has said, 'Then withdraw from anyone who turns away from Our remembrance and who desires but the life of this world' (Q. 53:29)."

He said, "I read one night during my private devotional exercises, 'Follow not the whims of those who have no knowledge, for never will they be a help to you in anything against God' (Q. 45:18-19). When I went to sleep, I saw the Apostle of God who said to me, 'I am one of the most knowing, but even I will not be a help to you in anything against God.'"

He said, "I sought the counsel of my teacher, saying to him, 'Give me your spiritual counsel.' He replied, 'Be not suspicious of God in anything, be sure to think well of Him in everything, and prefer not yourself to Him in anything.' Then I asked him concerning the saying of the Prophet, 'The believer does not abase himself.' He explained, 'To me it means his passion (*hawa*).'"

He said, "The man who is most compassionate toward human beings is a servant who shows compassion toward one who has no compassion for himself."

He said, "One night I read in my private devotions (*wird*) His saying, 'All who dwell on it (namely, the earth) will pass away, but the face of thy Lord, full of majesty and honor, will remain' (Q. 55:26-27). Then I saw Abu Bakr, the trustworthy, in a dream and he said to me, 'Unite with Him Who remains and forsake him who passes away. You will be exalted and honored. You will be too exalted to pass away and you will be honored with remaining (*baqa'*).'"

He said, "The religious sciences that are imprinted in the hearts are like gold and silver coins in the hands. If He wills, He benefits you by them, and, if He wills, He harms you by them."

He said, "The carpet of divine generosity are fourfold: a love that distracts you from the love of any except Him; a satisfaction through which your love is joined to His love; abstinence that really makes you abstain from His creatures; and a trust in Him that discloses to you His real power."

He said, "May your concern be with three things: repentance, piety, and vigilance. Strengthen them by three things: performance of the *dhikr*, seeking pardon, and silence in servantship to God. Fortify these six by four things: love, contentment, abstinence, and trust."

He said, "Whoever supplicates God for other than that for which His Apostle supplicated Him is an innovator."

He said, "I saw as if I were with the prophets and utterly sincere (*siddiqin*), and on awakening I had the desire to be one with them. Then I said, 'O God, make me to travel their road with security from that with which Thou hast tried them, for they are stronger than we and we are weaker than they.' Then I was told to say, 'Whatever Thou has decreed, aid us as Thou hast aided them.'"

He said,

> I saw as if I were in the highest abode of the heavens, and I asked, "My God, which of the mystical states is preferable to Thee, which of the religious works is most indicative of love to Thee? Help and guide me."
>
> I was told, "The state most preferable to Him is contentment with contemplation (*mushahada*) of God. The truest affirmation before Him is the saying, "There is no god at all save God" (Q. 37:35), while in a state of purity. The work most indicative of love to Him is disdain of the world and despair of its people though living in harmony with them."

He said,

> The utterly sincere (*siddiqin*) have five divine graces. The first of them is continual remembrance (*dhikr*) of God, and acts of obedience on the stipulation of performing them in the right way. The second is abstinence in respect of worldly goods with preference for having little. The third is a renewal of sure faith (*yaqin*) along with contrarieties (*mu'aradat*). The fourth is an experience of estrangement with people whose company is profitable, and of fellowship with people whose company is harmful. The fifth is physical manifestations, such as traveling over the earth, walking on water, the springing forth of water, and other occurrences that lie beyond the rule of natural law.
>
> This subject has its own times, individuals, and places. If anyone seeks them (namely, divine graces) in other than the proper moment for seeking

them, he is denied them. If anyone seeks them in other than their proper time, rarely does he discover them. On the whole, he who seeks them is not given them. Nor is anyone given them who resolves in his mind to have them, or plies himself in seeking them. They are granted only to a servant who considers neither himself nor his works, but who is occupied with the things that foster the love of God, beholding the bounty of God, despairing of himself and of his works.

These divine graces sometimes appear as in the case of one who does what is right outwardly even though inwardly his lower self (*nafs*) be faulty. They appeared in one who worshiped God with great clamor on one of the islands of the sea for five hundred years. He was told, "Enter Paradise by My mercy." But he replied, "Nay, by my works."

He related the story of a certain man who requested his teacher to assign him rites of daily worship and devotional exercises (*awrad*).

The teacher was angry with him and replied, "Am I an apostle to impose obligations? The divine ordinances (*fara'id*) are well known, and the acts of disobedience are common knowledge. Keep the divine ordinances and shun the acts of disobedience. Guard your heart from worldly desire, from the love of women, the love of high repute, and the predilection of appetitive desires. In all of that, be content with what God has allotted to you. Whenever it proceeds from the way of God's pleasure, be thankful to Him for it; and whenever it comes to you from the channel of His anger, patiently endure it."

The love of God is an axis upon which good deeds turn, and a comprehensive principle for the various kinds of divine gifts (*karamat*). All that is present in four things: true scrupulousness, good intentions, sincere performance of religious acts, and love of religious knowledge. You can achieve none of these except through the companionship of a worthy brother or a teacher sincere in counseling.

He said,

I exclaimed on the occurrence of some misfortune, "We belong to God, and we shall return to Him (Q. 2:156). God, reward me for my misfortune and cause something better than it to follow."

Then in my inner being I was inspired to say, "Pardon me by means of it, by whatever may be the consequences of it, by whatever may be implied in it, by whatever may be involved in it, by everything that has been before it and will be after it."

So I uttered it, and it became easy for me. Even if the whole world had been mine at that time, and if I had suffered misfortune to that extent, that would have been easy for me, and the consolation of contentment and resignation that I experienced would have been dearer to me than all that.

He said,

> Some of the most sublime bestowals of God are contentment with the occurrences of what He decrees, patient endurance when trials befall, reliance upon God in hardships, and recourse to Him in reverses of fortune. If anyone is the recipient of these four bestowals that issue from the treasuries of religious works by way of self-mortification, following the Prophet's example, and emulating the leaders, then his friendship toward God, toward His Apostle, and toward the believers is genuine. "If anyone befriends God, His Apostle, and those who believe—the party of God, they are the conquerors." (Q. 5:56)
>
> If anyone is the recipient of these four bestowals that issue from the treasuries of divine favors by way of love, then the friendship of God toward him is consummated through His word, and "He befriends the righteous." (Q 7:196) So make a distinction between the two friendships: a servant befriends God, and a servant is befriended by God. They are the lesser and the greater friendship. To explain, your friendship toward His Apostle issues from following his Prophetic example; and your friendship toward the believers issues from emulating the leaders. So get that understanding of His saying, "If anyone befriends God, His Apostle, and those who believe—party of God, they are the conquerors." (Q. 5:56)

He said,

> It is a part of what you may know intellectually with certainty (*'ilm al-yaqin*)[13] about God and about your standing with Him that, among creatures, you may engage in activities that will not belittle you before the True One, even though they may belittle you in the eyes of people. However, there must be no objection from the divine law and no conflict with the innate disposition (*tab'*).
>
> Indeed, it is a matter that you may know with the eye of certainty (*'ayn al-yaqin*) that you may be unmindful of the phenomenal world upon the assailment of the hardships of the succession of benefits (*fawa'id*) through the radiant [internal] witnesses (*shawahid*). Furthermore, it is the very truth (*haqq al-yaqin*) that you may immerse yourself in something as though you were in the very soul of the thing. It is like one who must embark upon the sea. He embarks, his ship breaks up, and the waves dash over him.
>
> Moreover, there are some who pass away, who are among those who die, and are transported to the degrees of *'Illiyin*.[14] There are some who live, and are among those who remain, and in whom there is no portion

at all of the prophetic model, but who are concealed from people altogether. There are some who remain in an intermediate stage (*barzakh*) between the True One and the creatures, manifest by epithets of both, perfect in respect of attributes of both, and the model of the two masses.

Among them are the Greatest Imam, the pattern (*qidwa*), the pole, the helper, the especially chosen compendium of the names, attributes, illuminations, moral characteristics, and others unbefitting for anyone to hear. Below them are saints, God-fearing people, servants, and ascetics who have no rank at all, and the people who speculate with proof and argument without having yet examined mystical revelation and spiritual ideas.

Below them are the people who use the means of religious works and ecstatic states, and the people who are confused in speech and action— and "he whom God disgraces will have no one to honor him, for God does what He wills." (Q 22:19)

Chapter in Love

He said, quoting from his teacher,

Remain in a constant state of purity from polytheism (*shirk*). Whenever you become defiled, cleanse yourself. Associate nothing whatsoever with God, and remain clear of the defilement of love of this world. Whenever you incline toward lust, repair by repentance what you corrupt by passion, or are on the point of doing. You must love God with due reverence and probity.

Drink unceasingly of its full cup with intoxication (*sukr*) and sobriety (*sahw*). As often as you recover or awaken, drink until your intoxication and sobriety are through Him, and until, on account of His beauty, you become unconscious of love, the drink, the drinking, and the full cup, through the light of His splendor and the faultless perfection of His majesty that appears to you.

Perchance I am speaking to those who know not the love, the drink, the drinking, the full cup, the intoxication, and the sobriety. "Certainly," someone remarked to him, "and how many are there who are engulfed in material things without being aware of their being engulfed? So teach me and inform me of what I am ignorant or of what He has bestowed upon me while I am heedless of it."

"Yes," I replied, "love is a seizure that God has granted to the heart of one who loves, through His beauty and the faultlessness of His perfect majesty which have been disclosed to him. The drink of love is a blending of attributes with attributes, characteristics with characteristics, illuminations with illuminations, names with names, epithets with epithets, and actions with actions. In this, there is ample room for reflection for whomsoever God wills.

Drinking is giving the heart, members, and veins to imbibe of this drink until one is intoxicated, and the drinking becomes habitual after practice and discipline. Now, each one is provided drink according to his ability. Some are provided drink without an intermediary, for God takes that upon Himself directly for them. Some are provided drink by way of intermediaries, through such intermediaries as the angels, the learned men and the most prominent of those who have been drawn near to God. Some are intoxicated by the spiritual consciousness of the cup without having yet tasted anything. What, then, do you think of tasting, drinking, satiety, intoxication with what is drunk, then of sobriety following that of varying measures? As is intoxication, just so is sobriety.

The cup is mystical knowledge of God, the True One. He imparts from that clean, pure, and clear drink to whatever chosen servants of His from among mankind He may desire. At times, the drinker sees this cup as external form. At times, he sees it conceptually. At times, he sees it intellectually. Form is the portion of bodies and souls. The conceptual is the portion of hearts (*qulub*) and intellects (*'uqul*); the intellectual is the portion of spirits (*arwah*) and inner souls (*asrar*).

O what a drink! How sweet it is! Blessings be upon him who drinks of it! May he always have it, and may he continue unceasingly. We petition God for a portion of His bounty. "Such is the bounty of God. He gives it to whomsoever He will, for God is possessor of great bounty" (Q. 57:21).

Sometimes a company of lovers assemble and they are given to drink from one cup, or it may be that they are given to drink from many cups. Sometimes, the one person is given to drink of one cup and more than one cup. It may be that the drinks will vary according to the number of cups. Or it may be that the drinking from any cup will vary even though a great number of friends drink from it.[15]

He was again questioned about love, and he said,

Love is a seizure that God grants to the heart of His servant and that distracts him from everything save Him, so that you see the soul inclining to obey Him, the intellect fortified by mystical knowledge of Him, the spirit rapt in His presence, the inner soul overwhelmed in contemplantion of Him. The servant asks for more, and more is given, and he enters into the sweetest of the delights of spiritual converse with Him. He is clad in raiment befitting approach to His proximity, and he comes to know chaste realities and virgin sciences. For that reason. one says, "The saints of God are brides."

The one speaking said to him, "Now that I have come to know love, what is the drink (*sharab*) of love, the cup of love, the cupbearer (*saqi*), the tasting (*dhawq*), the drinking, satiety, intoxication, and sobriety?"

He replied to him,

> The drink is the light radiating from the beauty of the Beloved. The cup is the kindness (*lutf*) that brings that light into contact with the mouths of the hearts. The cupbearer is He who befriends the greatest of the elect and His righteous servants. He is God, the One who is cognizant of the essential capacities and requirements for the good of His friends. If to anyone that beauty is disclosed, and if he enjoys it for one breath or two, and then the veil is lowered over it, he is the yearning taster. If that continues for anyone for an hour or two, he is the drinker in truth. If one's experience comes uninterrupted and the drink lasts until his veins and members become filled with the treasured lights of God, then that is satiety. Often in that condition, one becomes unconsious of sense and mental perceptions so that he knows neither what is said nor what he says, and that is intoxication (*sukr*). Sometimes, the cups circulate among them, religious states differ for them, and they come to perform the *dhikr*, to experience states (*halat*), and to engage in acts of obedience. They are not veiled from the divine attributes, in spite of the crowding in of their God-given human capacities. That is the time of their sobriety (*sahw*), of the broadening of their mental vision (*nazar*), and of the increase of their works. And so by the stars of knowledge and the moon of unity, they are guided in their night, and by the suns of the mystical sciences they obtain light. "These are the party of God. The party of God—are they not the ones who prosper?" (Q. 58:22)

Scrupulous Piety

Having been questioned concerning scrupulous piety (*wara'*), he replied,

> What an excellent way is scrupulous piety for those who consider their inheritance to be temporary and their reward eternal. Scrupulous piety leads them in the end to receive from God and on behalf of God, to speak by God, to act unto God and through God, upon clear proof and superior insight. In their general soul experiences and in the rest of their spiritual states (*ahwal*) they do not direct their own affairs, nor make

choices, nor travel, nor think, nor consider, nor speak, nor grasp, nor walk, nor make any movement except through God and for God.

With them (that is, scrupulous Sufis) knowledge has broken in inadvertently, according to the truth of the matter, and they are entirely of one accord, with no variance as to which is higher and which is lower. With regard to the lowest of the low, God causes them to abstain from that as a recompense for their scrupulousness along with His preserving them from coming into conflict with the divine law. He whose knowledge and religious works have no heritage is veiled by something lower, or is turned aside by some appeal, and his heritage is arrogance toward his fellow men, pride, effrontery with his knowledge, and being emboldened against God by his works. That is the evident ruin from which we take refuge in God, the Mighty.

The shrewd scrupulously avoid this kind of scrupulousness and seek refuge with God from it. If anyone does not increase, through his knowledge and religious works, in poverty to his Lord and humility toward his fellowmen, he is lost. Praise be to Him who cuts off many of the righteous people by their righteousness from the One who does what is right by them, as He cuts off the workers of corruption by their corruption from their Creator. So take refuge with God for He is the Hearing, the Knowing.

He said,

> I saw as if I were sitting with one of my companions before my teacher, and he said to me, "Learn from me four matters—three of them for you and one for this poor man. Make no choice upon your own authority in anything. Choose not to choose. Flee from that choice, from your flight and from everything to God, for your Lord creates what He wills and exercises free choice. They had no power to choose. All choices and provisions of the religious way are the choosing of God, with which you have nothing to do and from which you have no escape. Listen and obey. This is the position taken in divine jurisprudence and intuitive knowledge, and is an area for the science of reality received from God for anyone who is equal to it. So understand and recite, "Invite them to their Lord, for you are being rightly guided, but if they dispute with you, then say, 'God knows best what you do'" (Q. 22:67-68). It is incumbent upon you to renounce the world and trust in God, for renunciation is a fundamental principle in religious works and trust is a prime element in the inner states. Call God to witness and seek protection with Him in speech, actions, moral conduct (*akhlaq*), and inner states, "For if anyone seeks protection with God, he is led to a straight path." (Q. 3:101) Beware of doubt, associating others with God, covetousness, and finding fault with God in anything. Serve God by drawing very close to Him, and you will enjoy love, preferment, special

favor, and the patronage of God, "For God is the patron of those who fear Him." (Q. 45:19)

Then he said,

> That which has cut off the soul of this poor man from attainment (*wusla* or *wisal*) through obedience to Him, and veiled his heart from the realization of mystical knowledge of Him, and distracted his mind from the evidences (*shawahid*) of union with Him consists in two things. They are his entrance into the affairs of this world of his according to his own management, and into the affairs of his other world with doubt about the bestowal of his Beloved. So God has punished him with the veiling, recurring skepticism, and forgetting of the day of reckoning, and submerged him in the sea of self-management and self-determination, and he has become immersed in it with a dulled sense of scrupulous piety. "So will they not turn toward God and ask His pardon? For God is forgiving, merciful." (Q. 5:74)
>
> Therefore return to God at the first signs of self-management and self-determination, and you will obtain from Him the help you need to make easy the way, and you will be kept from finding things made arduous. Any scrupulous piety (*wara'*) that does not bear you the fruit of knowledge and light, reckon to it no reward. Any evil that is followed by fear (*khawf*) and flight to God, reckon to it no fault (*wizr*).

Then he pointed [to the poor man] and said, "Receive your sustenance from the stage where God has caused you to abide, with the use of knowledge and the following of the *Sunna*, and go no higher before He elevates you, else you will lose your footing."

He said,

> I was at al-Mansura,[16] and, on the night of the eighth of Dhu'l-Hijja,[17] I kept vigil in a state of anxiety over the affairs of the Muslims and the frontier (*thagr*). I mean Alexandria, in particular. I was making supplication and entreaty to God for the Sultan and the Muslims. Toward the end of the night, I saw a pavilion (*fustat*),[18] vast in expanse and mounting to the sky, over which a light was rising and toward which was pressing a throng of creatures of the inhabitants of the sky, while the people of the earth paid no attention to it.
>
> "To whom does this pavilion belong?" I asked.
>
> They replied, "To the Apostle of God."
>
> So I hastened toward it joyfully and met at its door a band of learned and worthy *'ulama*, about seventy in number, of whom I recognized the Jurists 'Izz al-Din ibn 'Abd al-Salam; Majd al-Din, a teacher of Qus; al-Kamal, son of the Qadi Sadr al-Din; the *muhaddith* [traditionist] Muhyi

al-Din ibn Sarraqa, and al-Hakim ibn Abi al-Hawafir. Together with them were two men than whom I have seen none more handsome and whom I would not have known had it not been that a thought came into my mind while I was in a visionary state that they were the jurist Zaki al-Din ibn 'Abd al-'Azim, the *muhaddith*, and the Shaykh Majd al-Din al-Akhmimi.

I desired to advance toward the Apostle of God, but I constrained myself to humility and the proper courtesies with the Jurist 'Izz al-Din ibn 'Abd al-Salam, saying to myself, "It is not befitting that you advance before the most learned of the *'ulama* of this time."

So the Jurist ['Izz al-Din] advanced, then all advanced as the Apostle of God motioned right and left to them to sit down.

Then I advanced weeping with anxiety and joy. Joy was on account of my nearness to the Apostle of God by lineage, and anxiety on account of the Muslims and the frontier. I felt a natural yearning for him. He extended his hand until he grasped mine, and said to me, "Be not anxious with all this anxiety on account of the frontier. You must be kindly disposed to the chief authority, meaning the Sultan. For if an unjust man governs them, then perhaps"—and he clenched the five fingers of his left hand as if to shorten the duration of his reign—"but if a God-fearing man governs them, it is well, for 'God is the Patron of those who fear Him.'" (Q. 45:19) And he opened out his right and left hands.

As for the Muslims, "your sufficiency is God" (Q. 8:64), His Apostle, and these believers. "For if anyone befriends God, His Apostle, and those who believe, it is well, for the party of God—they are the conquerors." (Q. 5:56) As for the Sultan, the hand of God extends to him His mercy so long as he befriends the people under his governance, is well-disposed in his governorship, and kindly disposed toward his believing subjects. So be sincerely disposed toward him, speak with persuasive words of the oppressor, the enemy of God, and write to him, "and be patient, for the promise of God is true, and let not those who have no firm belief disquiet you." (Q. 30:60)

"Our help," I said, "by the Lord of the Ka'ba!" And then, I awoke.

He said,

One of the poor devotees (*faqir*) asked my permission to attend the audition (*sama'*),[19] and I was on the point of granting it. Then I had a vision of my teacher who had in his right hand a writing containing the Great Qur'an and the Hadith of God's Apostle, and, in his left hand, pages containing verses of measured prose. He was saying to me chidingly, "Do you depart from the pure sciences to the sciences of those who follow their corrupt passions? Now if anyone indulges in this, he is a servant enslaved by his passions, a captive of his appetites and desires. Through these pages of verse, hearts given to heedlessness and forgetfulness, and the victims of misguidance and blindness become inflamed. They have no desire at all to do good and to procure forgiveness. On listening to these verses they toddle like [immature] boys. The evil-doer, if he refrain not, verily God turns his earth skyward and his sky earthward."

On hearing this, a state of ecstasy took hold of me, in which I said to him, "Indeed, O my master, but the lower self (*nafs*) is earthly and the spirit (*ruh*) is heavenly."

"Yes, 'Ali," he replied, "whenever the spirit is copiously watered with the showers of sciences and the lower self is firmly rooted in good works, then all good results. But whenever the lower self is dominant and the spirit subordinate, then drought and sterility result, the whole order is overturned, and every evil befalls. So heed the guiding Scripture of God and the healing word of His Apostle, for you will never cease to enjoy the good as long as you give preference to these two. But evil has already befallen him who turns away from them. The people of the Truth, upon 'hearing vain talk, turn from it' (Q. 28:55), and upon hearing the Truth, welcome it. 'Whoever commits a good deed, for him will We increase it with goodness.'" (Q. 42:23)

He said, "I saw in a dream my teacher beneath the Throne ('*arsh*). 'O, my master,' I said to him, 'yesterday I saw you beneath the Throne.'

"He replied, 'You saw no one except yourself, O 'Ali. If anyone is with God without a 'where' (*ayn*), how can he be seen? But whenever you come to inherit my station, you will see me.'"

One of His Devotional Recitations (Adhkar)

O God, the Praiseworthy, the Glorious!
O God, the Generous, the Just, the Compassionate!
O God, the Powerful, the Steadfast!

Grant me from Thy mercy the words wherewith to praise Thee, and so I shall be one of the true believers. Provide me with those inner subtleties of power that will make me strong, steadfast, a bearer and one borne in the worlds.

Grant me of Thy grace a gift whereby I shall be one of the just and pure devout.

O Compassionate One, O Kind One, be kind toward me with a kindness that the imagination of no one can comprehend. My God, I have found Thee compassionate beyond my hope in Thee. How should I not find Thee a Helper when my hope is in Thee? Whom have I if Thou sever me, and whom have I if Thou have not compassion on me?

So grant me help whence thou knowest, while I know not, for Thou art powerful over all things. May God bless our master Muhammad, his family, and his companions, and give them abundant peace.

Anecdotes

Our master Abu al-'Abbas al-Mursi said,

> When I traveled to Egypt in company with the shaykh, I was overtaken on the way by want and hardship. He said to me, "O Ahmad, God created Adam with His hand, caused His angels to prostrate themselves before him, made him to dwell in the Garden a half day, which is five hundred years, and then sent him down to earth. By God, He did not send him to earth to impair him. He sent him to earth for the sole purpose of perfecting him. And, by God, He certainly sent him down before making him a vicegerent, for He said, "I am about to place a vicegerent on the earth." (Q. 2:30)
>
> Now Adam had been serving God in the Garden with teaching the names of all things, and He sent him down to earth to serve Him with toil in order that the two kinds of servantship might be perfected in him: servantship of teaching and servantship of toil. On this account he deserved to be a vicegerent (*khalifa*). As for you, you were in the heaven of the mystical sciences and have been brought down to a place of weariness of soul and toil. Thus you deserve to be a vicegerent.

He [Abu al-'Abbas] said,

> I traveled in the company of the Shaykh Abu al-Hasan, and we stopped in Alexandria at Pompey's Pillar (*'amud al-sawari*).[20] We were hungry. An abundance of food was brought out to us, but he ordered us not to eat of it. When we had worshiped with morning prayer, he said, "Bring on what you have." We prepared the meal.
>
> Then he said, "I was informed yesterday of this food, for I was told, 'The most lawful thing is that which comes to you without asking, and you have asked no one for it, woman or man.'"

The worthy Shaykh Abu 'Abd Allah ibn Hariz related to me that one of the worthy and excellent men of the people of al-Jazira al-Qibliya[21] said to him,

> One night there occurred to my mind that there existed in our time someone of the men of eminence and miracle-workers who was worthy of imitation. I saw the Apostle of God who said to me, "The illuminations (*anwar*) of the Shaykh Abu al-Hasan al-Shadhili are gleaming in the world

of phenomena (*akwan*)," or, said he, "in the realm of being (*wujud*), and whoever persists in following any portion of them has a hold on every good."

He also related to me:

I saw in the book entitled *Kitab Lata'if al-Minan*[22] [by Ibn 'Ata' Allah] on the excellencies of the Shaykh and Saint Abu al-'Abbas al-Mursi and of his shaykh, my master Abu al-Hasan al-Shadhili, these words: "There came into my mind the question whether or not the Shaykh Abu al-Hasan lacked any portion of the sciences that were the special property of the angels." I went to him with the question and he replied, "The angels of the seventh heaven come to me, even the angels of the Lotus Tree, and I impart to them what God has imparted to me."

The worthy Shaykh Abu al-'Abbas al-Hammami related to me that he heard the excellent Shaykh and Saint Abu 'Abd Allah ibn Sultan say:

The shaykh [al-Shadhili] said one day in his assembly, "It does not pertain to any creature of God to bestow upon us any favor." In the assembly there was the jurist and chief judge of Alexandria, Nasir al-Din ibn al-Munir, who asked him, "What do you say concerning the statement of your ancestor, 'The hearts have been fashioned with a disposition to love him who has been beneficent toward them?'"

"As for us," he answered, "we consider no one beneficent toward us except God, praise be to Him. So our hearts have been fashioned with a disposition to love Him."

Then he added, "O Ibn al-Munir, you are finding fault with us. So, by God, you shall certainly die three deaths: the death of abasement, the death of poverty, and the death of effacement. However you will die a Muslim."

Consequently al-Munir was removed from the office of judge, afflicted with poverty until he found no barley bread with which to satisfy the hunger of his children, and with abasement until no one he met would greet him.

The learned Shaykh and Jurist Abu 'Abd Allah ibn Hariz related to me that, when the Shaykh [al-Shadhili] died in Humaythira,[23] the Jurist Ibn al-Munir undertook the journey to his tomb. He remained beside it some days, pled excuse before him, and recited verses of apology. In sleep, Ibn al-Munir saw the shaykh who said to him, "We have accepted your apology. Return now to your country and compose a commentary on the Book of God, and He will reveal to you how to do it." Ibn al-Munir returned to Alexandria and composed a great commentary, God having revealed to him how to do it, and it is now renowned as by him.

When he died, someone in a dream saw him in a goodly state and asked him, "How has God dealt with you?"

"I stood before Him," he replied, "and met the Shaykh Abu al-Hasan al-Shadhili who treated me as one of the virtuous (*akhyar*) and righteous (*abrar*) and interceded for me before God, and so He forgave me."

Verses of the Shaykh, Saint and Mystic Abu al-'Abbas al-Mursi

There are people who wander in a desert land, and others who
stray in the field of His love.
Pass away, pass away, and pass away. And abide ye in closest
proximity to Him.

The Shaykh Taj al-Din Abu al-'Abbas ibn 'Ata Allah said in his compilation, *Lata'if al-minan*, "I have found in the script of Abu al-'Abbas al-Mursi these words:

Have you a tale recorded of Layla, by the bringing forth of which the moldering bones come to life and are quickened? My pledge with her is the ancient pledge, but I, under any circumstances, am one who falls short in my passion for her. The specter of her was wont of old to visit me, but of late it has not come to visit. What had it in mind that it should make excuses? Is she miserly even with her phantom-form?[24] Or has it become so dim that her form is only indistinctly visualized?

It is from the face of Layla that the rising sun obtains light, and in the sunlight the eyes of men are dazzled. Certainly she has not been veiled except through the lifting of her veil, and what amazes me is that the appearing is a concealing.[25]

The following is also ascribed to Taj al-Din ibn 'Ata Allah:

I see all in need, while Thou hast the sufficiency. Such as I am to transgress, such art Thou to pardon.

It is Thou Who art the first to show affection out of kind generosity. Such as Thou art to tend gently, such am I to show aversion. Certainly no earthly living is agreeable with which Thou art not in continual relationship, nor is it unsullied. No, by God, but how can it ever be unsullied? I have resolved to quit this whole existence and to follow the path of love, and one who is chosen follows.

The vision of Thee is clear, as also the veiling, because whenever realization is attained, the veiling becomes the unveiling. How pleasing are the beloved of God in every state, for God is whatever they reveal, and God is whatever they conceal. But the hearts of those who have not seen Thee in any mode of manifestation have remained closed to the attainment of the mystery of spiritual passion.

It is Thou Who hast made manifest all that is and manifested Thyself in all that can be seen, just as it is commonly known [among Sufis]. Thou hast manifested Thyself to the universe, and so the universe becomes a theater of manifestation and all in it is His also, as the pages of Scripture have conveyed. What heart would recoil from Thy fondness? What eye, after Thy nearness to me, would slumber. What soul has Thy passion not caused to incline toward Thy love? Upon Thy love all the souls of mankind depend.

My Observation of His Salutation on the Apostle of God

Al-Shadhili was wont to wait at Bab al-Salam[26] and say, "This is a place of which our Lord said, 'O believers, enter not the houses of the Prophet except permission be granted you' (Q. 33:53), until he would hear the invitation, 'Enter, O Abu al-Hasan.' "

Al-Shadhili said, "Whenever I would greet him [that is, the Prophet], he would reveal himself to me, face-to-face, and return to me the salutation with his forefinger. His greeting was, 'Peace be upon you, O our master, O Apostle of God.' "

"The most excellent, the purest, the most sublime, and the loftiest prayer that he offered on behalf of any one of His prophets and chosen ones is this:

I bear witness that thou, O Apostle of God, hast conveyed that with which thou wast sent, and hast admonished thy people, and hast served thy Lord until the certainty (*yaqin*) came to thee, as God described thee in His Scripture: "An apostle from among yourselves has come to you for whom your adversity is hard to bear, who watches over you, and who is compassionate and merciful toward the believers." (Q 9:128) May the prayers of God, His angels, His prophets, His apostles, and all His creatures of the inhabitants of His heavens and His earth be upon Thee, O our master, O Apostle of God.

Peace be upon both of you, O ye two companions of the Apostle of God, O Abu Bakr and 'Umar, with His mercy and blessings. So may God recompense you two on behalf of the religion of Islam and its people with the most excellent reward that He has ever bestowed upon any two ministers of a prophet during his life, and for the excellence of your successorship to him over his community after his death. For you two were, for the Apostle of God, faithful ministers during his life, and you succeeded him with equity and beneficence among the people of his community after his death. May God reward both of you for that with His companionship in His Garden, and us together with you, by His mercy. He is the most Generous of the most generous.

O God! I call upon Thee to bear witness, upon Thine Apostle, upon Abu Bakr and 'Umar, upon the angels who descend to visit this noble garden and who abide here devotedly, that I testify that there is no god at all save God alone. No associate has He. I testify that Muhammad is His servant and His Apostle, the seal of the prophets and the guide (*imam*) of the apostles.

I testify that every command, prohibition, and information regarding the past and future which he brought is true, containing no uncertainty or doubt. I acknowledge to Thee my infidelity and transgression in walk, thought, will, and deed. Whatever Thou hast preferred for me, whether something for which Thou dost punish or pardon according to Thy will, or anything that is comprised in unbelief, hypocrisy, heresy, and error, or transgression, or misconduct toward Thee, Thine Apostle, Thy prophets, toward those who are near Thee, whether of angels, men, or *jinn*, and whatever creatures of Thine Thou hast especially favored— bestow upon me what Thou hast bestowed upon those near to Thee, for Thou art God the Bestower, the Generous, the Forgiving, the Compassionate.

One of His Devotional Recitations

God, I petition Thee by the high rank of our master Muhammad, the chosen one, and of Ibrahim who performed his vows, and by the veneration of every apostle, prophet, trustworthy one, saint, martyr, righteous and pious person, and by the sanctity of the Greatest of the names, and of all the names—God, I ask Thee to efface these creatures from our hearts and make them to be with respect to our innermost beings like dust in the air. Make us to walk the path of Thy prophets, Thy chosen ones, and Thy pious ones in secret and in open. Thou art powerful over all things.

A Devotional Recitation

May God help you and us to do what He desires and what pleases Him. May He be propitious to you and to us in whatever He has ordained by the particular and universal decrees. May He appoint you and us to be among the fortunate on the day of encounter.

God, may we die Muslims. Join us to Muhammad and his party according to Thy good pleasure and theirs, with security from shame, disgrace, and abasement because of the works of those who confuse evil with good that we have performed.

God, excuse us for our ignorance. Punish us neither for our negligence of Thee nor for our misconduct toward Thee and the noble recording angels.

God, forgive us our sins, our heedlessness, and our ignorance of Thy favors, and forgive us our paucity of reverence toward Thee. Turn Thy face toward us, and do not relinquish us to any of Thy creatures. Thou art powerful over all things.

God, forgive us for the evil that men know about us. Forgive us for whatever Thine angels know and have inscribed. Forgive us for whatever we of ourselves know without anyone of Thy creatures knowing it. Forgive us for what Thou alone dost know about us with regard to negligence of all Thy precepts, and kindly grant that we may dispense with all Thy creatures and that the veil of separation between Thee and us be lifted. Thou art powerful over all things.

God, pardon us as one beloved to another grants pardon that admits of no misgiving and in which there remains no blame or reproof. May what Thou dost know in us and about us be the best of everything that is known after the effacing and confirming, for with Thee is the Mother of the Book (*umm al-kitab*).

God, pardon all our sins, small and great, secret and open, former and latter. Pardon those of our friends who have departed from us on a journey of this world or of the next, and make their wandering to be a wandering of the God-fearing and their return a return of the successful. Appoint us all, by Thy mercy, to be of the acceptable ones, even though we be spurious, for the critics [of others] are tolerant. But Thou hast the greater right to do that, for Thou art the most Generous of the most generous and the most Merciful of the merciful.

Praise be to God, Lord of the worlds. No strength is there and no power except with God, the High, the Mighty. God, disappoint us not who hope in Thee. Deny us not who make supplication to Thee. We have supplicated Thee as Thou hast commanded us. So answer us as Thou hast promised us. Esteem not our humble entreaty lightly, nor unacceptable to Thee. As Thou hast rendered easy for us the favorable response, for Thou art powerful over all things.

A Devotional Recitation

O God, Thou Who hast given existence to the existing universe (*kawn*) through Thy sublime existence. O Thou Who dost control its states of movement and rest. I ask Thee, by Thine exalted name through which Thou dost quicken the dead, through which Thou dost exalt whom Thou willest, and through which Thou dost abase whom Thou willest, to assign me a happy issue and a way out from my affair. O what a great hope!

A Saying

He said, "The companions of the Apostle of God and the followers were distinguished by works that people might be imitators of them. But the people of our time are distinguished by mystical knowledge (*ma'rifa*), and I have been made the most knowing of them about God."

Verses of al-Mazduri

The following are verses of the Shaykh Abu Muhammad 'Abd Allah al-Mazduri about our master the Shaykh, Saint, and Mystic Abu al-Hasan al-Shadhili when he journeyed from Tunis to Egypt.

> I evoke the memory of the shaykh. How magnificat his sciences! Al-Shadhili is called the grandson of our Prophet. Long did he wander in Ifriqiya where he has sincere brethren among us. He built in Tunis a house that was well known, one finely constructed by our Suq al-Balat.²⁷

After the period of his wandering was the time of its construction, a house and porticoed structure²⁸ for our living. When he had it built, after his life of asceticism and after that of those persons who relied on him, the hand of discipline of the shaykh took them away forcibly from us as a protection for us, that our [Sufi] way might be safeguarded.

> No one knows the pain of yearning save those from among us who have been scorched by the fire of yearning.
> Ibn al-Bara' assailed him in due time, until he moved by permission [of God] from our region.

[And so], the Sharif [al-Shadhili] was rescued from the jurist, after his house was built and finished, and our edifice was brought to completion.

> So, he left the sciences early to spur on his white mounts toward the surety of God. How scanty is our narration!
> He dwelt thereafter in various places of the East for a time, and there built up renown unlike ours.
> The light of prophecy is in the course of his supplication. So may God have mercy upon him and us all.
> When his glorious life had spent itself, and the mounts drew near for the departure to our master,
> He was summoned, and he responded with the pilgrims hastening toward the gate of the Divine, and so he fled from our gates.

He left the children and everything immediately and came to
Humaythira where he obtained the object of his desires.

O would that I knew if with our friends we shall meet after the
long separation and all anxiety will be cast off from us!

The houses are deserted, and there is no kind person from whom is
to be hoped the favor, and no good person to share our
affection.

These abominations have declared our separation, but may God do
what is best for our welfare. May God have mercy on him with
His mercy that embraces all our wayward and our [true] guides.

Sayings and Anecdotes

The worthy Shaykh Abu al-'Abbas al-Jami related to me that explained in the
compilation of the Shaykh Taj al-Din ibn 'Ata' Allah, on the authority of Abu
al-'Abbas al-Mursi, was the latter's saying, with reference to His saying, " 'A crowd
of the former and a crowd of the latter,' (Q. 56:39–40) that they were the Shaykh
Abu al-Hasan al-Shadhili and his companions."

The Shaykh Abu al-'Abbas al-Jami also related to me that a certain man asked
my master Abu al-Hasan, "Who is your teacher (*ustadh*), my master?" He replied,
"In the beginning it was my master Abu Muhammad 'Abd al-Salam ibn Mashish.
At present, I dip up from ten seas, five Adamic and five spiritual."

"The Adamic are our master Muhammad and his companions Abu Bakr,
'Umar, 'Uthman, and 'Ali. The five spiritual are Jibril (Gabriel), Mika'il (Michael),
Israfil, 'Izra'il and the Spirit (*Ruh*)." May God bring benefit through the shaykh's
blessings (*barakat*) and assemble us with him by His grace.

He said one night, "I received my inheritance from my ancestor the Apostle
of God, a hidden treasure from the treasury of the names; and if men and *jinn*
were to write down the things heard from me to the day of resurrection, they
would be completely exhausted."

He also said one night, "I received my inheritance from my ancestor the Apostle
of God. My ancestor, al-Husayn,[29] took me and put his finger in my navel and
turned me around over his head until the heavens, the earth, the Throne ('*arsh*),
and the pedestal (*kursi*) became before me like the country round about."

Then I was told,

Say, "O God, I ask Thee for a portion of the light by which our master
Muhammad, Thine Apostle, saw what was and is to be, that the servant
may be described in terms pertaining to his master, not to himself; one
who finds sufficiency in Thee without repeatedly giving consideration
to what is relative to a sure means of livelihood, or suffering inability

to bear the overpowerings (*maqdurat*) that He has willed; one who encompasses his own inner being with all kinds of essence; one who sets the body in proper relationship with the soul, the heart to the mind, spirit to inner being, command (*amr*) to insight, and attributes to attributes."

He said, "I saw the Apostle of God, and I said to him, 'O my master, O Apostle of God, entreat God that He make me to be "a mercy (*rahma*) to all creatures"' (Q. 21:107). He replied, 'I am that, O 'Ali, but the saint is a mercy among all creatures.'"[30]

He used to say to his companions, "Be my companions and I will not prevent you from being companions of another; for if you find a drinking place more agreeable than this drinking place, go down to it."

He said, "I saw the Apostle of God who said to me, 'O 'Ali, in your age there is no assembly (*majlis*) dealing with the science of jurisprudence (*fiqh*) more splendid than the assembly of 'Izz al-Din ibn 'Abd al-Salam,[31] and none in the science of tradition (*hadith*) more splendid than the assembly of Zayn al-Din ibn 'Abd al-'Aziz, and none in the science of supreme reality (*haqiqa*) more splendid than yours.'"

My master Madi related to me,

> When my master Abu al-'Abbas al-Mursi sat sometimes discoursing in the meeting place, he would put his garment over his eyes to conceal them.
>
> One day I questioned him about that and he said, "O my brother Madi, whenever I was speaking, the veils would be torn apart so that I would see the Throne (*'arsh*) and its illuminations would spread over me until I was unable to see. By God, O my brother Madi, I fear nothing unless it be to be consumed by the intensity of the divine illuminations (*anwar*)."

The jurist and Qur'anic reader Abu Ya'qub Yusuf ibn Hayara[32] related to me that Abu 'Ali Jidar told him,

> I accompanied the Shaykh, Saint, and Gnostic Abu 'Abd Allah Muhammad al-Habibi to a threshing floor and, while we were in the midst of the forest, having with me a loaf of dry, hard bread, I desired a bunch of grapes to eat with it. He dismounted from his horse and said to me, "O 'Ali, go inside the forest and eat your loaf with what you desire, until I pray some cycles (*raka'at*)."
>
> So I went and saw hanging from every tree of the forest grapes of various hues and species. I ate until I was filled, and brought him two bunches, one white and the other black. I handed them to him, but he threw them on the ground and they were crushed.

One day, I was with him in the Jabal al-Julud, which is south of Tunis, and I became thirsty. "Are you thirsty?" he asked. I replied, "Yes." He handed me his jug, saying, "Go down to the spring that is at the foot of the mountain, fill it, pronounce the name of God, and drink."

I descended to the spring that is by the edge of the lake and that is salty and bitter. I filled the jug, drank of water that was fresh, and went back up to him.

"Did you drink?" he asked me. I replied, "Yes, fresh water."

He took the jug from my hand and poured it out. Then he said, "Because of the intensity of your thirst the water tasted good to you."

The *murabit*[33] 'Umar informed me, "One day I was in the neighborhood of the lime-burners. I saw my master Muhammad Abu 'Abd Allah al-Habibi on foot, and then appeared Abu 'Ali Jidar mounted on a stallion. The latter recognized him as my master 'Abd Allah al-Habibi and was on the point of dismounting for him, but al-Habibi said, "Do it not. You will be a rider (*faris*) in this world and the next, if God wills."

My master Abu al-Hasan related,

I saw as if a man came to me and said, "The sultan is coming to you. So pray, 'God, bestow upon me of Thy beauty, Thy love, and Thy special grace; and epithets of Thy lordship that abash the hearts, and before which souls are submissive, necks are bowed, eyes stare, thoughts are dissipated, every proud and haughty person becomes of little account, every impious oppressor prostrates himself. O God, O Sovereign, O Glorious One, O Mighty One, O God, O Unique One, O One, O Conqueror.' "

He related,

I passed the night in a state of anxiety on account of the Muslims—that is, the Turks[34]—questioning whether or not I should imprecate them. I saw in a dream my spiritual guide who was saying, "Wait. Be not hasty toward them. Be patient, give thanks, commit your affair to God, be content, be submissive, trust, fear God, do good, 'be not weak and be not sorrowful, for you shall be the superior ones if you believe.' (Q. 3:139) Is there a governor other than God in exercising jurisdiction over people who firmly believe?

"The companions and followers of the Apostle of God used to be ill-treated and suffer wrong, and how much less was their haste and their imprecation of the evil-doers? This was on account of their knowledge of God as Lord of all creatures. And if someone of them did offer an imprecation, it was with a permission from God and not out of straitened circumstance and anger."

He said,

Whenever man's heart is filled with the illuminations of God and the inner soul is filled with the most exalted light, his spiritual vision becomes blind to the deficiencies and defects attached to the observance of religious duties of the common believers, on account of the most exalted praise having no end in the endless space of time that has been bestowed on him.

But whenever the servant is veiled from the most exalted light and is confined to the lower light, is changed in disposition[35] because of the changeableness of the light, is perturbed on account of the inertness of his night and the dullness of his moment, it is enough for him to observe what the religious law prescribes and prohibits.

He said, "With God, love (*mahaba*) consists in casting off the appetitive desires (*shahawat*) and personal wishes. Never shall a servant attain [to union with] God while there remains with him any one of his appetitive desires and personal wishes."

He said, "I saw the Apostle of God and he instructed me, 'Tell so-and-so to recite these words, for, if anyone utters them, the mercy of God will be showered upon him as the rain. Praise be to God with Whom praise originated and to Whom all things return.' Also let him say, 'There is no god at all save God. God, pardon my association of others with Thee, my unbelief, my remissness. Pardon believers, both men and women.'"

Once, on beginning his worship, he declared,

There is no god at all save God, the All-Hearing, the Near, the Answerer. Thou dost answer the supplication of the petitioner whenever he supplicates Thee.

Thou dost respond to the destitute. Thou takest away his ills. Thou dost appoint as successor whom Thou willest. My Lord is one who harkens to supplication. "My Lord, make me and my children devoted to worship. Our Lord, wilt Thou accept my supplication? Our Lord, pardon me and my parents and the believers on the day when the account is taken." (Q. 14:40–41)

I ask Thee, with Thy blessing upon Muhammed, Thine Apostle, that Thou bless me and Thine angels with a blessing whereby Thou wilt bring me out of the shadows of darkness into the light.

Account me one of the believers, for toward the believers Thou art Merciful. God, make this worship a bond of union between Thee and me. Make it to be a worship that restrains from the obscene and the disapproved, and in it place me in Thy remembrance with the greatest remembrance (*dhikr*). Make me to see the embodiment of it [the (*dhikr*)] in my soul and in my knowledge. Let it accompany me as a divine gift to the end of my appointed time. "Verily Thou art powerful over all things." (Q. 2:20)

He said,

One of my companions, and the dearest of men to me, asked me to seek the divine guidance (*istikhara*) for him for some boon for which he was hoping. The first night, I made that the object of my request. I saw the same. Then on the third day, he asked me, and I appealed to God concerning what he desired of me.

Thereupon I saw my teacher who said to me, "He is a man who mingles with the people of the other world and relies on them for aid, and who mingles with the people of this world while his natural disposition recoils from them. If he is in straitened circumstances, he appeals to God. If He is gracious toward him, he proceeds to give thanks to God. So how do you think he stands in the eyes of God? Do you not understand? He has incited him to excellent religious works. He blesses him in what he desires in this life and stores up for him with respect to what remains eternally, and 'God will reward the thankful.' " (Q. 3:144)

He said,

I saw as if I were in the highest heaven ('*illiyun*) with the favorite angels in delights such that I desired no change. They said, "Proceed still farther."

I went on with them and entered a sumptuous abode that I am unable to describe, desiring earnestly the vision of God. Then I experienced a vision that I cannot describe, and a voice said, "He whose members I have kept from disobedience to Me, whom I have adorned with unfailing fidelity to Me, whose heart I have opened to contemplate Me, the tongue of whose inner soul I have loosened for spiritual communion with Me, between whom and My attributes I have lifted the veil, and whom I have made to see the inner meanings of the spirits of my words, such a one have I snatched from the fire and ushered into my Garden. He has attained nearness to Me, and My angels are his companions. 'If anyone is snatched away from the fire and is admitted into the Garden, he has already attained.' " (Q. 3:185)

This is a Garden prepared in advance for the people of faith who reach certainty. They will enter it on the day of requital with their bodies, tasting, feeling, and seeing. Then I will call out to them with word ('*ibara*) and sign (*ishara*), kindness (*lutf*) and truth (*haqiqa*), "O sons of Adam, let not Satan seduce you as he caused your parents to leave the Garden." (Q. 7:27)

He said, "He who is unmindful of God is one whom the difficulties of the present life have deluded with regard to the favors proceeding from God, and the corruption of whose lower self (*nafs*) has deluded with regard to the beneficence of God toward him. 'So remember the favors of God that you may prosper' " (Q. 7:69).

He said,

It is incumbent upon you to observe the five means of purification consisting in sayings and the five means of purification consisting in acts, and to remain clear of claiming the power and strength of God for yourself in all circumstances. Plunge with your mind into the inner meanings of the sayings subsisting in the heart, and emerge from them and speak directly to the Lord. Preserve God in the heart and He will preserve you. Keep God in mind and you will find Him in front of you. Worship God with these means of purification and be of the thankful ones.

The five means of purification consisting in sayings are Glory be to God; Praise be to God; there is no god at all save God; God is most great; and there is no power and no strength except with God the High, the Mighty.

The five means of purification consisting in acts are the five acts of ritual worship (*salawat*).

He said, "The spiritual truths (*haqa'iq*) are the meanings that subsist in hearts, and the transcendental verities that become manifest and are disclosed to them. They are bestowals from God and divine gifts (*karamat*) through which they have attained unto piety and the ability to accomplish acts of obedience. An indication of it is the saying of Haritha when he was asked, 'How are you this morning?' He replied, 'I am a believer this morning.' " (Read the tradition.)

A Daily Dhikr

He said, "On departing from my lodging for morning worship, a devotional exercise (*dhikr*) was suggested to me."

In the name of God, Lord of Gabriel,
In the name of God, Lord of Michael,
In the name of God, Lord of Israfil,
In the name of God, Lord of 'Izra'il,
In the name of God, Lord of Ibrahim,
In the name of God, Lord of Moses,
In the name of God, Lord of everything,
Who is "powerful over all things." (Q. 2:20)

He said,

Among the formulas that are fitting to be recited in the first part of the night, the first part of the day, and between times are:

"I seek refuge with God, with His power, with His complete and all-inclusive words, from the evil of whatever has been, whatever is this day, and will be in those follwing until the day of resurrection, both in this world and the next, from before the beginning of time until its close, eternity of eternity without end, and from the evil of whatever is not, even if it were as it might be."

"I take refuge in Thy might, Thy beauty, Thy greatness, Thy magnificence, Thy light, Thy splendor, Thy sovereignty, Thy power, Thy will, the execution of Thine eternal will, and in all Thy names, Thine attributes, Thine epithets, Thy characteristics, Thine illuminations, and Thine essence, from the evil of every knowing thing of Thine."

"Thou art my Lord and Thy knowledge is sufficient for me. So grant me mercy as broad as the breadth of Thy knowledge, for it is this mercy that has not ceased to be an object of quest for the good and a sanctuary from the evil."

"I believe 'in God, His angels, His scriptures, His apostles,' (Q. 2:285) the Last Day, the decree with its good and evil, and in His words that have branched off from His creative word that subsists in His essence."

He said,

The *dhikr* has four aspects: a *dhikr* meaning the act of remembering; a *dhikr* meaning the object of your remembrance; a *dhikr* that evokes your remembrance; and a *dhikr* that causes you to be remembered.

The first *dhikr* is the portion of the common people, that with which you cast off forgiveness or whatever you fear from forgetfulness. The second, concerning the object of your remembrance, is the object remembered, whether punishment or bliss, proximity or alienation, and so forth. The third, what evokes your remembrance, refers to four things remembered: the good things from God, the evils due to the lower self, the evils due to the Adversary, and these evils even if God be their Creator. The fourth, a *dhikr* that causes you to be remembered, is God's remembrance of His servants, in which nothing depends on the servant, although his tongue pronounces it. In this situation he is effaced in the act of remembrance or in the One remembered, the Lofty and Most High, for whenever you are admitted into this state, the rememberer becomes the remembered, and the remembered the rememberer. This is what one has to end with while following the [Sufi] way, and God is better and more abiding.

It is furthermore incumbent upon you, my brother, to perform the *dhikr* requisite for security from the punishment of God in this world and the next. It is also necessary for pleasing God in this world and the next. Hold to it and continue in it. That is, you should say,

"Praise be to God;
I ask pardon of God;
There is no force and no strength except with God."

You say, "Praise be to God," for favors and the bestowal of good are from God.

You say, "I ask pardon of God" upon encountering any evil from the lower self or the Adversary, even though the creation or willing of it be of God.

You say, "There is no power and no strength except with God" in the face of whatever influences may come over you from God or sentiments toward Him that may arise in you.

Know this matter well, for the central fact is that seldom any good or evil occur in the *dhikr*, thought, silence, or muteness unless it be in one of these four.

So say, "Praise be to God" and "I ask pardon of God." If something befalls you from God or from your lower self that has never yet been experienced, whether of good or evil, and you are powerless to repel it or attract it, then say, "There is no power and no strength except with God."

Recite these three *adhkar* together ordinarily, continue doing so, and you will experience their blessings, if God wills. Peace be to you.

He said, "Knock on the door of remembrance, seeking shelter and avowing your need of God, with continual silence toward your fellows and other men, watching over your innermost being to guard it from converse with the lower self with every breath if you desire to have spiritual sufficiency."

He said, "If anyone wishes to be delivered from dread of this world and the next, let him read [the Qur'anic chapter] beginning with, 'When the sun is folded up' " (Q. 81:1).

Trust

He said, "If you desire the good of this world and the next, the blessing of pardon and mercy, deliverance from the Fire, and entrance into the Garden, give up disobedience toward God and abide strictly by the command of God, for God loves those who put their trust in Him."

Someone said to him, "Explain to me how to trust in God, how to seek His protection, and how to ask His help." He replied,

> If anyone clings to anything, trusts in it, relies upon it, or stays himself upon anything except God, he is not one who trusts. Trusting is the resting of the heart, lower self, mind, spirit, inner soul, and external and internal parts upon God to the exclusion of every thing except Him, and seeking protection with God, clinging to Him, going to Him for shelter, and doing so from necessity.
>
> So be careful to seek protection with God lest you see any power of your own, will, judgment or resolve in anything, upon anything, from anything, or for anything. Then, as for seeking help with God, one should not take knowledge as a means, or the author of knowledge as a means, or a knowledge of the First and the Last. But submerge everything in the divine knowledge, power, will, and word as they submerged this world in the next, the next in the preeternity, the preeternity in the decree (*hukm*), and the decree in the eternal knowledge (*al-'ilm al-azali*).
>
> As for giving up (*hijran*) disobedience, give up until you forget. Real giving up is forgetting the thing given up. This is in the image of perfection. If you have not reached that point, then give up disobedience with struggling and fighting, for He will not allow those who perform good works to lose their reward.
>
> If anyone would abide strictly by the command of God, let him do it by remembrance, reflection, promptness, and submission to the command of God. Whenever some fault, deficiency, diversion, or act of forgetfulness befalls you, seek pardon of God for wrong done to yourself and for your evil conduct through your great ignorance, for if anyone commits evil or wrongs himself and then seeks pardon of God, he will find God to be forgiving and merciful.

Intention

He said,

> Religious works are valid according to the intentions (*niyat*). The validity of the intention is related to place (*mahall*), appropriateness, modality, and meaning. It is granted that freedom from impurities is required for the places in which the works are to be performed, that appropriateness refers to their proper times, that the modality alludes to their freedom from fault, and that their inner meanings must be real. One grants that the genuineness of the vow and the righteous of the purpose are to honor

the right of lordship and to obligate one's self to assume the quality of a servant. The place of the intention is the heart, and the time is at the beginning of the act. Its modality is the linking of the heart and the outward acts of the members.

Intention has a fourfold meaning: the purpose (*qasd*), the determination (*'azm*), the will (*irada*), and the desire (*mashi'a*). All these have one meaning. Intention has two aspects. The first is the strengthening of the act by keen awarenenss in the performance of it. The second aspect is sincerity (*ikhlas*) in performing the religious act unto God alone from the desire to obtain whatever reward He has to give and the desire to see His face.

A Dhikr of the Heart

He said, "The real devotional recitation (*dhikr*) has to do with what is tranquilized, that is, the heart, and what is revealed in the spiritual realities of the clouds of illumination, on the clouds[36] of the Lord."

Disobedience

He said,

Detach yourself from the love of this world by preference, and from disobedience with secrecy. Continue to implore divine mercy, and dispense thereby with the [divine] practical [mercy]. Allow not your soul to be attached to any thing, and you will be one of those well rooted in religious knowledge from whom no secret or knowledge is hidden.

If thoughts of disobedience and the world occur to your heart, cast them under your feet with disdain and indifference, and your heart will be filled with knowledge and right guidance (*rushd*). Act not by stealth to listen to the *khatarat*, lest their darkness cover you and your members become relaxed to their appeal. Then there will be no escape from embracing them, whether with the mental urge, the thought, the will, or physical movement. In that case, the mind becomes perplexed and the servant resembles him, "over whom the Satans have cast a spell of confusion in the land while companions with him call him to the guidance, saying, 'Come with us!' Say, 'The guidance of God is the true guidance.'" (Q. 6:71) But there is no guidance at all except for one who fears God, and there is no fear of God (*taqwa*) except for one who shuns the world. No one shuns the world except one to whom the lower self

(*nafs*) becomes docile, and the lower self never becomes docile except for one who knows it (namely, *nafs*). No one knows the *nafs* except one who knows God, and no one knows God except one who loves Him. No one loves God except one whom He has selected and chosen and between whom and whose lower self He has intervened.
Say,

"O God!
O All-Powerful,
O Willer,
O Glorious One,
O All-Wise,
O All-Praiseworthy,
O God, O Lord,
O Sovereign,
O Ever-Existing One,
O Guide,
O Gracious One,
Bestow upon me from Thy part a gift of mercy, for Thou art the Bestower.
Grant to Thy servant the favor of the true religion (*din*) and the guidance 'to a straight path, the path of God to Whom belongs whatever is in the heavens and the earth. Is it not to God that all things tend.' (Q. 42:52–53)
Hear my prayer for the honor of this greatest name. Amen."

Resolutions

He said,

Having been asked about resolutions ('*aza'im*), I replied, "If anyone is overcome by the spiritual consciousness of the divine will, his resolutions are dissipated on account of the rapidity and frequency with which the thing willed (*murad*) by God occurs to the mind, on account of its diversity in kind, and on account of whatever experience may completely engage him, so that no one loosens or binds, resolves or intends something pertaining to his own affairs, while his will is dispersed and his attributes disappear. Now, where do you stand in relation to the light (*nur*) of one who sees this matter with the light of his Lord, without the object of his reflection distracting him from Him by Whom he sees? So he (namely, the Prophet) has said, 'There is nothing that has been or that will be save that I have seen it.'"

Seekers

He said, "The gradations (*manazil*) of the seekers are three. They are the seeker who inquires about the essence of attainment of nearness to God by the lifting of the veil; the seeker who inquires about frequent occurrences of passing away (*fana'*) from self (*nafs*); and the third you have found [that is, the seeker who inquires about belief in real proximity to God]."

Spiritual Communion

He said,

> There are four planes of spiritual communion (*munaja*). First, either you call upon Him out of your attributes while you are looking toward His attributes, or you call Him out of His attributes while you are looking toward your own attributes. Second, either you are one passing away (*fani*) with His attributes from your own attributes, or one remaining (*baqi*) with His attributes while still in your attributes. Third, God makes you sit upon the plane of physical necessities whence you look furtively with the eyes of your heart at the supplying of needs and wants, or you recall to mind the way of the Prophet, in which case the plane is one of remembrance (*dhikr*). Fourth, He has made him to sit upon the plane of bounty, while the attributes of the servant are poverty, penury, impotence, weakness, necessity, indigence, ignorance, and abasement.

Satan

He said, "The shameful ways (*makhazi*) of Satan are four. Either he will cause you to sit reflecting on what draws you close to God and so you come to it; or [he causes you to sit thinking] about what alienates you from Him, and so you avoid it. Either you sit reflecting on your past sins, and so you seek pardon and are thankful; or you sit reflecting on the excellent religious works that you have performed, and so you are thankful and seek pardon."

Conversation

He said,

> Whenever you sit down to converse with the learned (*'ulama*), converse with them about the transmitted branches of knowledge and sound

traditions (*riwaya*). Either you will benefit them or derive some benefit from them, for that is all you can gain from being with them.

Whenever you sit down to converse with the devotees (*'ubbad*) and ascetics, converse with them on the plane of asceticism and devotion, sweeten for them what they find bitter, facilitate for them what they find hard, and give them a taste of mystical knowledge such as they have not tasted before.

Whenever you sit down to converse with the veracious mystics (*siddiqin*), put away what you know, make no reference to what you do, and so you will get possession of the hidden knowledge and of insights whose reward is unstinted.

Tranquility

He said, "Tranquility (*sakina*) lies in the being of the True One (*wujud al-Haqq*) without an intermediary, and resorting to the True One without the help of the members or God, except for the performance of religious service. In that case, the appointed lot of the soul becomes service (*khidma*), the lot of the heart is mystical knowledge, the lot of the intellect (*'aql*) is the unveiling (*mukashafa*), and the lot of the spirit is love."

Enigmas

He said, "If anyone has made real in himself the Being of God, he loses consciousness of every existing thing; and if anyone has his existence through Being, through him everything that has being becomes established."

He said,

How does one through whom the sciences are known come to have a knowledge of the sciences? Or how can one be made to know anything if his own existence precedes the existence of everything?

How can anyone be secure, in spite of His bounty, who knows His equity? Or how can anyone despair, in spite of evil, who knows His bounty? Or how can anyone be ignorant of God who considers the revolving of night and day, hearts (*qulub*) and perceptions (*absar*), stress and ease, or withholding and giving?

Miscellaneous Teachings

Quoting from his teacher, he said, "There are four things that, if enclosed within one, render other people needful of him while he can dispense with everything.

They are love toward God, finding sufficiency with God, sincerity (*sidq*), and certainty (*yaqin*). Sincerity applies to the judgements of lordship (*rububiya*), and who is better than God in judging people who firmly believe?"

He said, "He who neglects his heart despises his religion (*din*), and he who is preocucpied with his outer behavior is taking his religion as a jest."

He said, "The unity is the secret of God, sincerity is the sword of God, and the extending of the sword is 'In the name of God,' the interpretation of which is, 'Whatever God has willed is, and whatever He has not willed is not.' There is no strength and no force except with God."

He said,

> There are four punishments (*'uqubat*): punishment with torment (*'adhab*), punishment with the veil (*hijab*), punishment with being held back (*imsak*), and punishment with perdition (*ihlak*)—that is, perdition of the soul of the person interrogated. The punishment of torment is with reference to things forbidden. The punishment of the veil is for the people of obedient acts, and, in that case, the punishment is for misconduct. The punishment of being held back is with reference to haste or anxiety on the day of judgment. Often that happens to a person and the soul perishes.

He said,

> I was thinking seriously of imprecating a wrong-doer and, as I struggled with that idea, I saw my teacher who was saying to me, "If it is God who wills the destruction of a wrong-doer, be not hasty toward him, for hast toward enemies for their destruction and the desire of victory for friends come from hidden passion. And who is a greater wrong-doer than one who disputes the will of his Master and follows his soul's passion and whim? The man most divinely protected commanded and made prohibition by reciting His saying, 'Be patient as were those of the apostle who were endowed with resolution (*'azm*) and be not hasty toward them,' (Q. 46:35) and by His saying, 'So be patient; the favorable issue (*'aqiba*) is for the God-fearing.' (Q. 11:49) Now faith is the effacing of the attributes by the attributes, of the names by the names, and the submerging of the esences in the essences, in order to realize what is First, Last, Outer, and Inner, and what is the thing in relation to which He was Last so that He became First in relation to it, and what is the thing in relation to which He was Outer even so as to become Inner in relation to it. Whatever created thing is established is by His establishing it, and whatever is effaced is by His desire and will. Take that from His saying, 'God effaces and establishes what He wills, for with Him is the source of revelation (*umm al-kitab*),' (Q. 13:39) which is the first knowledge (*al-'ilm al-awwal*) from which all knowledge and Scripture have issued."

He said, "If you desire to look toward God with the sight of faith and firm belief continually, then be thankful for the favors of God and be content with His decree. Whatever favor you have is from God. Then, whenever evil touches you, entreat Him. If you desire it to turn away from you, or yourself to turn away from it, worship God lovingly, not barteringly; and knowingly, with due respect and modesty."

He said, "The grace (*karama*) of God in the matter of contentment with His decree is that it causes you to forget your misfortunes by looking forward to the day of rendezvous.

He said, "The understanding man is one who has an understanding from God of His signs (*ayat*) and whose occupation is recollection (*dhikr*) of and reflection upon His favors. To him is opened the way out of difficulties through taking refuge in and avowing dire need of Him, supplication and asking from Him, and seeking protection with Him. He appeals to God, and so God responds to him. No one knows what God wills to give him."

Then he recited, "In the creation of the heavens and the earth and in the succession of night and day" (Q. 2:164).

He said, "If anyone breaks away from the ordering of his own affairs to heed the ordering of God, from his own choosing of God, from his own regard to the regard of God, from his own interests to seek the knowledge of God with uninterrupted resignation to, contentment with, commitment to, and trust in God, He will endow him with sound understanding (*husn al-lubb*). This will result in the practice of remembrance, reflection, and other special virtues besides these."

With regard to the Prophet's saying, "If one's intention (*niya*) is valid, his works are valid," he [al-Shadhili] said,

> Good intention in relation to matters between God and you means turning the heart respectfully toward God, with respect for the commanding of God, and with respect for what He has commanded.
>
> Regarding affairs between other men and yourself, having good intentions means turning toward souls with a right disposition, fulfilling your obligations toward them, giving up your prerogatives, and dispelling difficulties with patience toward God and trust in Him.

He said,

> O servant of God, detach yourself from converse with the lower self (*muhadathat al-nafs*), the desire of Satan, obedience to lust, and emotion of chronic illnesses, and you will be righteous. Have a holy fear of God in times of the involuntary thoughts, mental urge, reflection, and agitation of the inner soul, and you will be utterly sincere.
>
> If any one of these things troubles you, forsake your means of livelihood, abodes, brothers, and tempting situations, and you will be

an emigrant. But if you give in to any of them, turn to God in repentance, ask pardon of Him, seek refuge with Him and call to Him, for help, and you will be a believer.

Take to yourself for armor (*sila*) ritual purification, fasting, worship, patience, performance of the *dhikr*, recitation of the *Qur'an*, and disclaiming the strength and power of God, and you will be in safety. If you are overcome, take to yourself faith for a stronghold, and, if you are prevailed upon, surrender the affair to God. Incumbent upon you are faith, the unity (*tawhid*), and love toward God. Submerge the world in the sea of unity before it submerges you.

He said, "The mystery of mysteries is the divine supplying of science (*'ilm*) and mystical knowledge (*ma'rifa*), comfort of proximity and love, and His choosing them, His separation of them from others for Himself, and His befriending them.

He said, "If anyone quits disobedience in his outward manners, and casts love of the world out of his inward arena, and persists in guarding the outward acts of his members, and in shepherding his inner soul, the increased blessings from his Lord come to him, and a guardian from His presence is set over him to keep him. God will join with him in his inner being and take him by the hand in all of his actions. The increased blessings are increases of religious knowledge (*'ilm*), certainty (*yaqin*), and intuitional knowledge (*ma'rifa*)."

He said, "Every desire that summons you to long for the thing represented in the mind is the tool and weapon of Satan; and every desire that summons you to obey God and long to perform good deeds is praiseworthy. Every good work that does not produce the fruit of light and knowledge reckon to it no reward; and every evil work that produces fear, fleeing to reward, and every evil work that produces fear, fleeing to God, and recourse to Him, reckon to it no fault."

He said,

> God, I repent to Thee. So give me refuge, hold me in rein, strengthen me, assist me, establish me, protect me from sin, shield me while I am in the midst of Thy creatures, and disgrace me not before Thine Apostle.
>
> I was told, "You are an associator (*mushrik*)."
>
> "How?" I asked.
>
> "You feared to be disgraced before men," I was told, "and your heart is attached to men and not to God. But you know that not one of them will either benefit or harm you. So long as your heart is attached to your knowledge and your striving, you are not as one going toward God, and you will not be such until you despair of everything, cleaving to hope in God with every breath. Then you will find comfort and help from God, even though you have not obtained what you want, even though He cut you off by that light from looking toward any other, and even though He put you in straitened circumstances."

He said, "The real significance of the remembrance lies in one's being detached from remembrance and joined to the One remembered in the *dhikr*, and detached from everything except Him."

He said,

> Whenever God honors a servant in his activities and moments of rest, He assigns to him service to perform (*'ubudiya*) and conceals from him his personal gratifications (*huzuz al-nafs*), makes him to live a life of servantship while the personal gratifications are concealed from him, and he looks not back on them, just as if he were in a place far removed from them. But whenever God looks with contempt on a servant with regard to his activities, He assigns to him personal gratifications and conceals from him his servantship, and he lives a life of gratification of his appetitive desires while servantship toward God is remote from him, even though he may engage in it to some extent with the exterior man.
>
> This is a chapter on contempt and friendship with God. As for the most magnificent state of utter sincerity and the greater friendship, the gratifications and the obligations in one endowed with spiritual insight are all the same, since whatever he receives or rejects is through God.

He said, "Steadfastness before God with a clear consciousness of Him is the fairest of obedient acts—that is, that he should admit you into His presence and lower over you the veil."

Someone commented, "If a person's volition is not strong, the passing of days upon him will increase for him nothing save retrogression." To this he replied,

> If a person desires that his volition should become strong, let him found his career on knowledge by the repudiation of ignorance, and upon the repudiation of this world by turning toward the other world, and let him persevere in the solitary life (*khalwa*) and the continuance of the *dhikr*. Then, there will appear upon him marks of the peculiar properties of Sufis, with radiance and splendor of countenance. People will approach him, men and women of the settled regions and the deserts who hasten to him to honor him with greetings and to present to him the homage of men. If he accepts that homage from them before he has reached the stages of composure and realization, then he falls in the regard of God, and he returns to the state whence he emerged. You see him at times praise this one, blame this one, nourish hatred toward that one. His degradation is already manifest by his turning of the back on the Lord and repudiating the things that foster His love for the sake of the things that foster love for himself. Beware of this great offense, for many men have been lost thereby. Seek protection with God, "for if anyone seeks protection with God, he has been led to a straight path." (Q. 3:101)

He said,

Know God. Then seek to be provided by Him from any source you will, save to stoop to anything forbidden or to covet what is unlawful. Act in good faith toward God among His servants, and be not unfaithful to Him with regard to what He has entrusted to you. Worship God with certainty and you will be one of the leaders (*imam*) of the religion. Rise above the knowledge possessed by the generality of Muslims to the knowledge possessed by the elect, and you will be one of the heirs [of the latter]. You have a model in one of the apostles, and one who has attained realization among the prophets. If anyone claims relationship to, inclines toward, loves, hates, shows affection for, approaches, fears, hopes in, trusts, or finds security in or with anything save God, or transgresses any one of the ordinances of God, he is an oppressor (*zalim*), and the oppressor cannot be an *imam*. God has said, "I appoint you an *imam* to men. He asked, of my children also? He said, My promise does not apply to the oppressors." (Q. 2:124) He about whom God spoke the truth regarding his certainty is an *imam*, however little or much has been related concerning it, and, if one is an *imam*, no harm is done him in his being by himself a community, even though his followers be few.

Desiring to go to a certain one of the oppressors to plead on behalf of one of the worthy men, he said,

God, make my going to him to be out of submissivenss to Thine Apostle. Adorn me with the adornment of "the poor emigrants who were expelled from their homes and goods, and who desired favor from God and His good pleasure, and to help God and His Apostle. These are the utterly sincere." (Q. 2:59) Favor me especially with the gift of love, preference for Thee, and the lifting of the veil from breasts (*sudur*), night and day.

Preserve me from my own niggardliness, and place me among those with whom it will be well. "Pardon us and our brothers who have gone before us in the faith. Put not in our hearts rancor toward those who believe. Our Lord, Thou art merciful and compassionate." (Q. 59:10)

He said, "He is described as niggardly and blameworthy who holds back his possessions on account of any one of these attributes: fear of poverty, wrong conjecture about God, contempt for the respect (*hurma*) due to the believers, predilection for the lower nature, and lust."

He said, "Whenever you find pleasure in any of your outer or inner states, say, 'Whatever God wills, there is no force except with God' (Q. 18:39)."

He said, "Whenever anyone, of *jinn* or men, intimidates you, say, 'Our sufficiency is God, and He is an excellent Protector' (Q. 3:173)."

He said, "Whenever anyone comes to you who prefers this world to the next, say, 'Our sufficiency is God. God will give us of His bounty, and so will His Apostle. Toward God is our desire' (Q. 9:59)."

He said, reciting with reference to the Eye ('*ayn*),[37] "The unbelievers almost cause you to slip with their looks when they hear the warning. They say, 'He is *jinn*-possessed.' Yet it is nothing other than a warning for all people (Q. 68:51–52). Recite, 'O Almighty, O All-Glorious, O All-Knowing, O All-Powerful, O All-Hearing, O All-Seeing!'"

When the people complained to him about wrong done to them, he said, "God, I am clear of the injustice of the unjust and of the wrong of the wrong-doers. We are created for the application of Thy justice, but apply it not to us with Thine anger. 'Thou art powerful over all things' (Q. 2:20)."

He said, "I met with a man in my journeying who enjoined me, saying,"

There is nothing in the way of spiritual utterances more helpful for doing things than "There is no force and no strength except with God" (Q. 18:39), and to seek the protection of God. So then, flee to God and seek protection of God, for "if anyone seeks protection with God, he has been led to a straight path." (Q. 3:101)

Then say,

"In the name of God,
I have fled to God,
I have sought protection with God,
'There is no force and no strength except with God.' (Q. 18:39)
Who forgives sins save God?"
My Lord, I seek refuge with Thee
From the working of Satan who surely is an adversary, a manifest
     misleader.

The utterance "In the name of God" is a saying upon the tongue issuing from the heart. The saying "Flee to God" is one descriptive of His sovereignty and command.

Then, you will say to Satan, "God knows all this about thee. My faith is in God, and in Him have I trusted, and with God do I seek refuge from thee, and if it were not for what He has commanded me, I certainly would not seek refuge from thee, for who art thou that I should seek protection with God from thee?"

He said,

All the instrumentalities (*wasa'il*) of religion are in four categories: bodies, goods, intellects, and hearts. God has said, "They said we were not of those who prayed. We were not of those who fed the poor. We used to enter into vain discourse with those who engaged therein, and we used to treat as a lie the Day of Judgement" (Q. 74:43–46). Prayer applies to bodies, feeding the poor to goods, entering into vain discourse to the intellects, and treating the Day of Judgement as a lie to the hearts.

He said, "Delay not your act of obedience beyond the proper time, for you will be punished for failure to perform it, or some other act, or some like act, as penalty for having delayed it beyond that time. For each time, there is an allotted portion for the duties of servantship that the divine obligation requires of you by the right of lordship."

I said within myself, "The very veracious (*al-siddiq*) put off the odd worship (*witr*)[38] until the latter part of the night."

Then a voice in my sleep said, "That is a custom and an established norm that God made obligatory for him despite his habitual observance of it. But how can you observe it along with your propensity for ease, enjoyment of the appetitive desires, commission of various kinds of remissive acts, and distraction from the contemplative practices? So beware, beware!"

So I said to myself, "Does this call for ordering my affairs to follow these prescriptions, or rejection of them entirely?"

He replied, "Nay, rather, it calls for an ordering of your life that necessitates the observance of proper conduct toward God and arousing yourself to what has been neglected. It is the injunction of God upon you, and an injunction from you upon His God-fearing devotees. So arouse youself to these injunctions and you will be one of the understanding persons."

He prayed, "God, we ask of Thee sound understanding; constancy of remembrance (*dhikr*) and reflection; refuge with Thee and need of Thee; supplication to Thee and the response from Thee; confidence in thee and reliance upon Thee; genuine asceticism practiced with unequivocal probity; and love and contentment. These are the religious works of the utterly sincere in the beginning of their careers."

He said,

> My teacher enjoined me, "If we fear God with a fear that makes us secure from everything, then there is no sense at all in having fear of anything, since He is by everything, with everything, above everything, below everything, near everything, enveloping everything. He is exalted above origination (*huduth*), places, and directions; and above love (*mahabba*), nearness (*qurb*) in space, and moving around objects of creation. Everything has been effaced virtually through the description of Him as 'the First, the Last, the Outer, the Inner. He is of everything cognizant.' (Q. 57:3) God is. Along with Him there is nothing at all, and He is now as He always has been.

He said, "The most firmly fixed of things with regard to attributes (*sifat*) is their being fixed before their actual existence (*wujud*). Then consider. Do you think that the essence (*'ayn*) has a 'where' (*ayn*), or that what exists (*kawn*) has a state of becoming (*ka'in*)?"

He said,

> Real knowledge (*'ilm haqiqi*) is the kind that contrary propositions and texts serving as evidentiary examples for the disproof of similars and equals do not challenge. Rather it is like the knowledge of an apostle, of one very veracious, or a saint (*wali*). He who enters this arena is like one engulfed in the sea whose waves break over him. In this situation, what partisans of the use of contrary propositions can dispute with him, or find him, or hear him, or see him? He who has not entered this arena has need only of the saying of God, "There is nothing like unto Him. He is the All-Hearing, the All-Seeing." (Q. 42:9)

He said,

> As for us, we look toward God with the eyes of faith and firm belief. Doing so has made us to dispense with proof and argument, and enabled us to draw inferences regarding the world of created beings. Is there in the realm of being anything beside the Kind, the True One (*Haqq*)? Of course not. But you do not see Him, even though He exists. This is necessarily so. Thus, you see them [mankind and all created things] like scattered dust in the atmosphere. Although you search, you find nothing.
>
> The Sufi celebrities taken together, and in epithets of the luminaries, are like the stars in relation to the satellite. That is, they [the stars] are without regency (*hukm*) despite their being (*wujud*). But they are useful for guidance in the darkness, for Scripture says, "And by the stars are they guided." (Q. 16:16) The greatest of the Sufi celebrities are like the suns (*shumus*) in relation to their satellites which are little in their significance. Such is the understanding of the similitudes of the prophets, apostles, the utterly sincere, and saints; and the comparison is applicable to any people who have points of similarity and equivalence. But to the Sufi travelers are given understanding, and their hearts are stilled by what they hear.

He asked,

> What is your position with regard to the unity that is stripped of attachment to both the name of God and creatures, while, by every name, you implore some grace or complain of some affliction? It is a veil separating you from the divine essence and from oneness with His attributes. But if one of the beautiful attributes should completely

envelope anyone, this fact causes him to dispense with seeking the help of the divine names and utterance. Relinquish not what is particularly yours for something that does not belong to you, and desire not the favor that God bestows upon another. May your servantship consist in resignation, contentment, acceptance of what is sent, good opinion of God in whatever you encounter, and being occupied with what is most worthy. "That is God's guidance by which He guides whatever servants of His He may will. But if they associate other gods with Him, futile for them is what they have been doing." (Q. 6:88)

He said, "God has men whose attributes He has wiped away with His attributes, whose religious beliefs He has made dispensable through His illuminations, whose resolves He has made of no effect by His will, whom He has made to dispense with His mercy by His essential mercy, whom He has chosen for communings (*munajat*) with Himself, and in whom He has established such secrets of His that the generality of the saints are unable to hear."

He said,

O you who pursue eagerly the way of your deliverance, yearning for the presence of His court, avoid constantly doing what God has rendered permissible for you, let alone whatever God has made lawful for you that does not come within the scope of your knowledge, and cease being occupied unduly with those things that occupy other men, for the sake of shepherding your inner soul. For in giving up excessive occupation with these things is renunciation of the world, and in letting alone what does not come within the scope of your knowledge is scrupulousness (*wara'*), by reason of the Prophet's saying, "Piety is that in which the soul becomes stilled and in which the heart finds rest, and sin is that which irritates the soul and brings agitation to the breast." If people give you another interpretation, understand. Occupying one's self with shepherding the inner man brings a comprehensive view of the inner truths of the faith.

So, if you are a shrewd man of affairs, leave what you desire for the sake of what He desires on condition of being contented with all of His judgments, "and who is better in judging than God for people who firmly believe?" (Q. 5:50) The forbidden things of the world incur punishment, and the lawful a reckoning, according to the tradition. Worldly goods, against which there is no reckoning in the future life and with which there is no veiling from God in the present, are those for which their possessor had no desire before obtaining them, for which he has no desire after obtaining them, and upon the loss of which there are no regrets. As for the noble and free man,[39] if anyone takes away his worldly goods from before his very eyes or leaves them with him before his very eyes, no trace of any other but God remains on his heart.

He said,

> I saw a person shouting to high heaven. So I commented, "You are driven only to your divinely apportioned sustenance, or to your term of life, or to whatever God determines for you. They are only five in number, not six. So fear God wherever you be, and make nothing the equal of fear, for 'the recompense is for the God-fearing.' (Q. 28:83) Of a truth, they love Him and He loves them. That is the favor of God that He gives to whom He will, for God is generous, knowing.
>
> So say, "I take refuge with God from the evil decree, from the fretting of the soul when the trial comes, from joy and sorrow, care and grief, in hardship and ease."

He said,

> I heard someone say, "He who is sensitive [to the first shock of misfortune] is not patient. He who burdens himself with trouble has not resigned his affair to God. He who asks is not contented with God. He who manages his own affairs has not committed them to God. He who calls for help has not trusted. These are five things, and how great is your need to be assiduous in these five!"
>
> Say, "My Lord, I stand in need of the good that Thou hast sent down to me. So increase for me Thy bounty and beneficence, and make me one of those who are thankful for Thy favors."

He said, "There are five things. He who possesses no particle of them has no faith at all. They are resignation (*taslim*) to the command of God, contentment (*rida*) with the decree of God, commitment (*tafwid*) to God, trust (*tawakku*) in God, and patience at the first assault [of misfortune]."

He prayed,

> "O Thou whose hand holds dominion over all things, who protects, but against whom no one is protected" (Q. 23:88), protect me from that into which Thou hast caused me to fall.
>
> Then I was told, "Sigh not to God with fretting and anger, else God will be displeased with you." So I answered, "This affair is difficult for me." He replied, "It is We who have decreed it upon you to train and teach you." Then He added, "Take away from them the responsibility for the things that are helpful and harmful, for they come not from them, and observe that they are from Me to them. Flee to Me from them while observing the decree as operative against you and them, or for you and

them. Fear them not so greatly that you become heedless of Me and forget and attribute the divine apportionment (*qadar*) to them."

If any fear drives you to other than He, its instigator is blameworthy, deficient, or reprehensible. He said that someone advised him, "If you contract a debt, put the debt upon God, for if you put it upon God, upon Him is the obligation to discharge it and He carries away from you its burdens. But if you contract a debt upon youself or against some fixed stipend that is yours, upon you is the burden of responsibility, even though you intend to repay it. Many a time you put it off, or you squander it, or you delay it, or you regard it lightly, or you pay too soon or too late, or you misuse it, or you lie, or you lose without having gained."

Then I asked, "How shall I charge God with the debt?" He replied, "Sever the lower self from regular means of subsistence, detach the heart from customary gifts, and attach it to Him who possesses the earth and the heavens. Say,

'God, upon Thee have I placed my debt.
By Thy name with which Thou hast borne me
Have I been borne.
In God have I trusted;
To Him have I committed my cause.
I seek refuge with Thee from entrance into the
Abysses of ignorance, the lower self,
Rebellion, defilement, and filth.'

"And if it should be your lot to receive some boon that comes to you as customary gifts after which your lower nature courses, flee to God from it as if you were fleeing from the fire and from the workings of the inhabitants of the fire. Say, 'Rescue me and pardon me, O Glorious one!' This is one of the wonders of the sciences of gnosis (*ma'rifa*) in comparison with the sciences of social relationships. So flee from your lower self and reckon on God for your compensation."

He said to one of his companions,

I saw you wearing yourself out and contending with your affair in struggle with your lower self. So I said to him, "O villain, O son of a villain—I mean by that, myself in the relationship of father, and you in the relationship of son—quit devising your own plans, even in the morsel that you eat, in the draught that you take, in the word that you speak or from which you refrain. Who are you compared with the Deviser, the All-Knowing, the All-Hearing, the All-Seeing, the Wise, the Informed? His majesty is too exalted and His names too sanctified for anyone to be associated with Him."

He said,

> When you desire to do a certain thing or abstain from doing it, flee to God therefrom as if you were fleeing from the fire, and make exception for nothing. Call to God for help. Accustom yourself to this. He is "thy Lord who creates what He wills and exercises free choice." (Q. 28:68) No one is ever firmly established in this matter except a veritable mystic or a saint. Now the veritable mystic is one who has judgement, and the saint is one who has no judgement; for the veritable mystic judges with the judgement of God, while the saint passes away with God from the consciousness of everything.
>
> The *'ulama* devise plans, make choices, speculate, scrutinize, persisting in their own intellects and attributes. The *shuhada'* (martyrs) endure, strive, fight, are made to live,[40] are caused to die, and they have been assured a restoration virtually, even though they have not been assured it with the senses and the body.
>
> As for the meritorious ones, their bodies are venerated, but their inner souls are shriveled and in the throes of death. It would not be befitting to expose their inner states, except to a veritable mystic in the beginning of his career or to a saint at the end thereof. It is sufficient for you to know their merits that are manifest and to be content with that without exposing their hidden inner states.
>
> Whenever you desire to do a certain thing or abstain from doing it, flee to God, as I have told you, and call to Him for help. Accustom yourself to that, and say,
>
> "O First, O Last, O Outer, O Inner,
> I ask of Thee the effacing of my names through Thy names,
> Of my controlling through Thy control,
> Of my choosing through Thy choosing.
> Be for me as Thou wast for Thy saints.
> Cause me to enter into affairs 'with a true entry, and cause me to leave with a true exit, and appoint for me from Thy presence a helping power.' (Q. 17:80)
>
> Take heed not to lose confidence in God. Trust in God, for God loves the trustful.

He said, "Knock on the door of the *dhikr*, seeking shelter with God and avowing your need of Him, with continual silence toward your fellows and the shepherding of your innermost being to guard it from converse with the lower self with every breath, if you desire to have spiritual sufficiency."

He said in prayer,

God, enlarge our means of subsistence (*arzaq*), multiply our guests (*adyaf*), make us to be among the God-fearing, walking the path of Thy good pleasure, without prodigality and without parsimony. Help us to that end, and direct us by thy guidance. Purify us from our own effort to be sincere through Thine act of purification. Preserve us from avarice, niggardliness, reproachfulness, suspicion with regard to sustenance, distrust, wrong opinion of Thee, and from relying on any other, from opposing Thy will in speech and action, from claiming to trust in Thee and to commit matters to Thee while the inner man is void of the contemplation of Thy power, of showing regard to Thy will, and of looking unceasingly toward Thy knowledge.

The most hideous of men is he who uses cunning devices against God through allowing worldly interests to sever him from God while courting His good disposition through the making of supplication, humble entreaty, and performing the rest of the religious works. The pen is dry from writing down what he is.

He said, "Sustenance is divinely apportioned. It is not the piety of a pious man that increases it. Nor is it the impiety of a impious man that diminishes it. So make us sincere toward Thee with respect to sustenance through Thy unity, and, in religious works, through supplication, humble entreaty, and seeking shelter in Thee, by genuine servantship performed solely unto Thee. 'Bestow upon us mercy from Thy presence, for Thou art the Bestower' (Q. 3:8)."

He said,

If anyone guards himself against association with regard to the divine unity and to love during the beginning of his involuntary thoughts, God will bring him speedily the mighty help in whatever later thoughts may pass through his mind. Then he will not be veiled from God and no flaw will occur in his performance of the religious ordinances. But if anyone does not guard himself against associations with regard to the divine unity, and if the inclination toward certain appetitive desires takes hold upon him, he will be veiled from divine aid.

This is a clear statement of God to the people who have aroused themselves from heedlessness. God has said, "By the soul and what fashioned it, and inspired it with its wickedness and its godly fear." (Q. 91:7-8) So, have a holy fear of God in the matter of association with regard to the divine unity, hold yourself to this, and depart not from it either by diminution or addition. Beware of sharing your love for God with any other through inclination toward the appetitive desires, whatever desire it may be.

If anyone is a servant of God, fearful of Him, apprehensive toward Him, and on his guard against Him in the time of His beneficence, he is in security from God, whatever severe affliction of His may come upon him. The proof of it is the saying, "If anyone is for God in time of ease, God will be for him in distress."

He said, "Mystical knowledge, love, and genuine states of ecstasy have driven away from you misfortunes and the causes of illnesses."

He said,

There are four things. Abide by them and enter whenever you will. Take not one of the unbelievers for a friend, nor one of the believers for an enemy. Be removed in your heart from this world. Reckon yourself one of the dead. Testify to His oneness and to the apostleship of the Apostle. It is sufficient that you do this. Say, "I believe 'in God, His angels, His scriptures, His apostles' (Q. 2:285), His decree in its entirety, and in all of His words that have branched off from His Word. 'We make no distinction among any of His apostles.' (Q. 2:285) You should say as they said, "Thy pardon, O our Lord, for unto Thee do we return." (Q. 2:285)

If anyone observes the preceding four things, God guarantees for him four things in this world and four in the next: truthfulness in declaration, sincerity in the performance of religious works, sustenance like the rain, and preservation from evil. These pertain to this world. For the world to come, they are: the greatest pardon, the proximity and place of rank, entrance into the Garden of the Abode, and attainment of the highest degree.

Four things are related to the requital: entrance before the presence of God, sitting down to converse with Him, the salutation of peace from God, and satisfaction on the part of God, which is greatest of all.

If you desire truthfulness in declaration, seek help against your lower self by reciting, "We have caused it to come down." (Q. 97:1) If you desire sincerity in religious works, seek help against your lower self by reciting, "Say, it is that God is one." (Q. 112:1) If you desire sustenance, seek help against your lower self by reciting, "Say, I take refuge with the Lord of the dawn." (Q. 113:1) If you desire security from evil, seek help against your lower self by reciting, "Say, I take refuge with the Lord of men." (Q. 114:1)

He said,

Whenever you ask, ask of God. If He responds to your needs, render thanks. If He denies you, be contented with Him. Beware of the hardening of the soul, of being distrustful of God, and of the dominance of the appetitive desire, lest you be denied mystical knowledge, contentment, and pardon. Thus, you will be veiled from God, and be rejected from the highest place to one lower than that, and, you never know, He may cast you down to the very limits of the lowest of the low.

He said,

> If you desire to ask men for something you need, submit it to God before submitting it to them. If He decrees that you should have it from them, thank Him and thank them. If He has not decreed that you should have it from them, be content with God, and lay nothing to their charge. Blame no one, except for what God has blamed him. Commend no one, except for what God has commended him. If it is otherwise, refrain from blame or commendation, for this is safer for you, and more suitable for your obtaining the satisfaction of God. Serve God with sure faith, and you will be elevated to the loftiest stages, even though your religious works be few.

He related,

> I saw as if I were in the highest heavenly realm beneath the Throne in a certain place where there were many people. A dog was set loose upon some game that was there, and he caught the game. A man came and took the game from the dog. He said, "The *'ulama* of the community are entirely agreed upon the lawfulness of this game.[41] Therefore, it is licit. That is only by reason of the dog's attachment to its master."
>
> Then, I slept and saw as though we were assembled in another place, and I saw as though I had been singled out to appear before the King, the True One, and as though I were before Him in the realm of spacelessness. I said, "O my Lord, this man"—referring to a person who desired something of him—"brings me nothing to consider without my finding in it confusion and entanglement." Thereupon the voice said to me, "This is a servant who is seeking understanding on God's authority in matters of natural intelligence. It is conceded that he has shrewdness of intellect (*kiyasa*), but he did not know that that legal understanding comes from the same mold as a sense of superiority."
>
> The utmost that emanates from the most eminent of the utterly sincere (*siddiqin*) is contained in four spheres: knowledge (*'ilm*), works (*a'mal*), neediness (*faqr*), and acquitting one's self of the strength and power that rightly belong to God. Know that religious knowledge is the most excellent of the stages, and ignorance is the most abominable of the attributes. Now, they had knowledge and acted according to their knowledge. Indeed, they knew that that knowledge became perfected only by standing in need of God in everything. So have knowledge and act. Although they possessed legal understanding, they acted according to what God knows about them. But the dog was more understanding

than they, because he set about to perform the will of his master, and not his own will. So the leaders of the community (*fuqaha'*) are agreed that his game is lawful. They were accordingly priviledged to follow the way of grace to God. Someone has said, "Consider your own coming into existence. Were you of any help to yourself? No, but it was God Who was for you with His superabundance. Whenever you come to know the superabundance of God on you in the case of the least movement of your knowing and acquisition (*kasb*),[42] submerge the movement in the grace of God upon you before it submerges you.

He related,

I came upon a group of jurists from among the companions of Ibn al-Bara'. I greeted them and they turned away from me. That was a painful experience. Then I heard the voice saying to me, "O 'Ali, indeed you have exaggerated your own importance and overestimated your worth, since you were sensitive to their turning away from you. But who are they when they turn toward you, and how is it when they turn the back? If you were one divinely assisted, you would be distracted through your turning toward God from their turning away from you; and if you were under right guidance, you would be distracted through God's turning toward you from your turning toward Him."

He continued,

I was told, "Imprecate Ibn al-Bara'."
"O my Lord," I replied, "I will make supplication in his favor for reconciliation and repentance."
Then I was told a second time, "Imprecate him."
I responded in like manner, and I was told a third time, "Imprecate him."
So I said, "O my Lord, teach me how to speak."
"Say," I was told, "O God, cut off the blessing from his knowledge and his life, and cut off his posterity by an evil end. Make him and those who come after him to be a warning for the firm believers."

He said, "One day, the thought came to my mind that I was nothing, and that I had none of the mystical stations (*maqamat*) and states (*ahwal*). I plunged into a musk house and became immersed in the odor of musk. But as long as I was immersed in it, I did not detect that odor. Then I was told, "The sign (*'alama*) of abundance is the loss of the sense of abundance on account of the greatness of the abundance."
He said,

I was told, "If you desire My good pleasure, know that it derives from My name and from Me, not from your name or from you."

"How is that?" I asked.

He replied, "My names (*asma'*) preceded My gift (*'ata'*). My names derive from My attributes, and My attributes subsist in My essence (*dhat*), and My essence is not subject to obliteration. The servant has lowly names and lofty names. God has attributed to him the lofty names, according to His saying, 'The repentent, the worshipers, the praisers, and other.' (Q. 9:113) And His saying, 'The Muslim men and the Muslim women, and others.' (Q. 33:35)

"The servant's lowly names are known, such as 'the disobedient one,' 'the sinner,' 'the corrupt one,' 'the wrong-doer,' and others. So as your lowly names are obliterated by your lofty names, in like manner your names are obliterated by His names, and your attributes by His attributes, becasue the newly existent, whenever it is joined to the eternally preexistent, has no continuance at all. Whenever you address Him by His names, as you say, 'O Forgiving One, O Relentent One, O Near, O Bestower,' you ask the gift of them for yourself, and, indeed, to yourself do some of His names come down. In like manner, whenever you set your gaze on your lowly names—such as those for disobedience, wrong-doing, and corruption—you are taking upon yourself alone their covering and pardon, and you are abiding by yourself instead of with God. But whenever you address Him with His lofty name and direct your gaze to His lofty attribute subsisting in His essence, all your names become obliterated and your being comes to nought. So you become completely effaced, having no being whatsoever. That is the place of passing away (*mahall al-fana'*), and after the passing away comes the abiding (*baqa'*).[43] 'That is the grace of God that He gives to whom He will, for God is possessor of great grace.' (Q. 57:21)"

Section on the Commonality and the Elect

He said,

Know that the sciences whose masters are the recipients of encomium are darkness as compared with the sciences of those who have attained reality (*tahqiq*). These are the ones who have been submerged in the waves of the sea of the Essence of God and in the depths of His attributes, so that they were there, but they were not they. They are the exalted elect (*khassah*) who have become heirs of the prophets and apostles in respect of their hidden qualities. Even though the ranks of the prophets and apostles be very illustrious, they have a share in them, since there is no prophet and no apostle without an heir (*warith*) from among this *umma*. Now every heir has rank according to his inheritance from his testator.

The Apostle of God has said, "The '*ulama* are the heirs of the prophets." One is not an heir unless he has an assigned share from his testator, whose place he takes in respect of attainment of reality with station and state. Indeed, the stations of the prophets are exalted, lest others catch a glimpse of their true natures. Every heir occupies a rank commensurate with his testator, because God says, "We have been bountiful to some of the prophets above others" (Q. 17:55); and, as God has been bountiful to some above others, He has been bountiful to some of the saints above others. Now, the prophets are the quintessences of mankind, and each individual essence imparts some endowment according to its natural ability, and every saint has some endowment which has been made particularly his.

The saints are divided into two categories. One of them is substitutes of the apostles, and the other is substitutes of the prophets. The substitutes of the prophets are the righteous ones (*salihun*) and the substitutes of the apostles are the utterly sincere (*siddiqun*). The difference between the Righteous ones and the utterly sincere is like the difference between the prophets and apostles. There are some of one, and some of the other—except that, among them, there are a number who exclusively enjoy the endowment from the Apostle of God that they testify to be an essence of certainty, but they are few. Yet, in respect of mystical realization (*tahqiq*), they are many. Every prophet and saint has some endowment from the Apostle of God. There are some saints who witness his essence, and there are some from whom his essence and his endowment are hidden, and who, therefore, become absorbed in whatever experiences may come to them. They are not engrossed in seeking an endowment. Rather, they are completely over-whelmed by their spiritual state, considering only their present religious experience. There are others who have received the endowment of divine illumination by which they have pondered until they have come to know intuitively, thereby, the meaning of mystical realization (*tahqiq*). That is a grace (*karama*) to them which no one will disbelieve, except one who disbelieves the validity of the divine gifts of the saints. We seek refuge with God from disbelief after having received divine knowledge ('*irfan*).[44]

They are the ones who have followed a way that no others have followed, since the Way [consists in] two roads, the "elect" road and the "common" road. I mean by the "elect" the beloved who are substitutes of the apostles, and I mean by the "common" the novices who are substitutes of the prophets, upon all of whom be peace.

The road of the elect is a sublime road, the least explanation of which would frustrate the mind. However, you should know the road of the commonalty ('amma), which is the road of ascent from one stage to another until you reach a stage that is a goodly resting place in the presence of a powerful sovereign.

The first stage upon which the beloved devotee sets foot to ascend therefrom to the higher [stages] is the lower self. He occupies himself with watching over and training it until he finally comes to know it, and, if he comes to know it and to understand it thoroughly, at that point the [divine] lights shine upon it.

The second stage is the heart (*qalb*), with whose tending and knowing he occupies himself, and, when he perfects himself in this so that no [deficiency] remains, he ascends to the third stage, the spirit (*ruh*). He occupies himself with tending and knowing it, and, when knowledge of it is achieved, the illumination of certainty dawns upon him little by little. This continues until, his inner sight, becoming familiar with the succession of lights upon it, certainty breaks forth upon him with such force that he does not understand [with the intellect] anything because of the lights of the three states that he had previously experienced. At this point, he understands what God wishes [him to understand].

Then God endows him with the light of the original intelligence (*al-'aql al-asli*) amidst the lights of certainty, so that he sees it to be an object without limit or end, by comparison with this servant, and into which the totality of created things disappears. Sometimes, he sees these created things in it, as he sees dust particles in the air through the medium of the light of the sun, and, whenever the rays of the sun turn away from the window, he sees no trace of the dust particles. The sun that he sees is the Essential Intelligence (*al-'aql al-daruri*), which he sees after the endowment of the light of certainty; and, whenever this light of the sun disappears, these created things depart. A summons proceeds from it—one of a suppressed nature, without a sound, which imparts an understanding of all that he sees, except that, what he sees other than God, is not from God in the least.

Thereupon, he arouses himself from his stupor (*sakra*) and says, "O Lord, help me, for I perish." He knows, for a certainty, that no one, save God, will rescue him from this sea. At that time, he is told that this object is the Intellect of which the Apostle said, "The first thing God created was the Intellect"; and, in another tradition, when He said to him, "Advance."

So, this servant was given to be submissive and tractable to the light of this being, because he was unable to perceive the limit and end of it, and was incapable of having knowledge of it. Then he was told, "Indeed, you have no knowledge of it without it." So, God endowed him with the light of His names. That passed before him like a twinkling of the eye, or as God willed [when He said], "We raise to grades whom We will" (Q. 6:83).

Then, God endowed him with the light of the Lordly Spirit (*al-ruh al-rabbani*) by which he came to know this being, and ascended to the field of the Lordly Spirit. All that adorned this servant departed, and he relinquished it of necessity. He said, "Everything has being." Then, God caused him to have life with the light of His attributes, and made him rise gradually by this life to the knowledge of this Lordly Being, and, when he scented the pasture lands of His attributes, he was about to say, "It is God." But the Eternal Providence (*al-'inaya al-azaliya*) overtook him and called out to him, "Is not this Being the One Whom no person is allowed to describe, and any of Whose attributes no one is allowed to explain to other than His people? But, by the light of another, is an explanantion given."

Then, God endowed him with the light of the [divine] Mystery of the Spirit, and, thus, he sat by the door of the circle of the divine Mystery. So he pondered and came to know the attributes of the Lordly Spirit through the light of the [divine] Mystery. Then his spiritual urge was aroused to know this Being, which is the Divine Mystery, but his sight failed to discern it, and all of its attributes vanished as if they were nothing at all.

Then, God bestowed upon him the light of His Essence and quickened him with a life that was eternal and endless. Thereupon, he looked upon all objects of knowledge (*ma'lumat*) through the light of this life. So he became the source of all beings, his light radiating in everything of which only he [the servant] had knowledge. Nearby a voice proclaimed, "Be not deceived about God, because the one truly veiled is he who is veiled from God through God, since it is inconceivable that any other should veil him, for he is quickened with a life that God has deposited in him."

Then he said, "O my Lord, [I am] with Thee, from Thee, and unto Thee. So make little of my error, for I seek refuge with Thee from Thyself in order that I may see none but Thee." This is the path of ascent to the presence of the Most High, the Most Lofty. It is the way of the beloved, substitutes of the prophets, and of what is accorded any one of them beyond this, no person can describe a single particle. Praise be to God for His favor, and blessing be upon our Master Muhammad, seal of His prophets, and abundant peace.

Now, the way that is peculiar to the beloved is from Him, unto Him, and by means of Him, because it is impossible to attain unto Him by means of any other. The very first step for them, before any other, was His bestowal upon them of the light of His essence. Then, He withdrew them from among His servants and caused them to desire the solitudes (*khalawat*). Religious works became of little importance in their eyes, but of great importance with them was the Lord of the earth and the heavens. While they were thus, lo, He clothed them with the garment of nonbeing (*'adam*); and they looked, and behold they were not they [themselves].

Then, He caused them to be overwhelmed by the obscurity of their conceal-ment from their own sight. Indeed, they became nonbeing (*'adam*), having no cause (*'illa*) at all. All causes disappeared, and every phenomenon ceased to be. There was no phenomenon and no being at all, but only the sheer nonbeing that had no cause. There was no knowledge attached to it. Objects of knowl-edge vanished. Objects, whose characteristics are predetermined, passed away completely with no cause at all. There remained one who should be referred to as having neither description, nor attribute, nor essence.

Thereupon, there became manifest One Who has never ceased to be manifest in which there was no cause. Rather, He became manifest to His divine consciousness, through His essence, in His essence, with a manifestation that had no anteriority (*awwaliya*). Yea, rather, He looked out of His essence, to His essence, through His essence, and into His essence.

So this servant became alive through His manifestation with a life without a cause, [and He became manifest with beautiful attributes, all of which were without a cause]. Thus, He was the first to become manifest. Absolutely no one was manifest before Him. Things came into being through His attributes and became manifest through His light, in His light.

The first[45] to become manifest was his [the servant's] consciousnes, through which his heart became manifest. Then His command became manifest through His consciousness, in his consciousness. By His command, the essences became manifest in the light of the pen. Then his intellect became manifest through His command, in His command; and by it, it became manifest in His Throne, in the light of His tablet. Then, His spirit became manifest through his intellect, in his intellect, and, through His spirit, His footstool (*kursi*) became manifest in His light through the light of His Throne.

Then his heart became manifest through His spirit, in his spirit, and, through his heart, His veils became manifest in the light of His footstool. Then his soul became manifest through his heart, in his heart, and, through his soul, the sphere (*falak*) of good and evil became manifest in the light of His veils through the light of His veils.

Then his body became manifest through his soul, in his soul, and, through his body, the bodies of the coarse world, such as the earth and the sky, became manifest, and on the whole, every coarse thing was through the light of the sphere. In that case, the first step of this individual beloved one was the soul's casting off of nonbeing, which was a casting off without a cause, a confronting of the nonbeing with the falling away of the divine attributes of firstness, lastness, outwardness, and inwardness. So it becomes a nonbeing attribute confronting a nonbeing [entity]. The meaning of the nonbeing attribute [confronting] and the nonbeing [entity] is as follows: When the servant had arrived at evidence of the cause, which was the actual vision of the True One (*shuhud al-Haqq*), just as there is no continuous witnessing without some interruption, a witnessing with no moment of inattention whatsoever, an evidence of the cause was supplied in which, and on account of which, there was no cause, which [evidence] was the consciousness of the sheer nothingness. The meaning of the supplying of the evidence in which there is no cause whatsoever is the indispensable condition that no observable objects of creation existed.

So it was that there came successively upon him the evidence of pure nonbeing, which was the intoxication of everlasting forgetfulness, so that he lived the life to which allusion has been made in previous discourse upon that station.

Thus, the Way of this servant is a sublime Way. First of all, he is cast into the sea of the [divine] essence. He becomes as nothing, and then is quickened into pure life, is removed without change of place to the sea of the [divine] attributes, then to the sea of the dominical command, then the sea of the divine Mystery, then the sea of the original intelligence, then the sea of the spirit, then the sea of the heart, then the sea of the soul, and then the sea of sensory perception.

Then, he encounters the sea of the [divine] consciousness, and is cast into the sea of heedlessness (*ghafla*), then into the sea of the quality of the tablet, then the sea of the Throne, then the footstool, then the veiledness (*mahjubiya*), and then the sea of the spherical. Then he encounters the sea of the enveloping [divine] consciousness, and he is cast into the sea of the Gardens [of Paradise], and then into the sea of the fires.

Then, he is cast into the sea of [divine] envelopment, which is the sea of the [divine] consciousness. There, he is submerged completely in a way which affords him to all eternity no escape.

If He wills, He appoints him a substitute for the Prophet through whom He gives life to His servants; and, if He wills, He conceals him, for He performs in His dominion what He wills. Each one of these seas includes diverse seas. If the righteous saint, who is the substitute for the Prophet, enters the least of these seas, he will be completely submerged with no way of escape for him. This is a word of warning in connection with the exposition of the way of the elect and the way of the commonalty. Praise be to God in abundance.

Display of Knowledge

He said,

> Display not your knowledge in order that (*li*) men may consider you to be sincere, but display your knowledge in order that God may consider you to be sincere. Even though the letter *lam* be [construed to indicate] the reason [for displaying your knowledge], a reason advanced to justify an affair between you and God with regard to something that He has commanded you to do is better for you than a reason advanced to justify an affair between you and men in respect of [something that] He has forbidden you to do. For certainly a reason that turns you back to God is better for you than a reason that severs you from God. On that account, He has fastened upon you rewards and punishment, because

one does not hope for rewards or fear punishment save as these come from God. God is sufficient as One Who is sincere and as One Who credits with sincerity. God is sufficient as Knower and as Teacher. God is sufficient as Guide, Helper, and Friend. That is, as Guide Who guides through you and Who guides to you; as Helper Who helps you, Who helps through you, and Who does not lend help to oppose you; as Friend Who befriends you, Who befriends through you, and Who befriends not in your disfavor.

Good Breeding

He said,

Good breeding (*ta'dib*) and learning (*ta'lim*) are from God for those who use insight in the practice of the religion of God. It is said that there are only two [categories of] things: one, a thing that I have allotted to you; and one, a thing that I have turned away from you. If anyone meddles with both or one of them, little is his understanding and great is his ignorance, forgetful is his mind, and vast is his thoughtlessness. He is hardly conscious of anyone who would awaken him from his slumber. So, if a friend comes to you with a question of religious law or the proper manner of doing something, or with both, or if you go to him, that is a matter of the first category. In that case, be with Me and for Me in whatever I have allotted to you, and I will be for you with mercy in whatever I have turned away from you and in whatever disapproved thing is sent to you.

God is not pleased with a servant who exerts himself to turn away what has been turned away from him by God and to repel what he cannot escape. So, act toward God with certainty. Stand fast where He has established you, abstain from the forbidden where He has forbidden you, with true insight (*basira*) in the matter of religious certainty, and be not one of the heedless.

Love for God

He said,

If a person loves God, and if He loves him, his friendship is brought to perfection. The lover in very truth is he over whose heart there is no authority belonging to any one except his Beloved and in which there is no will other than His will. So then, he whose friendship in relation to God has been established for him feels no aversion in meeting with God [on the day of judgement]. He knows that from His saying, "If you allege that you are friends of God, exclusively of other men, then desire death, if you are men who speak the truth" (Q. 62:6). In that case, the veritable friend [of God] is not averse to death if it comes to him, since certainly one who has no beloved except God loves Him, and he who loves nothing of his passions has love for Him, and one who has tasted of intimacy with his Master will love meeting with Him. Love expresses itself for you in its purity in ten instances. Ponder over them for, beyond them, there are no others. [They are] in the Apostle, the Veracious, the Distinguisher, the companions, the followers [of the second generation] (*tabi'un*), the friends of God, the *'ulama* who guide to God, the martyrs, the righteous ones, and the believers. Afterwards, one must have [religious] faith for ten things: the prophetic way and innovation, right guidance and error, obedience and disobedience, justice and injustice, and truth and falsehood.

Whenever you love or hate, love for His sake and hate for His sake, without being concerned with which state you are in, for it may be that the two qualities are united for you in one person, so that it becomes incumbent upon you to fulfill the right of both of them together.

So then, love for God has been manifested in the first ten mentioned. Look now. Do you see any trace in [human] passions there? [Certainly not]. In like manner, consider that love for Him is part of the lot of your righteous brethren, of the utterly sincere masters, the rightly guided men of learning, and the remainder of those present [among you]. Therefore, if someone leaves you or dies, and if consequently you find that your heart has no attachment for that person because of those who are present, just like one who has no attachment for the latter because of him who is absent or who has died, then love is purified of [human] passions and love for God has sprung up.

But if you discover anything cleaving to the heart such as [the thought of] someone or something you love, resort to [religious] knowledge, and consider well the matter in relation to the five categories [of legal prescriptions]: the obligatory, the approved, the disapproved, the forbidden, and the allowable.

Sin and Pardon

He said,

I was worried about meeting with a certain king. Then, my sin rose up before me. Whenever I prayed for pardon and repented, I weakened. So I was told to say:

"O God, I ask of Thee strictness in fulfilling
My religious duties, and the performance
Of good works with certainty.
I seek refuge with Thee from the facing of my
Sin, for that is something that weakens my heart.
Cause me to bear witness to Thee with the witnesses,
For it is this that is the ultimate strength of my soul and innermost
being."

God, cover me with Thy forgiveness, have mercy on me with Thy mercy, empower me with Thy power, aid me by Thy will, teach me knowledge that is comfortable to Thy knowledge, and grant me judgement that concurs with Thy judgement.

Provoke in me veracious speech among Thy servants, and be for me hearing, sight, tongue, heart, mind, hand, and strengthener.

Preserve me from mistakes, deviation, rebellion and falsehood in speech, action and vows, in mystical states, suppositions, and imaginings, in insights and sights of the eye, in involuntary thoughts and cognitions, in the least perceptible suggestions and whisperings, anxiety and meditation, [acts of] determining and willing, movements and moments of quiescence, and in whatever Thou knowest, O Thou Knower of hidden things.

Thou art my Lord, and Thy knowledge is sufficient for me. I make no request and have no preference. Verily, my Lord is self-sufficient and generous. Servantship is only that which is performed as Thou wilt—in supplication, beseeching, and preferring; in states, utterances, actions, and vows; and yet other [actions] that Thou dost cause [the servant] to acquire or that Thou dost bestow without acquisition or asking. Verily, my Lord is cognizant of all.

He said,

I saw [in a dream] a man who sought my injunction. I said to him, "Take not disobedience as your abiding place, for the world with love for it as an idol. Break away from the lower self and lust; seek the help of God, for how excellent is the Master. It is incumbent on you to have real faith, and to sense [God's] presence in well-doing. Hold fast to that with knowledge, and you will experience the increase in wisdom. Await the increase from God, and hope for nothing except God. 'Is there a god with God? Exalted be God above what they associate with Him.'" (Q 27:63)

Knowledge

He said,

On a certain night I had been meditating absent-mindedly and, with thought transcending the realm of the cognitional, when God bestowed upon me exalted knowledge, and I penetrated into the unseen in delightful manner. I said within myself, "Is not this better than entering into the ordinary affairs of creatures, [that is], being with the Creator? And is not being with God more perfect than being in the midst of concerns common to men, even though this be clearly permitted according to the religious law?"

While I was thus, I went to sleep, and I saw, as if a torrent surrounded me on every side, carrying along scum on my right hand and on my left. I began to wade through [the water] to get out of it, but on all four sides I saw no land to which I could escape. So, becoming resigned, I remained standing in the torrent like a post or firmly rooted palm tree, and said to myself, "This is by the bounty of God that I have stood firmly in this torrent without being touched by the least bit of the scum."

Then, there approached me a person of handsome form who was saying to me, "Certainly it is on account of being a Sufi that one becomes exposed to human necessities that are required by the King, the True One. If God ordains anything, you are thankful. If He ordains nothing, you acquiesce. The ordaining of them, which obliges you to give thanks, is not more perfect than their not being ordained, which obliges you to acquiesce. The ordaining of them, which obliges you to give thanks, is not more perfect than their not being ordained, which obliges you to acquiesce. God has taught me knowledge that subsists in my very self, leaving it not, but adhering to it like the whiteness in white and the blackness in black. He is God. There is no god except Him, "the One, the Irresistible, Lord of the heavens and the earth and what is between them, the Mighty, the Forgiving." (Q. 38:65–66)

Consider the divinity, uniqueness, oneness, irresistibility, lordship, might, and forgiveness, and how all of these are joined in one statement. Forgiveness descends upon the person who has mystical knowledge of God, like the torrent bearing scum, and God causes whom He will to stand firm in the midst of it, and remain there, without a bit of the scum touching him."

I awoke from my sleep, having been apprised of the great secret. Praise be to God!

A Remedy

He asked,

Do you know what is the remedy for a person who severs himself from [the obligations of] social relationships before becoming adept in the realities of mystical contemplation? The remedy for him consists in four things: casting himself on God with an abandon that is unaccompanied by [claims to] the power and strength [that rightly belong to God alone]; and resigning himself completely to the command of God with a resignation that is unaccompanied by personal volition along with God's [will]. These two are inner remedies. The outer remedies are: restraining the members from misdemeanors, and fulfilling the duties of the legal prescriptions. Then you will sit on the carpet of recollection, devoting yourself wholly to God exclusively of all other, by reason of His saying, "And remember the name of thy Lord and devote thyself to Him completely." (Q. 73:8)

Trustworthiness

He said, "Let no one be solicited [for a blessing or a favor] except a trustworthy person. How many servants are trustworthy in respect of worldly goods without being trustworthy in moral relations? Many a time a servant is trustworthy in respect of goods and moral relations without being trustworthy in the matter of religion. He who is trustworthy in religion is the one who receives from God with the insight of certainty and the comprehensive view over all the circumstances and issues of affairs in this world and the next."

Worldly Goods

He said,

Whatever bit of worldly goods God bestows on me, I rejoice in it, in order that I might use it or give aid, and proceed to praise God and thank Him. Thanksgiving is acknowledgment subsisting in the heart and an expression rising on the tongue. I had been joining the two, and I applied myself to that for a while during the night. I went to sleep and dreamed that I saw my teacher who was saying, "Seek refuge with God from the evil of this world whenever you advance, from its evil whenever you turn back, from its evil whenever you spend, and from its evil whenever you withhold." I began to make such utterance and my words reached the master who continued to say, "[Say], and from misfortunes, calamities, and illnesses of body, heart, and soul, all of them collectively and separately. If Thou hast decreed anything at all, clothe me with the garb of contentment, love, and resignation, and the garments of pardon, repentance, and satisfying contrition."

Gazelles

He related,

> I saw in my sleep a herd of gazelles being hunted by men whose aspect was uglier than any I have ever seen. Boys caught them and began to play with them. Then I awoke and marveled at them. I slept [again] and saw a man of handsome mien who was saying to me, "The swiftest and least approachable of the wild animals are the gazelles, but you have seen them taken in captivity and boys playing with them. In like manner the men most advanced in their pursuits are the adepts of [religious] knowledge and the mystical sciences, but you have seen women and the worldly life seize their minds and Satan play with them. So beware of women and the world. Cling to sincerity and godly piety, and forsake the abodes of evil, and you will attain the loftiest degrees."

Religious Acts

He said,

> There is nothing more difficult and more arduous in the accomplishment of obedient acts, the performance of the *dhikr*, and the recital of the *Qur'an* than maintaining a firm hold on the lower self, keeping the heart present in them, understanding their inner meanings, and giving to the letters their due value, and, at the same time, preserving the will to do it for the honor of God. This is the occasion above all for sincerity and determination to perform the religious works according to His injunctions. It is the proper place for veracity and for lifting the inner soul away from the world and from everything other than God; and it is the right occasion for the intention.

Realization

He said, "There are four things. If anyone becomes involved in them, he has not experienced mystical realization (*tahqiq*). [They are] seeking [Paradise or rewards], fleeing [from the fire], repelling [evils or wrong-doers], and attracting [benefits]."

Sure Pardon

He related, "I saw [in a dream] a person who was saying to me, 'Good news for you, goodness for you! There are four things [to say to you]. We have pardoned the sin. We have dismissed the fault. The hidden has become manifest, and [all] misgiving has been taken away. [Let there be] no doubting or uncertainty. So judge according to the will of God, and dispute not with the deceivers.' "

Security

He said, "If anyone desires to be secure from the inhabitants of this world and the next, let him recite [the *Sura* beginning], "When the sun is folded up" (Q. 81:1), to the end."

A Request

He said,

My request of Thee is obedience and a love for it; aversion to disobedience and hatred of it; an eschewing of the world while remaining faithful to the religious law with regard to it; confidence in what is in Thy hand and contentment with what Thou hast meted out from it. Dispose us to render thanks when in a state of gain, to be contented when in loss, and to spend freely when in abundance (*fadl*). Make the compensation for what departs from us dearer to us than the benefits of what remains for us.

Bestow upon us sincerity in our very essence, the performance of pious works, pure knowledge, and a guiding light, for thou leadest whom Thou wilt to a straight path.

Anxiety

He said, "If anyone recites [the *sura* beginning], 'We have sent it down on the night of the decree' (Q. 97:1), he will be spared anxiety of the inner domain [of human mystery]."

A Petition

He said, "God, I petition Thee to grant me attentiveness and a turning of the regard to Thee, knowledge of Thee, actions in obedience to Thee, longing to meet Thee, fear of Thee, hope in Thee, reliance upon Thee, contentment with Thee, with thine Apostle, and with what has come from Thee. I ask of Thee to be joined with him, to attain reality through his light, to see with his sight, and to have mastery of his knowledge, for 'Thou art powerful over all things' (Q 2:20)."

Divine Management

He said, "I saw the straitened and difficult circumstances of the poeple, and it occurred to my mind to supplicate God for them. 'Leave your management of affairs to the management of God, and be content with Him as the one responsible, for the people have become weary of divine favors and have been secure for punishment, and I have deprived them of [My] mercy. God prescribes what He wills.' So I desisted from supplication."

Final Injunction

He said,

> Desiring of my teacher his final injunction when I was on the point of leaving him, I requested, "O my master, give me your injuction. "O 'Ali," he replied, "God is God and men are men. Keep your tongue free from the mention of them, and your heart from inclining before them, and be careful to guard your bodily members and to fulfill the divine ordinances. Thus, the friendship of God is perfected in you. Have no remembrance to them except under obligation that duty to God imposes upon you. Thus, your scrupulousness is perfected. Say, 'God, relieve me from remembrance of them and from matters that expose [me] to them. Save me from their malice, enable me to dispense with their good through Thy good, and make me to be an elect saint among them.' Verily, 'Thou art mighty over all things.'" (Q 2:20)

Qualities of the Sincere

He said, with reference to the qualities of those who are sincere,

They are men whom He has created with a disposition to irreproachable servantship to Himself, whom He has made sincere for the purpose of purifying their holding to the oneness of His lordship and following His law in so far as He has endowed their inner beings with the illuminations of His presence.

He has provided their spirits with the inner meanings of the mystical sciences and with the peculiar manifestations of His providence. He has caused their minds to ponder the beneficences of His greatness. Their souls He has purified, guarded, and brought out of the darkness of ignorance. He has guided them by the stars of science and the sun of mystical knowledge of Him; and He has confirmed their beliefs by the proof of His Scripture and [the] *Sunna* [of the Prophet]. They are men whose resolves He has wiped away through the realization of His overpowering will, and whose will He has brought to an end by making it absolutely dependent on His will.

He has bedecked them with the adornment of world-renunciation, the ornament of trust, the dignity of scrupulousness, the light of knowledge, and the luster of gnosis.

He has recalled to their minds His bounty and superabundance, and He has drawn them near to Himself so that, with Him, they are made to dispense with all others. Some of them He has appointed to be keys for the hearts of men and fountainheads of the greatest wisdom that they learn according to the divine law and communicate secretly and openly to those who are capable of receiving it. Some of them, the decrees have concealed and veiled from others in order that they alone may become the masters of the reality of the hidden mysteries.

They are not at all recognized by their distinguished mark. In their inner life, they are with the True One, while in their external life, they are with men. They are they, and not they. They are in the realm of being, appearing to have passed away [from it]. In outward appearance they have aligned themselves in ranks, but in their manner of living they have customarily gone their separate ways. Externally, there is poverty. Internally, there is a sufficiency. They have assumed the characteristics of their Prophet, as the Most High has said, "He found you destitute and enriched [you]." (Q. 93:8) Do you think that He enriched him with worldly goods? By no means, for he pressed the stone over his heart, but he nourished the army with a measure. He departed from Mecca on foot, but mounted al-Buraq and ascended thereon to the highest heaven, to the Lotus Tree of the Limit (*sidrat al-muntaha*). He saw what he saw, "and the heart did not falsify what he saw." (Q. 53:11)

Therefore, consider the state of the enriched in his two aspects, and witness the nobility of his qualities in the two states. If you say, "They are [but] human beings," I will say, "Yes, but not like human beings." As you say of the ruby, "a stone, but unlike a stone." Among men was a Prophet and an Apostle who summoned [them] in truth to the True One. Then the friends of God were given from Him a heritage of the prophets among mankind, since they are a people who set out to imitate [him] earnestly and minutely. They believed in the saying, "He is God, and there is nothing with Him. He is now existing as He has been." They have taken their places in the station of unity (*tawhid*), resting on the foundation of detachment (*tajrid*) from the gratification of self (*huzuz al-nafs*) and from taking notice of [such] gratifications, and of following the example of those who have gone before.

This is the goal and fundamental principle of the [Sufi] people with regard to sincerity and attainment of the status of the elect. How wonderful [it would appear to you] if you were to look into the real nature of their humility and poverty, which is the very essence of dignity and affluence with their Master. To realize perfection in their state is difficult, except in the case of a friend of God in the last state, or of one utterly sincere, even though he be in the beginning [of his career], for the goals reached by the friends of God correspond to the starting point of the utterly sincere. So, take the secret openly to yourself, and keep hold of it with both of your hands.

Mind not those who are envious of you, for He said to His Prophet, Say, "I seek refuge with the Lord of the daybreak," as far as His saying, "and from the evil of the envier when he envies." (Q. 113:1–5) Ask me not that I cut them off on your account. It is as if He were to say to him, "Ask me to protect you from the evil of those who are envious of you, but do not ask me to cut them off from you, for the envious person [must be expected] along with [divine] favors, and [divine] favor must necessarily rest upon you."

So be patient, O wretched man, if you desire to be healed, and perchance it will occur through the revelation of a [divine] message. Yearn not for its coming when you are in a veiled state.

Among his injunctions [are these words]:

"O, my son, cleave to one door, not that necks may bow in obedience to you. God has said, 'Return to your Lord and resign yourselves to Him before the punishment comes upon you.'" (Q. 39:55)

Be not heedless of God. Neither consider yourself secure from His cunning. Look to no one except God, and you will acquire sciences, gifts, and understandings, and you will obtain from God an unceasing reward. (Q. 68:3)

He said, "He who considers carefully my teaching [does so either as] a believer or as a critic. Each of the two is divided into two classes. One believer gives verbal expression to it without understanding its meaning, while the other believer understands both its meaning and verbal expression. One critic, who distorts both its verbal expression and meaning, loses both this world and the next, while the other critic construes correctly its verbal expression and meaning. Blessed is he! Yes, blessed is he!"

Chapter Five

— —

Al-Shadhili's Death and the Appointment
of Abu Al-'Abbas al-Mursi as Successor

One in whom I have confidence related to me that he (*al-Shadhili*) said,

When I entered the land of Egypt and established my dwelling there,
I prayed, "O my Lord, Thou hast caused me to dwell in the land of the
Copts to be buried among them so that my flesh becomes mingled with
their flesh and my bones with their bones."

A reply came to me. "Nay, O 'Ali, but you will be buried in a land
that God has never compressed at all."

My master Madi ibn Sultan related to me,

When he (*al-Shadhili*) set out on the journey on which he passed away,
I was married to a woman of the people of Alexandria who, being with
a child, began to weep and to plead. "Are you leaving me, when I am
on the point of giving birth to a child, to go away on a journey?"

I informed the shaykh of that, and he said, "Call her to me." I brought
her to him and, upon my entering with her before him, he said to her,
"O mother of 'Abd al-Da'im, leave Madi to me to travel with me, and
I shall hope for something better from God for you."

She replied, "O my master, I hear and obey." He invoked a blessing
upon her and she left. While we were jouneying, she gave birth to a
male child whom she named 'Abd al-Da'im.

Having made travel preparations, he [al-Shadhili] ordered, "Carry with
you a pickax and shovel, in case one of us should die and burial should
be necessary." That had not been for him a previous custom in all of
my travels with him, and so it was an intimation of his death.

Testimony of Sharaf al-Din

His son, the worthy Shaykh Sharaf al-Din, related to me in the city of Damanhur, in the year A.H. 715,

With us was a youth who was studying the *Qur'an*. As an orphan without father and whose mother was one of our household, he was raised with us. When the shaykh [al-Shadhili] was about to go on the voyage, he commanded us to depart with him, together with all the women folk and the children. The youth showed great desire to accompany us. The shaykh instructed, "Carry him with you." His mother came to the shaykh and said, "O my master, perchance you will look after him." "We will look after him," he replied, "if God wills, as far as Humaythira."

We set off and, on entering the desert, the shaykh and the youth fell ill. The youth died one day's journey before reaching Humaythira. We wanted to bury him, but the Shaykh said, "Carry him to Humaythira."

We halted and washed him, the shaykh prayed over him, and we buried him there. He was the first to be buried in that place. It was during that night that the shaykh was to pass away.

That evening, he assembled his companions and gave them various final injunctions. He enjoined upon them the "Litany of the Sea" (*Hizb al-Bahr*), adding, "Teach it to your children, for in it is the Greatest Name of God." He talked in private with my master Abu al-'Abbas al-Mursi, gave him injunctions, and made him to be the especially favored possessor of the blessings with which God had favored him. He said to his companions, "When I am dead, look to Abu al-'Abbas al-Mursi, for he is my successor. He will have an exalted station among you. He is one of the doors of God, praise be to Him."

Between sunset and dusk he said to me, "O Muhammad, fill for me a receptacle with water from this well."

"O my master," I replied, "its water is salty and bitter, but the water that we have with us is fresh."

He said, "Give me some of it [water from the well], for what I have in mind is other than what you think."

So we brought him a receptacle of water and he drank of it, rinsed his mouth, and spat it into the receptacle. Then he said to me, "Pour it back into the well."

I poured it back, and the water of the well turned sweet and fresh and became abundant, by the permission of God.

He passed that night in devotion to God and the recitation of the *dhikr*. I heard him saying, "My God, my God."

When day broke, he became still. Thinking he was asleep, we shook him, and found him dead—may God have mercy on him. We called my master Abu al-'Abbas al-Mursi and washed the shaykh. We prayed over him and buried him in Humaythira.

This place is in the desert of 'Aidhab, in a valley on the Sa'id road. I have drunk of its waters, I have visited his tomb, and I have seen blessings attributed to him.

After they buried him, continued Sharaf al-Din, his companions differed in determining whether to turn back or proceed.

My master Abu al-'Abbas al-Mursi said to them, "The shaykh ordered me to perform the pilgrimage and promised me divine gifts." We went forward, saw [the way] made easy and divine blessings, and returned in company with him."

He [al-Mursi] became thereafter the possessor of great celebrity, and many of his miraculous powers were manifested, of which I shall mention those learned from reliable sources, if God wills.

A Premonition

Al-Shadhili said,

When I fell ill, I prayed, "My God, my God, when will the encountering [with Thee] take place?"

"O 'Ali," I was told, "when you reach Humaythira, then will the encountering be."

I saw as if I were being buried at the base of a mountain before a well containing a little salty water that was becoming more abundant and fresh."

Testimony of Abu Ishaq Ibrahim

Abu Ishaq Ibrahim ibn 'Abd al-Rafi', the shaykh and excellent jurist, preacher, *mufti*, and chief judge in Tunis, related to me,

When the Shaykh Abu al-Hasan set out to perform the pilgrimage on the journey during which he passed away, he said to his companions, "This year I shall perform the pilgrimage of substitution." He died before accomplishing the pligrimage. When his companions returned to Egypt, they questioned the Mufti 'Izz al-Din 'Abd al-Salam and informed him of what he had said. He wept, and then said to them, "The shaykh, by God, informed you that he would die. Do you not know by that he has instructed you that the angel is the one who will perform the pilgrimage in his stead? For a tradition relates that the Prophet said, 'If anyone leaves his home for the purpose of performing the pilgrimage, and dies before accomplishing it, God deputizes an angel to take his place in the performance of the pilgrimage each year until the day of resurrection.' "

Testimony of 'Imad al-Din

The most equitable, accomplished, and excellent jurist, and judge 'Imad al-Din, chief judge of Alexandria, related to me in the year A.H. 715,

In Alexandria died a woman of questionable character. While in a pleasing mystical state, I had a vision in which someone asked her, "What has God done with you?"

She replied, "The Shyakh Abu al-Hasan al-Shadhili died today and was buried in Humaythira. He [God] has pardoned every Muslim buried today in the lands of the East and the West, and He has pardoned me on account of him, in honor of him, and for his sake."

When the pilgrims arrived, they made known his death, and so the date was found to be exact. He died in the year A.H. 656, at the age of sixty-three or thereabouts. May God be merciful to him, be pleased with him, and be pleased with us through him.

Personal Description

I heard my master Madi say with regard to his description, "He was dark-complexioned, lean of body, tall of stature, thin-bearded, long-fingered, as if he were from al-Hijaz, eloquent of tongue, suave of speech."

He [Madi] was wont to declare, whenever he became absorbed in profound disclosure, "Is he not one of the choicest of men, who has a far better understanding of these secrets than we? Come to a man whom God has made to be a sea of illuminations."

Excellences of al-Shadhili's Successor

He is the saint, the righteous, the mystic, the Shayk Abu al-'Abbas al-Mursi. His name is Ahmad ibn 'Umar ibn 'Ali al-Ansari al-Mursi. He was raised by the shaykh [al-Shadhili], having reached [North Africa from Spain] in a ship that foundered in the sea off Bonah.[1] [There] his mother and father died, and he with his brother Abu 'Abd Allah Muhammad reached Tunis where the Shaykh [al-Shadhili] received them. They accompanied him to Egypt. 'Abd Allah became a tutor of boys, and one of those who had memorized the *Qur'an*. Abu al-'Abbas gave himself to a life of worship and devotion until he attained the rank of successor and pole.

Testimony of Madi ibn Sultan

The Shaykh Madi ibn sultan related,

> A dispute arose between him [al-Mursi] and myself. The shaykh [al-Shadhili] heard him and said, "O Madi, you must treat Abu al-'Abbas with deference for, by God, he knows the lanes of heaven better than you know those of Alexandria."
>
> Then the shaykh [al-Shadhili] summoned Abu al-'Abbas and said, "O Abu al-'Abbas, go speak among the people." So he sat down in the 'Attarin Mosque of Alexandria [to teach], while the shaykh discoursed at the Citadel, which was his residence. About this we have already spoken. So al-Mursi was contemporary with the shaykh [al-Shadhili] in teaching, with the latter's authority.
>
> After the sight of the shaykh [al-Shadhili] became dim, Abu al-'Abbas came to him and the former said, "O Abu al-'Abbas, my outer sight has been turned back to my inner sight, but I have become one who perceives wholly by God, than whom there is no other, that as long as I live I will not leave behind more excellent men than my companions, and you, by God, are the most excellent of them."
>
> Then al-Shadhili asked him, "How old are you, O Abu al-'Abbas?"
>
> "Thirty years," he replied.
>
> "Ten years more," said al-Shadhili, "and you will inherit the rank of accomplished sufi after me."

Testimony of Yaqut al-Habashi: The Story of the Raisins

The worthy teacher Yaqut al-Habashi, one of his [al-Mursi's] companions and servants, narrated to me in the city of Alexandria in A.H. 715,

> I was giving myself to worship in a mosque outside of Alexandria, and I continued to do so without interruption some days. On becoming very hungry, I entered Alexandria to go to the shaykh [Abu al-'Abbas

al-Mursi], and on the way I found a *dirham*. I wanted to use it to purchase bread. In the market, I saw delicious raisins and, knowing that the shaykh likes them because he was from al-Andalus [Southern Spain] where they grow in abundance, I bought some for him, giving preference to him over myself.

Going to him, I found him seated in the Citadel where he was residing after [the death of] the shaykh [al-Shadhili]. I placed the raisins before him, sat down a while, and was on the point of rising [to go] when he said, "Sit down."

I sat down. Just then a person arrived with a low table on which were a fat roasted sheep and thin baked bread.

The shaykh said, "This is [God's] gift to you because you showed preference to me over yourself even though you were hungry. So eat."

I ate alone until I was filled. Then he ordered the poor devotees [*fuqara'*] to eat of it.

"Take away the raisins," he then ordered, "and offer them as alms, for what is found and picked up is not permitted to us."

Story of Fishing

He (Yaqut al-Habashi) also related to me,

I was at Nastaraq, outside of Alexandria. Fish there were plentiful, and from there they used to be brought into Aledandria. A Sufi came from his house with money to purchase fish. I searched for some but failed to find a single one. I met the captain of the fishing crew and asked him about fishing.

"With this wind," he replied, "not one fish can be caught."

This person was a Christian. So I said, "Enter [the water] with the blessing of God, for the shaykh enjoys favor with Him."

"God does not diverge from the customary way," he responded.

"I will give you and your men a fair recompense," I promised him. "So go in with the blessing of the shaykh [al-Mursi]."

I gave him the money, and he entered the sea, spread the net, drew it in to shore, and took from the net an abundance such as they had never seen.

The people present were astonished at that. The captain exclaimed, "This is a mighty blessing! I will enter with the blessing of such-and-such a monk." He entered with his net, but took in it only small flying fish that are inedible and useless.

Among the fish [of the former catch] was one bigger than any I had ever seen. A Jew came up, grabbed it, and sought to buy it. I prevented him from doing so, and sent all the fish to the shaykh [al-Mursi]. When it arrived, he ordered [the porters], "Pick out that [big] fish and take it to Yaqut to give to the Jew, for he has a wife with a child who was hungry for fish. There is none today, and he had his eye upon it."

So I took the [big] fish and gave it to the Jew and informed him of what the shaykh had said. He became a Muslim, together with a group of Jews, the captain of the fishing crew, and a number of Christians.

Testimony of 'Abd al-Da'im: An Abundant Harvest

Abu Muhammad 'Abd al-Da'im, son of the worhty Shaykh Madi ibn Sultan, related to me in Alexandria in A.H. 715 the following:

I had gathered together in my possession the full sum of nine hundred dirhams, and set out for Cairo to engage in trading with it. On the way I met my master Abu al-'Abbas al-Mursi in the town of Laqana, and so I joined him.

"Where do you intend to go, O Abu Muhammad," he inquired.

I informed him of my situation and purpose. Then he asked, "How much money do you have?"

I told him nine hundred dirhams.

"Return to your father's service," he said, "and nine hundred dinars will return to you."

Now, Madi was in Alexandria. So I returned in the company of Abu al-'Abbas. On appearing before my father, I informed him of my meeting with Abu al-'Abbas and of what he had said to me.

"O my son," he replied, "if you seek what will remain [eternally], that will be better for you. Do not count on [gaining the nine hundred dinars] except in your own parcel of land." With the dirhams, I plowed beside the Nile and we reaped a good harvest of grain, although the Nile had not risen that year. "Sell the produce," the shaykh said, "and distribute it to the people."

So I would sell produce and exchange dirhams for dinars and put them in my money chest, leaving out sufficient for my family. When I opened the chest, I found within nine hundred gold dinars, and the year was not yet finished, and, by God, it neither exceeded nor fell short [of nine hundred dinars] by the weight of a date stone.

Testimony of 'Imad al-Din on Taj al-Din

The chief judge in Alexandria, 'Imad al-Din, related to me that Taj al-Din ibn 'Ata' Allah al-Maliki² informed him of the following:

> The shaykh [al-Mursi] desired his son 'Ali to read *al-Tahdhib*.³ He requested of us [a copy of] *Kitab al-Tahdhib* that his son might read it in clear Arabic script. Not finding such a book, I made a copy for him in a clear Arabic script and brought to him the first volume of it.
>
> The shaykh examined it and found it to be good. He drew me to him and shook me energetically. "O Taj al-Din," he said, "these [other people] have made you prominent in exoteric knowledge, but we will make you prominent in esoteric knowledge."
>
> He [Taj al-Din] left his presence uttering words [divinely] bestowed, and he composed on that [subject] many works.

Story of Two Jars of Honey

The worthy teacher Abu 'Abd Allah ibn Sultan, brother of my master Madi, related to us the following:

> A pilgrim of the people of al-Manqub arrived from the East. I went to him, accompanied by al-Hajj Abu Hilal Iyad al-Qirjani to greet him and to inquire about our master Abu al-'Abbas [al-Mursi].
>
> He informed us that Abu al-'Abbas sends us his salutations and requests us, that is, his companions in general, to send them two jars of honey. Al-Hajj Iyad said, "I have one jar of honey," and I provided another jar.
>
> Al-Hajj Iyad had a devout daughter who possessed some dirhams. She placed them in a purse that she put in the jar, saying, "When the jar reaches the shaykh, the mendicants, if God wills will eat fritters with the honey."
>
> Now, the ships did not travel [with pilgrims] that year. However, I saw him [Abu al-'Abbas] in a dream and he said to me, "O Abu 'Abd Allah, send us the two jars that you have."
>
> I replied, "O my master, up to the present the ships have not set out to come your way."
>
> "Cast them in the sea," he answered, "With my name written on them, and, if God wills, they will reach me."
>
> So I wrote his name on them, and swam with them quite a distance out into the sea where the water was deep. I exclaimed, "My God, it is Thou Who hast spoken, and Thy word is true. "God commands you

to restore objects left in trust to their owners." (Q. 4:58) This is my trust with Thee for my master Abu al-'Abbas al-Mursi."

I released them into the sea, but, by God, as soon as my hand let them go, a hand seized them from me. That happened in the afternoon.

The worthy teacher Yaqut al-Habashi informed me in the city of Alexandria as follows:

In Alexandria, after the afternoon prayer, while sitting with the shaykh [al-Mursi], we were reciting the sevenfold supplications [*al-musabba'at*]⁴ and the devotional exercises appropriate for that hour. Before the customary ending, the shaykh arose and went out to the seaside. We accompanied him as far as the lighthouse where we sat down.

He was talking softly as if he were making supplication or saying something. Suddenly, a huge wave as large as a mountain broke, and we thought it would drown Alexandria. But when it reached him, it receded, and there, standing before him in the sand, were the two jars.

"Take them," he said. "This is a gift of your brother Abu 'Abd Allah ibn Sultan from Tunis." That occurred on the same afternoon of the day mentioned.

When we entered the house with them, he ordered, "Open this jar and empty it."

We took out of it a purse containing dirhams, fifty to be exact. "Buy fritters with them," he said, "according to the intention of the person who put them in the jar."

The worthy teacher Madi ibn Sultan related to me what follows:

At that time I was in Alexandria. The Shaykh Abu al-'Abbas came to me with some fritters and honey. "This honey came to me as a gift from your brother Abu 'Abd Allah from Tunis," he explained. I found that hard to understand since my brother had sent nothing to me in particular.

Later, I went to the the Shaykh Abu al-'Abbas. He said, "You grieved because your brother failed to send you the least bit of honey. Yesterday that honey was in the possession of your brother in Tunis."

"I am one resigned to God," I confessed, and recognized the situation as it was and how it occurred.

Statement of Abu Zayd ibn 'Abd al-Rahman: Pilgrimage with the Apostle

In Egypt I met the worthy teacher Abu Zayd ibn 'Abd al-Rahman who lived at al-Rawda near the two hills of [Cairo]. He was one of his [al-Mursi] companions. I asked him how he had met the shaykh [al-Mursi].

He replied thus:

> I was settled at Mahallat al-Marhum,[5] a village in the district of Alexandria, engaged in weaving. I was asking God to grant me to see the *qutb*, to receive from him some blessing, and obtain every good. So I saw [in a dream] as if I were at Bab al-Sidra.[6] The gate opened and a man was coming out. At his head were two unfurled banners.
>
> A voice said to me, "He is the *qutb* and his place of residence is Alexandria."
>
> I set out for Alexandria and went to see one of my companions who was a mendicant and whom I had known as one of the pious men. After telling him my story, he conducted me to the pious men of Alexandria, among whom were the teacher Abu al-Qasim al-Kari and others. I recognized none of them until we came to my master Abu al-'Abbas. On presenting myself to him, he said, "I am he whom you were seeking."
>
> He was indeed the one I had seen while asleep. I desired to perform a prayer cycle of the greeting of the mosque. He was seated in the niche of the mosque. So I asked myself, "Where should I perform the cycle?"
>
> The shaykh answered my query by saying, "My teacher [al-Shadhili] told me that, when he went to see his teacher Abu Muhammad 'Abd al-Salam ibn Mashish and wished to perform a cycle of prayer, the latter instructed him saying, 'O Abu al-Hasan, whenever you see the *qutb*, greet him with peace and perform two cycles of prayer at his right.'"
>
> So I went forward and performed two cycles of prayer on the right of him [al-Mursi]. Thus it was that he disclosed [himself] to me and enabled me to know that he was the *qutb*.

The author continued,

> This blessed Shaykh 'Abd al-Rahman, bent assiduously on what was good, would leave his house only for the Friday worship. I used to visit with him frequently. He performed the pilgrimage to Mecca with us in company with the congregation in A.H. 715.
>
> I had heard that he had a vision that provoked him to make the journey. On asking him about that, he explained as follows:
>
> "When the pilgrims went to al-Birka and I remained behind, I saw as if I were in the midst of the caravan. Suddenly, there was high tent surmounted by a great light.
>
> 'To whom does that tent belong?' I asked.
>
> I was told, 'To the Apostle of God.'
>
> On approaching it, the door opened, and my master Abu al-Hasan al-Shadhili emerged. I greeted him with peace. 'O 'Abd al-Rahman,' he said, 'do you wish to see our master the Apostle of God?'

'Yes,' I replied.

[Al-Shadhili] entered to ask audience for me. Appearing again, he told me to enter. I did so and found the Apostle of God seated in the center of the tent.

I greeted him with peace and stood in my place. The shaykh [al-Shadhili] went forward, conversed with him, and then turned to me, saying, 'Our master the Apostle of God—or my ancestor, I am not sure about it—tells you to go on pilgrimage with us this year, for he will perform the pilgrimage with us.'

I asked him, 'O my master, the Apostle of God, is it this year especially that you perform the pilgrimage with people?'

'Every year,' he answered me, 'I stand with my people at the place of standing, and this year I have come to accompany the caravan from this place.'

I awoke and praised God; and, by God, whatever I lacked for the journey, god made easy for me, and I passed that night with the pilgrims on journey. He [Abu Zayd] mentioned to me things he had seen on the journey. These would take too long to relate.

Testimony of Jamal al-Din Yusuf

I received the following information from the worthy teacher, scholar, and mufti Jamal al-Din Yusuf, son of the late Shaykh Abu Muhammad 'Abd al-Karim al-Wadashi al-Maliki, known as al-'Iraqi, in the city of Cairo—God protect her—in the beginning of the month Jumada al-Akhira in A.H. 716.

After the death of my master Abu al-Hasan, my master Abu al-'Abbas used to go up to Cairo, at the time of the flooding of the Nile, to take charge of a mosque at a place called al-Maqs bi'l-Dikka outside Bab al-Bahr of Cairo. Our master Abu al-Hasan used to do that every year, and the teachers of Cairo, and of that region used to gather with him to receive his blessings and catch from him something of his profound sciences and noble mystical states. So my master Abu al-'Abbas continued to follow his example.

He [Jamal al-Din Yusuf] related to me the following story in this blesssed mosque that contained a dwelling in its upper part where this jurist was living, because he was judge, mufti, and chief personage of the place:

> My master the Shaykh Abu al-'Abbas arrived there according to his custom. A group of dignitaries and scholars of Misr [Cairo] met with him and said, "O shaykh, whenever our master Abu al-Hasan came to this place, he would come to us in Misr that we might learn from him some of the bestowals of the True One—He is exalted—and be blessed

by his visit to us. Now that God has assigned you to fill his place, we desire to be blessed by your teaching and recall the words of the shaykh [al-Shadhili]."

"When early morn of the morrow breaks," he replied, "if God wills, we shall come to you."

Early morning of the next day, he commanded us to set forth to Misr, and to take with us the *Risala* of al-Qushayri.[7] So I took it, and we reached the congregational mosque of 'Amr ibn al-'As. We discovered that it was filled with the dignitaries and scholars of Egypt.

He commented to me, "A critic and a believer!"

We seated ourselves on the east side of the mosque. Then he instructed me, "Take out the *Risala* of al-Qushayri."

I did as he said.

"Read," he then ordered.

"What shall I read?" I asked.

"That which appears before you," he replied.

So I opened the book and found the chapter of "penetrating insight" (*firasa*). I read the first part of the chapter. On my finishing a prophetic tradition (*hadith*), he said, "Close the book."

Then he went on to explain, "*Firasa* is in four categories: *firasa* of believers; *firasa* of men of true faith; *firasa* of the saints; and *firasa* of the utterly sincere. With regard to *firasa* of believers, its state is like this and its extent is like that."

Thus, he continued to teach with weighty words. Then, proceeding to the subject of the *firasa* of men of true faith, he taught on a higher plane. Concerning the *firasa* of the saint, it is like this and like that, and on that subject he spoke with words divinely bestowed, not of his own acquired learning, such as to bewilder the hearts of persons present. He became absorbed in that subject until the call for noon worship was given and men were weeping. I saw the perspiration roll down from his forehead, flowing over his beard—and he had a large beard.

On recovering from the emotion of his theopathic state, he continued, "Regarding the *firasa* of the utterly sincere, it is like my experience with my teacher [al-Shadhili] from whom I received what he had received. On that occasion, I was before the Throne [of God] and I saw Shaykh Abu Madyan[8] to whom I said, 'Who are you, and what sciences do you possess, and what has God imparted to you?'"

"'I,' he replied, "am head of the seven and one of the four;[9] and seventy-one sciences are mine."

"Then I asked, 'What has the Shaykh Abu al-Hasan al-Shadhili done?'"

"He excelled me," he answered, "by forty sciences."[10]

"When morning came, I went in to my teacher [al-Shadhili].

"Abu al-'Abbas," he said, "yesterday you were in the highest kingdom and you saw the Shaykh Abu Madyan. You asked him, 'Who are you? What sciences do you possess? What has God imparted to you?'

"He replied to you, 'I am head of the seven and one of the four, and I possess seventy-one sciences.'

"You asked, 'What has the Shaykh Abu Muhammad ibn Mashish done?' That is, his teacher also.

"He replied, 'Indeed, he has excelled me by forty sciences, for he is the sea that cannot be encompassed.'"

Then he [Abu al-'Abbas] raised his hands and began to make supplication. Men crowded to touch his garments and receive his blessing. They marveled at the divine esoteric doctrines that they had heard.

[Jamal al-Din Yusuf] also related that he had heard [al-Mursi] say, "For the last twenty years, I have not been veiled from God, and for the past twenty years I have possessed [wealth] and I have possessed [it] in order to put it in the possession [of others]."[11]

He [Jamal al-Din] also said that he heard him [al-Mursi] say, "By God, I know the Throne [of God] as I know this my palm of the hand."

He, the writer may God pardon him—says, "I heard him give this account in the upper room that was the place of residence of this excellent scholar in the year mentioned, and he has authorized me to relate it."

Correspondence of al-Mursi

In one of his letters from Alexandria, he responded to a certain companion in Tunis. I have examined the very script of his writing. It was a long letter in which he inquired about the situation and commented at the end,

The state of affairs is not as you know. For I have accompanied one of the leaders of the utterly sincere and have learned from him a mystical doctrine that cannot be received except individually. To explain it would require a long time. Of him I make my boast, and to him I trace my lineage. I refer to Abu al-Hasan al-Shadhili.

It used to be that no one accompanied him without God revealing something to him in two or three days. If after three days he experienced nothing, that was a sign that he was false, or that, even though he was sincere, he had taken the wrong road. There is an indication of that in the Book of God in which He said, "My Lord, appoint for me a sign." He said, "The sign for you is that you will not speak to men for three days except by gesture." (Q. 3:41)

He [al-Shadhili] used to say, 'Whenever some need to ask of God occurs to you, invoke Him by me.'

It has been my experience, by God, that I would not mention [or remember] him in times of hardship without it being dispelled, or on the occasion of some difficult matter without it becoming easy.

And you, O my brother, whenever you experience hardship, invoke God by him. Now I have counseled you, but God knows all. Peace be to you."

Statement of Abu 'Abd Allah Muhammad ibn Hariz

The Shaykh, Lawyer, and Scholar Abu 'Abd Allah Muhammad ibn Hariz related, on the authority of the worthy and excellent teacher Abu 'Abd Allah al-Shatibi, the following:

I used [to supplicate God] to be pleased with the shaykh [al-Shadhili] every night so many times and make request of God by him for all my needs, and the response would come to me speedily.

I saw [while asleep] the Apostle of God and said to him "O my master, O Apostle of God, I [supplicate God] to be pleased with the Shaykh Abu al-Hasan al-Shadhili every night after my prayer in your favor, and I make request by him for my needs. Do you see in this that I am in any way acting wrongfully toward you?"

He answered, "Abu al-Hasan is my son, physically and spiritually. The son is a part of the father, and if anyone partakes of the part, he partakes of the whole. So, whenever you make request by Abu al-Hasan, you make request by me."

Letter to Shihab al-Din on the Soul

In his correspondence with Abu al-'Abbas Shihab al-Din Ahmad, son of my master the Shaykh Abu al-Hasan, there was a letter toward the end of which he wrote:

May he continue to be a protective veil surrounding the utterly sincere who have attained realization, a lofty pattern for the saints who have been drawn near to Him, a distinctive image for the firmly believing martyrs. May He make the creaturely letter *lam* to be obedient to his control, and the merciful letter *alif* to have rule over his spirit, and the divine point a link from Him to join Him to his inner being through the illumination of the *qutb*, the assistance of the three, and the sciences of the seven.[12] So now—may God be graciously inclined to yur spirits and make spacious in His secret retreats your resting place—someone asked me about rhymed poetry that gives expression to the soul, how it is accommodated to the body, shackled with personal gratifications, provoked by desire, and brought to self-realization in the unitive state [with the divine]. So I responded with these verses:

"If you were to ask us as a pure favor about the accommodation of
    the soul itself to the body;
And about its being shackled with personal gratifications
You have become acquainted with its filth; you have remained at a
    distance complaining of its putridity;
And about its impulses by nature inclined [toward evil], causing
    [you] to fall through its evil desires into sorrowful gloom;
And about its descent to its dominion, while it possesses knowledge
    to enable it to distinguish between fair and foul;
And if you ask about its true nature in the pristine state of the
    mine of its origin [where] the quality of the soul turns not away
    from its true nature to face toward an idol;
Then heed—may you be guided—the sciences the perception of
    which the knowledge-seeker has difficulty in grasping.
Let not the uninformed person allure you.

As you direct your steps toward the True One, the divine proofs of these sciences become readily obvious. So, he who takes hold of them is remote from grief.

O my inquirer about sciences, the "thinking" man apprehends them not with understanding, nor the clever man, but with sublime and all-pervasive illumination that subdues to slumber the reasonings and all natural dispositions. Receive [these sciences] for yourself by a truth that they do not gainsay. This is the starting point of the matter, but the limits make me refrain. From explaining the [full] truth.

Take hold of the science of souls, and let not their external form veil you [from God] in the world of the [final] abiding place. The evolvement (*tatawwur*) [of the stages] of the soul is a mystery which a mind fettered with fancies and filth fails to comprehend.

But [the soul] emerged, subsisting with knowledge [in itself alone] until
    it became accommodated [to the body] like dwellers to a dwelling;
And in order to speak of servants fulfilling the [divine] command
    issued before the creation and trials,
The soul was in process of descent into its worlds, like Adam and
    Eve conjoined;

And the spirit was in process of ascent into its mystical sciences
that are the penetrating insights for enabling mankind to
recognize the divine graces.
The illuminations [of the spirit] drew near to the veil and shone
forth, a light descending between the water[13] [above] and the foul
earth.

The prototype [of the soul] is in the heights, a mirror of its mine of
origin; its subtle qualities are concealed like the covert within the overt.

[It is like] an olive tree whose oil is liquid for one to drink; its real
properties subsist in its roots and tree tops.
[Its is like] a fire calling for liquid [fuel] to consume, offering
guidance for the universe and all being.
The all is you, with a meaning unconcealed; but the [divine]
illuminations veil it [i.e. the all] like water in milk.
So the servant is veiled within the glory of his Owner;
His spiritual knowledge is too subtle [for ordinary perception] in
this life time and age.

Eulogy of Shihab al-Din[14]

He [al-Mursi] used to eulogize my master Shihab al-Din in the following ode:

Peace be upon him whose light has risen high over us, and prompts
[us] to desire to be like him.
He is noble; his virtues are abundant; on the True One he builds
without fear.
And why not, since his ancestor was the best of men? He had from
him a sword with which to strike,
And to judge as he willed in his time with the light from God
which does not delude.
He [Shihab al-Din] is the light that vivifies by virtue of its own
qualities; and a sea of sweet water for anyone who would drink.
He is the secret with whose assistance you strive, a lover who flees
not from the Truth.
So contemplate him as a spirit for your very self, if you desire the
things you seek.
You see the folk like stars in the magnitude of his sea, but to his
zenith they pursue their course.
He surpasses folk in knowledge—with it he excels humankind—and
[that knowledge cannot] be taken away.

In his time God inspired hearts that were not veiled from the
Truth;
But how wretched before Him the envious and obdurate man! Far
from the Truth, distressful!
I am one who acknowledges that he has been especially favored.
Who among men compares with him as companion?
Upon you be our salutations of peace with which we shall meet the
enemies and not be overcome.

Correspondence with Jamal al-Din

This is from one of his letters to his brother Abu 'Abd Allah called Jamal al-Din.

If you desire the finest from your chosen way (*suluk*), renunciation of
the world along with your pursuits is best. Serve thy Lord wherever you
may be with contentment, and you will enjoy what the people of
beneficence have obtained. The people of [divine] friendship, guidance
and holy fear—these are my masters, and with them I overcome life's
vicissitudes.

O Muhammad, forget not, the sustenance that you have comes from
them. Let your spirit be a witness to this, since by it your body subsists.

Make this your course of action for the sake of him who has prescribed
it, and you will find confirmation in your private and public life.

God knows that I am giving you good counsel; for that I desire no
praise or reward.

God is my sufficiency, and our Lord is the Helper. It is He who lends
aid for all matters as He has warranted.

The writer—God's pardon be unto him—affirms that this poetry that I have
collected as being from him [al-Mursi] was transmitted by the learned Shaykh
and mufti Jamal al-Din al-'Iraqi previously mentioned.

Death of al-Mursi and His Grave

He [al-Mursi] resided in Alexandria and there died in the year A.H. 685 or 684—I
am uncertain—and was buried outside the Gate of the Sea (*Bab al-Bahr*) in front
of the tomb of al-Maghawari in one of the cemeteries of al-Manar.

I used to visit it frequently and pass the night in that cemetery. Often, I went
out early in the morning to visit his grave to make request of God for [certain]
things, and, by God, I have never approached God for anything pertaining to
this world without obtaining it. I am hopeful that God, the Generous, will grant

what I have requested with regard to the next, and that He will gather us with them under the standard of the faithful and honored Prophet and beloved, the greatest of means of divine access for us before God, our master Muhammad.

A Sea Rescue

The jurist and *mufti* of the city of Tunis, al-Hajj Abu Muhammad 'Abd al-Kafi, related to me on the authority of the honored teacher Abu Muhammad 'Abd al-Malik al-Murjani[15] in Mecca, who was told in al-Haram al-Sharif by my master Najm al-Din al-Isbahani, the following:

> I left my country to seek the *qutb* and entered a ship. The ship broke up, and I was there struggling in the water. A hand grasped me and threw me up on the beach. I was so thirsty that I thought I would die, when suddenly a person handed me a leather bag of fresh water and departed toward the west. I drank until I had enough. Then I entered Egypt to seek him until I came to Alexandria, and into the presence of my master Abu al-'Abbas.
>
> "Who handed to you the bag?" he asked.
>
> I was silent.
>
> "He who brought you out of the water is so-and-so," he informed me.
>
> A month did not pass before I obtained from him the ability to look at people and distinguish by their mark (*wasm*) the distressed from the happy.

The Grave: A Theriac

The chief judge of Alexandria related to me,

> The grave of our master Abu al-'Abbas with us is a tried remedy (*tiryaq*). No one presents to God [a petition] for anything at the grave without God responding to it. It is similar to the comments of the people of Baghdad with regard to the grave of my master Ma'ruf al-Karkhi. I shall tell you something to strengthen your belief in that.
>
> A group of merchants and people of affluence related that a certain merchant of Alexandria, one of the wealthy named Zayn al-Din al-Qattan, suffered from fox disease on his face. His beard and eyebrows fell out, and his face appeared ugly in public. Every physician in Egypt had tried to cure him, but without success.
>
> One of the pious men told him about the qualities of the grave of my master Abu al-'Abbas al-Mursi. He, therefore, applied himself in

supplication at his grave and in rubbing his face with its soil. He continued to do that some days and his beard and eyebrows grew out again as they had been, by the permission of God—He is glorified.

Tomb and Mosque of al-Mursi

That [the building of al-Mursi's mosque] occurred ten years or so before the date of the writing of this account. Al-Mursi's tomb was in a burial plot surrounded by a low wall about three cubits high. On the side of the burial plot facing Mecca there was a niche for prayer. On his tomb was a metal board inscribed with the text, "They rejoice at God's favor and bounty, for God does not allow the reward of the believers to fail" (Q. 3:170), as well as His saying, "They have followed after what is pleasing to God, and He is the possessor of great bounty" (Q. 3:171).

A certain Zayn al-Din, upon seeing this act of divine intervention and God's restoration of what had been lost, constructed over [the tomb] a magnificent building, and a mosque for worship with a minaret for the call to prayer, one of the finest of Alexandria. He also endowed it munificently to provide a person to give the call to prayer, for the *imam*, and for the caretaker. It became a most important center of visitation and noble shrine. May God bring benefit to us through his blessings in this world and the next. He hears all and is ready to respond. "Praise be to God, Lord of the universe" (Q. 1:1).

Attainments of Abu ʿAbd Allah Muhammad ibn Sultan, Brother of Madi

Our master Abu al-Hasan [al-Shadhili] used to come to al-Masruqin, a Tunisian village where Madi and his brother were born. The shaykh would observe him [Abu ʿAbd Allah] while the latter was in school and prognosticated for him a favorable future.

Madi served the shaykh and accompanied him to the Orient, while Abu ʿAbd Allah remained in al-Masruqin, a young lad who had been circumcised before the shaykh. When the latter established residence in the Orient, he sent Abu ʿAbd Allah al-Qurtubi, one of his leading companions, to him saying, "Go to Tunis to raise Abu ʿAbd Allah ibn Sultan."

So Abu ʿAbd Allah al-Qurtubi came to al-Masruqin and took the lad from there to Tunis. There, they employed themselves as tailors while giving themselves to devotional recitations and the recital of the *Qurʾan* in an upper room within the city of Tunis. There he raised the lad and taught him the Sufi Way.

A Dhikr is Given

He [Abu 'Abd Allah ibn Sultan] related,

> One night I sat down before him [al-Qurtubi] and Abu Muhammad al-Habibi. They asked, "From which one of us do you choose the Way?"
>
> Embarrassed, I thought to myself, "If I say one of them, the other will be hurt." So I replied, "[Wait] until I ask God's preference."
>
> That night I dreamed, and in my dream I saw my master Abu al-Hasan [al-Shadhili] who said to me, "O Abu 'Abd Allah, you are [to give allegiance] to neither one of them. You are [to give it] to me. [Instruction will come] from me to you."
>
> I awoke despondent because he had given me no *dhikr* by the [repetition] of which God would awaken my spiritual insight (*basira*).
>
> I went out to the lighthouse with Abu Muhammad al-Habibi and stayed in a room while he remained in another. In the middle of the day I had a dream in which I saw the shaykh.
>
> "O Abu 'Abd Allah," he said, "I have ordered Abu Muhammad al-Habibi himself to give you the *dhikr* you were seeking of me."
>
> I awoke. Abu Muhammad was knocking on the wall. Going to him I found him writing something. Then he handed it to me
> saying, "Take what you sought."
> I found in [the writing these words]:

O Opener, O knower, open to me Thy door;
Assign to me power from Thine illumination.
Cleanse me thereby from involuntary thoughts, [satanic]
whisperings, and glances [away from Thee].
Bestow on me [the privilege of] sitting [in Thy presence] and
conversing with Thee.
Cause me to see with spiritual insight and clear vision.
Render me innocent of creaturely side-glances.
Grant me mystical knowledge from Thy presence, with which Thou
wilt enable me to dispense with traditional learning (*naql*) and
proof (*dalil*).
By it guide me to a level road.
Place me among those who have been drawn near [Thee], who have
attained to reality through the light of certainty.
Allow me to occupy the stage of the rightly guided leaders [of the
faith]. "Thou art powerful over all things." (Q. 2:20)

> When I read it to him, and recited "Allow me to occupy the stage of the rightly guided leaders," he commented, "That is a big demand."

"My master," I replied, "I have received what you have given me."

"By God," he said, "I have given it to you only by permission of the shaykh while I was asleep."

He [Abu 'Abd Allah] continued to relate,

I saw the Apostle of God and said to him, "O Apostle of God, you said that in every century there will be foremost (*sabiqun*) until the day of resurrection."

"That is right," he replied.

I continued, "My master, in this century, are there foremost?"

"Yes," he answered, "and you are one of them."

So I said to him, "By your light, those of us who are foremost became foremost. God's blessing be upon you."

A Case of Exegesis

Abu 'Abd Allah also said,

I saw in a dream as if I were among a group of learned men who were engaged in an exegesis of His saying, *K h y ' s h m ' s q* (Q. 19:1). One of them said something, and I made a remark about it, but they did not give in to me, and I did not yield to them. We walked away until we came to the Apostle of God. After greetings, we sat down before him and informed him of the matter that had arisen between us.

He said, "Let each one of you make his own comment."

Each one repeated what he had said. Then he turned to me, saying, "Repeat what you commented to them."

I repeated, "You are the person addressed, and you are the one intended.

"*Kaf*: O thou art the totality of being, thou art the cave (*kahf*) of the being in which every being takes shelter.

"*Ha*': We have prepared (*hayya'ana*) for thee the dominion, and we have prepared for thee the kingdom.

"*Ya*': O (*ya*) [thou] spring ('*ayn*) of springs and mine of the concealed secret.

"*Sad*: My attributes (*sifati*) thou [possesseth]. "If anyone obeys the Apostle, he has obeyed God." (Q. 4:80)

"*Ha*': We have made Thee to be endeared (*habbabnaka*).

"*Mim*: We have given thee the kingdom (*mallaknaka*).

"'*Ayn*: We have given thee knowledge ('*allamnaka*).

"*Sin*: We have spoken secretly with thee (*saramaka*).
"*Qaf*: We have drawn thee near [to Us] (*qarrabnaka*)."

Turning toward them, the Apostle said, "What Abu 'Abd Allah ibn Sultan has said to you is correct."

He [Abu 'Abd Allah ibn Sultan] continued, "Whenever I saw him [that is, the Apostle], he usually addressed me, 'O my son.'"
He said,

I saw as if someone were saying to me, 'O thou traveler (*salik*) to the King (*malik*), desist from your speaking and works.'"
Thus, if the King asks you about your possessions, [reply] that you possess nothing. Then keep the Being Himself in your mind, and abandon to Him all your resources.

He said,

One night I praised God for a boon that had fallen to me, and I saw in a dream as if I had rendered thanks for it. I slept again and dreamed that I saw someone saying to me,

"O Muhammad, who is He Who in His house has lodged you?
Who from His fruits has nourished you?
Who from His rivers has quenched you thirst?
Who of recollections [of His name] has taught you?
Who with His secrets has clothed you?
How ignorant you are of His ability [to care for you]."

Al-Yafruni: The Murabit

Abu 'Abd Allah al-Yafruni, one of the pious men, related,

I spent eleven years asking God to enable me to meet my master Abu 'Abd Allah ibn Sultan. [He, al-Yafruni, lived in a mosque near the limekilns in Tunis].
One night, after the sunset worship, there he was, having entered and sat down before me. "I am he," he said, "Muhammad ibn Sultan whom you have been asking of God to see."
I fell down at his feet. Now, I was used [to feeding myself] on pieces of bread and various bits of food, [and so had nothing to offer him]. A certain person of the mosque went out carrying a platter and circulated among the inhabitants of the quarter until he had collected in it a sufficient quantity [of food] to bring to me. According to custom, he came and placed it before me.

I wept.

"Why do you weep?" he asked.

"Because of this condition," I replied. "I subsist by these morsels from the rubbish of men."

"Place your hope in God from this night on," he said, "that a better state than this will be yours."

He passed that night with me. After morning worship he departed. At that moment, a man from the limekilns approached me and said, "O *murabit*, let no one beg any food whatsoever for you. Your food is my charge until one of us dies."

Another time, [Abu 'Abd Allah ibn Sultan] came to visit me. The congregation of the mosque saw him and commented, "We were unaware [of the importance] of this man whom our master Abu 'Abd Allah ibn Sultan comes to visit."

They had him [al-Yafruni] marry a pious woman and purchased a house for him. He enjoyed well-being through [ibn Sultan's] showing regard for him, and blessings came upon him outwardly and inwardly. May God give benefit through him in this world and the next.

Other Anecdotes

A person in whose word I have confidence related to me the following:

There was a certain poor beggar whose house rent was long overdue. He was at a loss to know what to do about it.

[He said] "I took the matter to God and, in my sleep, I saw a man of dark complexion and handsome mien who said to me, 'Abu 'Abd Allah ibn Sultan will pay what you owe.'

"When morning came, there was my master Abu 'Abd Allah who had arrived. He gave me money and put food before me. When I informed him of my vision, he said, 'The man whom you saw was my master Abu al-Hasan al-Shadhili. He was the one who ordered me to bring this money to you.'"

He said,

One evening I went out by Bab al-Bahr[16] to visit my master, Abu 'Abd Allah al-Kumi,[17] who was buried by the mosque al-Ra's. Many people performed the visitation to him.

[After my visit] I walked in the middle of the salt marsh toward my house. Seeing people sitting together, I approached a group of them and discovered goblets and the men drinking wine. I cried out against them and broke the goblets. That troubled me greatly. They fled from before me, and I returned to my lodging inwardly perturbed.

"Thus," I said, "the people of our master Muhammad are flagrant in their disobedience."

That night, in my sleep, I saw Jesus who was saying to me, "O Muhammad, if you desire peace, then you must reprove your self and desire not praise upon it."

He said,

When the worthy teacher and eminent scholar Abu Muhammad al-Murjani set out on the pilgrimage, I desired to go along with him. I went and told him so.

"How much [money] do you have?" he asked.

"About fifty dinars," I replied.

"It is not licit for you," he explained, "to set out on the pilgrimage unless you have sufficient to get you to Mecca and return to your homeland, according to the accepted stipulation of the juridical school of Malik."

Therefore that year I remained behind. When the night of 'Arafa arrived, however, I saw as if I were standing on 'Arafat with Shaykh Abu Muhammad [al-Murjani]. I was saying to him, "O my master Abu Muhammad, this is the pilgrimage of spirits (*arwah*). So remain for me until I perform with you the pilgrimage of bodies."

The following year I set out [on the pilgrimage]. I found him in the sacred precincts of Mecca and appeared before him. On seeing me, he stood facing me and declared, "Here I am, awaiting you, to perform the pilgrimage of bodies with you."

He said,

When I started out for the Orient with the purpose of visiting the Shaykh Abu al-'Abbas al-Mursi, my son asked me, "O my master, how is it that you give precedence to him over the pilgrimage?"

"My son," I replied, "the *qutb* is the locus of blessings and mine of miraculous works, and the secrets of God are gathered in him. So, if you look toward him, you are looking toward the locus of [divine] secrets. Therefore I shall find mercy in looking toward him."

On approaching Alexandria, I saw [in a dream] as if I were in a house the size of the Zaytuna Mosque. On its walls was written the inscription "the good pleasure." I awoke and said to my companions, "I saw so-and-so, and it seems to me that my master Abu al-'Abbas has died. This 'good pleasure' refers to what has been apportioned to you. That is, you see it only before God."

When I reached Alexandria, I learned that he had died that very night.

Wajih al-Din

He[18] said,

> In Cairo I met one of God's saints called "Wajih al-Din," and I stayed with him. But I was inwardly troubled over preparation for the journey.
>
> "O Abu 'Abd Allah," he said to me, "one like you troubled over preparation for the journey! I lived near [the tomb of] the Apostle of God for many years during which I prepared no food at all. Whenever hunger came upon me, I would enter the sacred place and greet the Apostle of God. Then I would find by the *Rawda*[19] food all prepared and I would eat of it until I was filled and then leave. I know not, by God, who placed it there or who took it away."

He continued,

> Then I saw [in a dream] the Shaykh my master Abu al-Hasan [al-Shadhili]—O Muhammad! What a remarkable man was he!—who said to me, "I have been ordered to take you with me."
>
> So he carried me with him[20] in one half of an oyster shell until I had performed the pilgrimage, and he returned me to Cairo.

Wajih al-Din told me,

> I saw the Apostle of God [in a dream]. He said to me, "Want of reputation is a divine grace, but everyone disdains it. Public esteem is a disgrace, but all people want it. Yet, in public esteem is the breaking of the back.
>
> "One who has not considered [his own] shortcomings falls short and if anyone falls short, death is more fitting for him, or, he said, death is better for him."

Al-'Awfi

The Shaykh and Preacher Abu 'Abd Allah al-'Awfi, known as ibn al-Qasir, related to me,

> When Shaykh Abu Muhammad al-Murjani and the religious leaders of that time desired to build a mosque for preaching at Bab al-Sawayqa in Tunis, they decided that it be [at the] caravansary of the vegetable market (*Funduq al-Baql*). There they gave the call to prayer and performed the worship.
>
> Shaykh Abu 'Abd Allah [ibn Sultan] passed by while I was teaching the *Qur'an* to the boys in the school opposite the congregational mosque

(*jami' al-khutba*)[21]—today by the aforementioned Bab—and I stopped in his presence and greeted him.

He looked at me and said, "O Abu 'Abd Allah, the market will always sell vegetables, and this is the mosque for preaching, and you are its preacher."

As he declared, so it was, and this jurist continued to be its preacher until he died.

Story of the Crow

A person in whom I have confidence related the following:

I was sitting with him[22] one day when he quickly arose. I followed him. He came to the arches that were near the cisterns (*Bi'r al-Ahwad*) and stopped. A woodcutter came along with a basket load of wood. Tied on top of it was a crow.

"How much for that crow?" he asked the woodcutter.

"One dirham," he replied.

He gave the woodcutter a dirham, took the crow, untied it and let it go.

"This crow," he explained to me, "is grown and has little ones. She feeds them and raises them. I feared lest they die of hunger and thirst. So I restored her to her children."

Story of the Beard

My father related to me,

The son of one of his brothers named Sultan came to him. He was living at Sijum.[23]

He said, "A dispute arose between so-and-so—that is, one of the teachers of the town and myself. He swore up and down that he would pluck out the beard of my paternal uncle Abu 'Abd Allah of whom I am proud."

"Let him pluck it out," he replied, "if he finds a way to do so."

[The nephew] proclaimed loudly before him and then departed. What he had in mind was to lay charges against the treatener to someone who would punish him.

The next day the shaykh [Abu 'Abd Allah Muhammad ibn Sultan] journeyed to Sijum. The elders of the village came out to him. The man in question, however, on hearing about him, hid himself in his house.

"Where is so-and-so?" inquired the shaykh.

They sought him, but he would not come out.

"He must come here," the shaykh insisted.

So, confused at the predicament in which found himself, he appeared.

"Grab my beard, O my son," ordered the shaykh, "and, to please me, pluck it out."

"God forbid, O my master," he exclaimed.

The shaykh continued, "You swore up and down, and I fear lest you violate your oath."

The shaykh did not cease [to urge him] until the man shot out his hand [to seize] his beard.

He began to kiss the shaykh's hand and weep. All those present wept. It was a tremendous hour. He turned away and went back to his family.

When the nephew heard about the scene, he came to the shaykh to remonstrate on what he had done.

"I am deficient in nothing," he told him. "Muhammad ibn Sultan and I went away, and I have returned."

Then [the shaykh] went on to say, "O son of Sultan, if the Apostle of God were in the world, he would say 'my people,' and at death he would say, 'my people,' and on the day of resurrection he will say, 'my people.' So how can I harm them or correct them while he is my means of access and intercessor before God? My God, forgive the people of Muhammad. My God, have mercy on the people of Muhammad."

True Worship

He said,

In the beginning of my worship I used to ask God to show me a miracle. I saw [in sleep] as if I were standing before the King.

I was told, "Recite."

So I said, "Praise be to God, Lord of the Universe." (Q. 1:1)

"You have spoken truly," I was told.

So I continued, "The Merciful the Compassionate." (Q. 1:3)

Again I was told, "You have spoken truly."

I continued, "King of the judgement day." (Q. 1:4)

I was told again, "You have spoken truly."

So I went on, "Thee we worship." (Q. 1:5)

"You have lied," I was told. "Repeat."

I repeated it three times, each time hearing the same.

Then I was told, "You worship only miracles."

The King then said, [referring] to me, "Lift him up."

So I was lifted up as a boy is raised for the teacher, and a person was on the point of whipping my feet.

I exclaimed, "The Lord is Lord, and the servant is a servant. If I have done what is appropriate to servantship, do with me what is appropriate to lordship."

The King ordered, "Release him."

I was released. Then I imposed upon myself [the duty] to worship God with worship directed uniquely to His noble face and abandoned all requests that I used to make. Then, with the opening of my inner sight, I saw things I had been unable to see. For example, raising my feet, I would see the whole earth as a single step. Or I would walk among graves, and the graced and the punished would appear to me. Likewise, whenever I faced in the right direction for worship, I would be looking toward the Ka'ba with my eyes.

Then he mentioned seven supernatural occurrences (*khawariq*).

Again I asked God about overlooking faults [in worship]. I said, "O Lord, make my worship to be directed solely to Thy noble face, laid up in store for the day of encounter." So [my faults] were overlooked.

Al-Murjani: Fear and Hope

My father related to me the following:

> One day, I set out to visit the Shaykh Abu Muhammad al-Murjani. I wanted to visit him incognito. I sat down in a dead-end lane near his home and lowered my garment over my face. Suddenly, he was there shaking me. I raised my head and faced him standing bare-footed. He took my hand and said, "You have exhausted me, O Mubarak!" He then took me to his home.

He also related that, when Shaykh Abu Muhammad al-Murjani fell ill and his state became critical, Shaykh Abu 'Abd Allah ibn Sultan visited him and asked, "How do I find you, O shaykh?"

"I fear death," he replied, "for I have been remiss in [religious] practice and am therefore ashamed [to appear before] God at the encounter."

"By God," he assured him, "if we were to hear of a bountiful sultan who makes generous gifts, we would willingly journey to him and expend every effort to encounter him. On arrival, we would rejoice in meeting him. How much more so on encountering God the Generous in a real way, [God] Who has given you...?"

He went on to mention [God's] bounties and to talk about teachings from the mystical truth to the point of making him weep.

"May God reward you with good," uttered al-Murjani, "since you have brought me back to a testimony of the reason." Fear had overpowered the Shaykh al-Murjani at a moment when hope was subdued, and he restored him to [a spirit of] hope.[24]

I ask God not to sever our hope from His mercy and forgiveness, and that He do with us in this world and the next whatever befits His bounty.

House of Evil

One whose word I trust related to me what follows:

A certain house was provided by the Sultan as a resting place for Arabians of the desert. There, they committed acts of disobedience and deeds that contravened the law.

The shaykh passed by that place and the people of the quarter complained to him about it. He stood before the door, his lips quivering. "I hope God will take away this evil from you," he said.

From that day henceforth, not one [of the evil-doers] frequented the house, but pious people inhabited it.

Ibn al-Mu'addib: the Sultan, and the Well

My father related to me,

When the Sultan [of Tunis] was on the point of seizing Ibn al-Mu'addib[25] with whom my master Madi was staying, he [Ibn al-Mu'addib] rushed to him [Abu 'Abd Allah ibn Sultan] and his brother Madi, and these two interceded for him before the Sultan. The latter assuaged his fears. Consequently he [Ibn Sultan] took my master Madi to his home to protect him from the Sultan and others, for he was alone. He remained with [his brother] until he passed away.

Now, when my master Abu 'Abd Allah [Ibn Sultan] had traveled to the East and found that my master Abu al-'Abbas [al-Mursi] had passed away, he said to him [Madi], "We are two old men, and I cannot be separated from you after having seen you. This, my master Abu al-'Abbas, whom I had taken as my intimate friend after the death of the shaykh [al-Shadhili], has died."

My master Madi was alone, his family and his aforementioned son, 'Abd al-Da'im, having passed away in Alexandria. So he [Madi] had said, "O my son [Ibn al-Mu'addib], I look upon you as a substitute for my brother Abu 'Abd Allah [Ibn Sultan]. So they journeyed together to Tunis.

When Ibn al-Mu'addib was made safe from the Sultan, he complained to Madi that he had a chest containing considerable money that he had thrown into the well out of fear of the Sultan. The water of the well was so deep that no one could reach the bottom without plunging into it and swimming hard. He feared to tell this to any person, but made it known to Madi.

Madi said to him, "My brother Abu 'Abd Allah will arrive, if God wills, and we shall look into the matter."

So, Abu 'Abd Allah came, and Madi informed him of what had taken place. "What shall I do?" he asked.

"Write something," he replied, "and throw it in the well to make the water sink away."

So he [Abu 'Abd Allah] wrote names on pieces of earthenware and threw them into the well, and the water sank away.

Ibn al-Mu'addib then descended [into the well] and brought up the chest. The well remained a hole without water. "How can you leave this well with no water in it?" [Ibn al-Mu'addib] asked.

Madi instructed, "Write, O brother, something and throw it in the well, and, if God wills, the water will return."

Abu 'Abd Allah wrote on a piece of earthenware and threw it in the well, and the water returned as it had been.

My father asked him, "My master, what did you write to make the water disappear and to bring it back?"

He replied, "[I wrote] 'In the name of God the Merciful, the Compassionate. *Allahumma!* By Thee, from Thee, to Thee.' By these [words], O my son,[26] the water sank away, and by them the water returned."

Story of the Grape Thief

I received the following tale from a person who had heard it from one of the men of al-Masruqin:

This man had a small garden with trees and grape vines in the place mentioned.

A man from that locality came in the middle of the day, when no people were present, to steal the grapes that were in the vineyard. When he extended his hand to pluck the bunch, his hand withered, and he had to sit down without being able to rise.

At that moment, while he was in a stupor, the shaykh [Abu ʿAbd Allah ibn Sultan] appeared before him, took him by the hand and made him stand up.

The shaykh said to him, "You have troubled me [to come] in this heat."

"I repent to God," he confessed. "I will not put my hands on the goods of a Muslim."

Story of the Cattle Thief

He [the author's father] also told of the following incident:

A thief wished to enter a house in which we were dwelling in al-Masruqin. At times, it sheltered a few heads of cattle, and he was on the point of stealing some of them.

He became glued to the wall and unable to reach [his objective] or retreat, so that he remained until morning where he was. The shaykh came [Abu ʿAbd Allah ibn Sultan], took his hand, gave him hospitality, and brought him to repentance. So he turned to God.

My father moved with us to a house in front of his, seeking to be near him and see him at all times. So God rewarded him with good on our account.

Carbuncles Healed

I fell ill with carbuncles that attacked my eye. It is an awful malady! If it attacks the eye, it cracks and bursts, and renders the features ugly. I endured great suffering because of it.

Several times [the shaykh] came to me, placed his blessed hand on the affliction, and cast a charm over it, reciting, "In the name of god the Merciful the compassionate" (Q 1:1) three times; "In the name of God the Living the Self-Subsisting" (Q 2:255) another three times; "In the name of God, with which nothing on earth or in the heavens can do harm, for He is the Hearer, the Knower" for three times; and "In the name of God I place on you this charm, and may God heal you from every ill that besets you, and drive away misery, Lord of men, and heal. Thou art the Healer, there is no healing save Thy healing."

He would also pray, "My God! By the high rank of Muhammad [the Apostle], may the eye of Muhammad not be distressful to him. Remove from him [the plight] that he is experiencing, through the supplication of Thy Prophet, the truthful, the excellent, the blessed, the one carrying weight with Thee. Exalt the name of thy Lord the Highest (Q 87:1) in comparison with Whom nothing is high, and on account of Whose manifestation nothing remains fixed."[27]

So, by God, my eye healed and returned to its normal state without disfigurment or defect. "Praise be to God, Lord of the Universe" (Q. 1:1).

On Learning the Qur'an

I had attended school until I reached maturity. Then, my father took me out of school. So, I was learning none of the Qur'an and was writing with a terrible script. That was a source of chagrin to my father, and he complained of it to the shaykh [Abu 'Abd Allah ibn Sultan]. The latter ordered me to read in the Book [the Qur'an] one portion and explain it to him each day until I finished it. I completed it in four days. Then, he ordered me to copy the book of the *Risala* [of al-Qushayri]. I did that and improved my penmanship. Thus, God established the great Qur'an in my heart. Praise be to God in abundance.

The Orange Tree

When we went to dwell in the house previously mentioned in front of his house, by it stood a bitter orange tree whose branches had withered and whose leaves were few. We worked [the soil about] it, watered it, gave it our attention, and it flourished, its leaves increased, and it bore fruit and became beautiful.

The shaykh used to come into our house almost every day and sit a long time with us. This lasted for a year or longer. One day, my father said to him, "O my master, look at this tree, how the children have taken care of it, and how it has revived after it had withered."

He raised his head and looked at it. "By God," he exclaimed, "I did not know whether or not there was a tree at this house." That was because he was deeply submerged in thought of the True One.

It is as our master said—"Their outward behavior conforms to that of the creatures; [but] their inner reality is with the True One. So they are they, and they are not they."

Fasting and Feasting

When the month of Ramadan arrived, my father called for him [Abu 'Abd Allah ibn Sultan] the first night of the breaking of the fast. After breaking the fast, [my father] said to him, "O my master, the Apostle of God said, 'If anyone gives to one who has been fasting wherewith to break the fast, he will receive the reward of one who fasts.'[28] Where will such a one as I receive the reward of one who fasts such as you?" So he wrote to [my father] by oath that he would break the fast at our house every night. Thus, it was.

One night, we prepared food for him. On top of it was a chicken. The one who had prepared it was my paternal grandmother, a pious and blessed woman. The part she liked best was the breast of the chicken. Now, when she placed the meat on the platter, she chose a big chicken breast, the finest there was. Then she said to herself, "The shaykh, by God, is more worthy of it than I."

We brought on the food. He looked over the platter. Then he lifted the chicken breast and handed it to me. "O Muhammad," he said, "return this chicken breast to your lady who prepared this food."

We did not know what thought had gone through her mind. Weeping, she told us these thoughts.

The Fig

The worthy teacher Abu al-'Abbas al-Jami related to me that he was sitting beneath a fig tree. The owner of the garden saw a fig that had ripened early. He said to [Abu 'Abd Allah], "O my master, climb up and pluck it for yourself."

"We have nothing to do with it," he replied, "the name of 'Abd al-Rahman is written on it."

Just then a lad climbed up, plucked, and ate it.

I asked him what his name was, and he answered, "'Abd al-Rahman."

Unveiling Secrets

Another time he [al-Jami] said,

> One night in the beginning of my career, I passed the night at the home of my master Abu Muhammad al-Habibi. A man without knowledge of the [Sufi] masters came to him. He said to al-Habibi, "I have heard that you unveil secrets for men. So do so for me."
>
> Al-Habibi replied, "[It is better] to conceal the concealed things of God."
>
> "My master," he repeated, "I want you to disclose secrets to me."
>
> Al-Habibi turned away from him, but the inquirer persisted. Al-Habibi finally ordered him to blow out the candle, and began to disclose to him [many] things. He would say, "My master, stop, enough," while the shaykh continued to pour out instruction.
>
> Then al-Habibi said to him, "You youself requested this and allowed yourself to get in beyond your depth."

Al-Habibi turned toward me, and I became afraid of him. He reassured me, "You have nothing to fear except your lower self, for it is that that has caused your trouble."

He then passed his hand over my chest (*sadr*)[29] and said, "Would to God that it perish."

So it was that his self perished to the point that no bit of it remained perceptible.

This shaykh was of the people of Shadhila, the first to accompany the shaykh [al-Shadhili] in Ifriqiya, from whom he received great gifts. I have mentioned this in the beginning of the book, and how they met.

The Viper

He [al-Jami or al-Habibi] said, "I saw as if I were sitting before my master Abu al-Hasan [al-Shadhili]. With him were a number of his companions. On his lap was a viper which he was stroking with his hand.

" 'My God,' he exclaimed, 'this is the soul of Abu 'Abd Allah ibn Sultan. I will show it to him.'

"Thereupon, he threw it away. The ground split open and swallowed it."

Translevitation

One whose word I believe related to me that the worthy teacher Jarar had informed him that, when he first began to experience the mystical state, he would ask himself how the saints were able to practice translevitation. He pondered over that.

I set out to visit Abu 'Abd Allah al-Habibi whose residence was in Tunis outside Bab al-Jazira.[30] I found him standing in the doorway of his house and greeted him.

He took my hand and said, "You are the one I have been awaiting."

He came out, and together we went away [from the city] toward the south—that is, in the direction of Jabal Hamza, passing by people of Morocco on the right side, until we came in sight of a seashore.

Suddenly, there appeared a city built up, and two young men who looked as if they were Andalusians were coming toward us. They joined us and were happy to be with the shaykh. We entered the mosque [or the garden] outside the city, and we sat with the two until we performed the worship of noon and afternoon. They wanted him to pass the night with them, but he declined.

We left them [and returned] until I recognized Jabal Hamza, which I knew to be in Ifriqiya. Before the yellowing of the sun, we arrived [back in the city] and, when we reached the door of al-Habibi's house, he took hold of my ear and asked, "O Jarar, what did you think of the translevitation experience? Do you know where you were today?"

"No, by God," I replied.

"In Tangier," he said, "and the two young men whom you saw are saints of God. I visit them and they come to me frequently. I wanted to show you what God is able to do for whomsoever He may will of His servants."

A Heritage

A person in whom I have confidence related to me that this blessed Shaykh Abu Muhammad al-Habibi had a daughter married to a companion of my master Abu Muhammad al-Murjani. When he [al-Habibi] fell ill and his condition worsened, he gathered his sons and divided among them his heritage. But he willed her nothing.

Her husband complained to Abu Muhammad al-Murjani. The latter came and spoke to him [al-Habibi] about it. His answer was, "I shall inherit from her, and she will receive no heritage from me."

That very day toward afternoon, she died without having been ill. The shaykh [al-Habibi] died toward the latter part of the evening. His miraculous interventions (karamat) were many, and I have written briefly about some of them. I did not wish to omit from this volume [mention of] her excellence as a means of access and of her drawing close to God.

Testimony of al-Himyari

Shaykh Abu Ishaq Ibrahim al-Himyari related to me that he heard him say, "While worshipping at 'Asqalan [north of Gaza] in Syria, I heard a sound behind me and someone saying, "O Abu Muhammad, these children, move with them to Ifriqiya to raise them there."

Accordingly, he traveled to Ifriqiya and there boys were born to him, among whom I have known Shaykh Abu 'Abd Allah Muhammad and Shaykh Abu al-'Abbas Ahmad. These were excellent men. The former died many years before his brother. The latter died later. Both were buried in al-Masruqin. They left behind them their blessed children, to one of whom divine blessings were attributed along with supernatural deeds (kharq 'adat).

Story of the Rent Money

A pious woman related to me this account:

> As a servant for the family of my master 'Abd Allah al-Habibi, I washed the room where he dwelt. I was owing ten dirhams as rent on the room in which I was living. On that account, I was troubled, for I had absolutely nothing with which to pay.
>
> The shaykh entered while I was in the midst of washing [the room]. He sat down before the door of the room until I finished the washing. I spread for him something on which to sit. Then I went out and said, "Enter, my master, for I have completed the work."
>
> "O Umm al-Salam," he said to me, "enter and take up from under the rug that you have spread the ten dirhams that you owe."
>
> I entered and found the ten dirhams, even though I had just finished washing the spot and had left nothing there.

Tombs of Saints

He [al-Habibi] died in the city of Tunis—may God protect it—and was buried in the southern part of al-Zallaj, a blessed cemetery in which were buried together four excellent and divinely [Sufi] teachers, all of whom were companions of the shaykh [al-Shadhili].

Among these were this blessed shaykh, my master Abu 'Abd Allah ibn Sultan, my master Abu Muhammad Abd al-'Aziz al-Zaytuni, and my master Hilal al-Masruqi—may God be pleased with them all.

One of my companions, who had suffered some misfortune, saw my master Shaykh Abu al-Hasan [al-Shadhili] in a dream. He complained of that to the shaykh. The latter replied, "Whenever some misfortune befalls you, go the the grave of Abu Muhammad al-Habibi and cry to God there, and I will be the one to cry to God for you."

Another companion of the shaykh [al-Habibi] in Tunis was the teacher Abu 'Abd Allah al-Qurtubi whom I have previously mentioned. He was buried in the Zallaj (cemetery) in a burial plot in front of the slaughter house. By the head of the grave is a small palm tree. One day I was sitting by his tomb when a group of people from al-Damus passed by.[31]

"Whose tomb is this?" they questioned.

I told them.

"When we pass by in the early morning or in the early part of the night, we see something like light burning by it," they said.[32]

Story of the Cripple

Shaykh Abu 'Abd Allah ibn Sultan related to me the following about associating or sitting with him [al-Habibi]: "You are unable to disobey God when you are with him even for a single moment. Whenever you say, [for example], that you saw such-and-such a person, or such-and-such a person says [it], he will say, "There is no god save God," rather [than anything else].[33] So nothing is spoken in his presence except [true] knowledge, mention [of God], or some spiritual truth."
He also said,

> I kept company with him [al-Habibi] for a time in self-mortification (*mujahada*) on Jabal Makut in al-Jazira al-Qibliya. One Friday, we went down to one of the nearby villages for the worship. On entering the mosque—or, he said, on leaving it—there was a crippled man in the courtyard of the mosque. Looking toward us, he exclaimed, "O poor men (*fuqara'*), raise me up, O my masters."
>
> The shaykh [al-Habibi] did not wish to disappoint his expectation of the poor devotees. So he took him by the hand and said, "Arise."
>
> The man arose and walked.
>
> The people of the village, seeing this and astounded, asked him [about it].
>
> "That poor man," he explained, "took me by the hand and made me stand up."
>
> At that moment he fell to the ground, a cripple on the spot. People picked him up and carried him to us.
>
> "You have revealed the secret of God," the shaykh told him.
>
> He wept and clung to the borders [of the shaykh's garments].
>
> The shaykh ordered, "Bring me an inkwell and a sheet of paper."
>
> [They did so] and he wrote for the cripple an amulet (*hirz*), saying, "Put it in a little oil, apply the oil, and hope in God for some good."
>
> So he applied the oil and became cured. Praise be to God.

Al-Habibi said to me, "O Abu 'Abd Allah, I dealt with him [in the first instance] directly as between myself and him. But when he revealed the secret of God, he became crippled [again]. So I dealt with him in a way to conceal myself by the names of God."

Al Bija'i

Among the companions of al-Habibi was Abu 'Abd Allah al-Bija'i the tailor. He worked at his trade inside Bab al-Jazira in the neighborhood of the dyers. He was also buried in the Zallaj Cemetery to the west of al-Habibi.

Christians Enter Tunis

My master Abu 'Abd Allah ibn Sultan related to me the following: "When the Christians were on the point of descending on Tunis in A.H. 668,[34] I saw in a dream someone saying to me, 'O Muhammad, leave my city until I chastise my servants.' So he left and went to the region of the Jarid [in southern Tunisia]. Then, the enemy descended on Tunis and remained there until he [ibn Sultan] was instructed to return to Tunis. When he entered Qayrawan, the enemy withdrew from Tunis."

Light from the Grave

My father told me what follows:

A man was building a tower near the grave of al-Habibi. He was in a state of confusion in his work for, one night, he saw a light rise up from his grave so bright that it illuminated the heavens, and the illumination of the sky remained as if it were sunlight.

In the morning, he went to inquire about the person buried in the grave and his lineage. [On being told who he was], he turned to God, jouneyed to the East, and became a firm follower of the shaykh.[35]

The Tailor Shop

My father related to me about Abu 'Abd Allah al-Ra'is [the captain] who was near the Sur mosque and was one of the pious.

He used to sew in the shop of my master 'Abd Allah al-Bija'i. Shaykh Abu Muhammad al-Habibi was sitting in the shop with him. Abu 'Abd Allah al-Ra'is, on seeing the sun alight on the face of my master Abu Muhammad al-Habibi, would take his hiram (blanket) to place it in the window-frame to shade him.

Whenever he did that, the shaykh would say, "The captain has arisen to spread his sail." By so doing, he obtained many blessings, was called "shaykh," and established for himself a good reputation.

One day, he [al-Habibi] called me, [recounted the captain], and said, "O Abu 'Abd Allah, you will not die until you perform the pilgrimage. And when you die, people will say about you, 'How he glorified God!'" Just so it happened.

Anecdotes about Madi

With regard to my master Madi, it is sufficient to mention his high consideration in the service of the shaykh, the *Qutb* [al-Shadhili], the latter's showing to him special favors, and taking him into his family. Many of his miraculous interventions remain unpublicized.

[For example], one in whom I have confidence related to me that a certain man had lost a donkey. He searched, but could not find it. He came to him [Madi] weeping and imploring him to make supplication [to God to find it].

Looking at him, he said, "Your donkey is in Qayrawan."

Again, one of our companions saw Madi in a dream, and the latter said to him, "Whenever you need to ask something of God, ask it of Him at my grave."

I replied, "O my master, but you are dead."

"I have not died," Madi responded, "and I have not absented myself from my companions. If dust [of the grave] darkens the sight of any man, he is not a [Sufi] master."

He [Madi] used to say, when he was enjoying good health among us, "By God, I will not enter the Garden [referring to the Garden of God] until none of my companions remains [alive]."

He [Madi] died in the city of Tunis on a Wednesday of A.H. 718 [A.D. 1318–1319] at the age of 116 or approximately so.[36]

He also used to say, "I heard the shaykh [al-Shadhili] say, 'I was told, O 'Ali, one who has seen you will not suffer misfortune, nor [will] one who has seen one who has seen you. If you were to desire it, I would make this applicable to the day of resurrection.' We have seen him with the eyes of love and veneration.[37] 'Praise be to God, Lord of the worlds' (Q. 1:1)."

My master Shaykh Yaqut al-Habashi—May God benefit us through him— also told me about that in the city of Alexandria in A.H. 716 [A.D. 1316–1317], on the authority of my master Abu al-'Abbas al-Mursi, who received the same from the shaykh [al-Shadhili]. So I said to him [Yaqut], "O my master, I have seen you with the eye of real love and veneration. Therefore invoke God for my sake."

"May God accord you the good fortune of eternity," he replied.

When I arrived in Tunis from Egypt, having visited the [grave of the] shaykh in Humaythira [previously], and after having seen some of his children and grandchildren, and met my master Madi and told him all that I saw, he said to me, "Not one of the followers of the shaykh [al-Shadhili] has comforted me as you have done." He would reiterate that to me every time I went to visit him. He would weep and say to me, "Well done, O Jamal[38] al-Din, may God beautify and adorn you as He has adorned His most sincere saints. I beseech God to strengthen you, enrich you, enrich [others] through you, and make you to be a leader whom others will imitate in this world and the next."

I hope from God, the Generous, His acceptance of that out of His bounty and goodness. "Praise be to God, Lord of all things" (Q. 1:1).

This is the declaration of the poor and the needy servant [of God] who makes entreaties to God—He is exalted—through these eminent [Sufi] masters for the good of this world and the hereafter, its author Muhammad ibn Abi al-Qasim al-Himyari, known publicly as Ibn al-Sabbagh, who desires from God that He accept his [work] and that He make it a work sincerely devoted to Him alone.

When all of this had been gathered in my mind—and I feared lest I forget it—I compiled it for myself and for those who loved the blessed shaykh and his companions.

I have transmitted these accounts from reliable sources, persons of excellence, and good men.

All of this I have gathered without benefit of aptitude for grammar or language out of love for this blessed shaykh, for his resplendent and praiseworthy brotherhood, for his companions, and for those who love him.

May God assemble us with him beneath the banner of our faithful and noble Prophet Muhammad before God—He is exalted. Prayers and peace be upon him, his family, his followers, his wives, his children, and the people of his household. "Praise be to God, Lord of all things" (Q. 1:1).

There is no force and no strength except in God, the High, the Mighty.

Notes

Editor's Introduction

1. P. Nwyia, *Ibn 'Ata' Allah (m. 709/1309) et la naissance de la confrerie sadilite* (Beirut, 1972) 4.
2. The following quotation illustrates the high level of Hasan al-Basri's devotion and piety: "Hasan of Basra, hearing mention made of the man who shall only be saved after having passed a thousand years in Hell-fire, burst into tears and exclaimed, 'Oh, would that I were like that man.'" R. Nicholson, *The Idea of Personality in Sufism* (Cambridge, 1923) 8.
3. Ibid., 5.
4. Ibid., 7.
5. A. N. al-Sarraj, *Kitab al-luma' fi'l tasawwuf*, ed. R. A. Nicholson. Gibb Memorial Series, no. 22 (Leiden, 1914).
6. A. B. al-Kalabadhi, *Kitab al-ta'arruf li madhhab ahl al-tasawwuf*, ed. A. J. Arberry (Cairo, 1934). Translated by A. J. Arberry, *The Doctrines of the Sufis* (Cambridge, 1935).
7. A. T. al-Makki, *Qut al-qulub fi mu'amalat al-mahbub*, 2 vol. (Cairo, 1893).
8. A. R. al-Sulami, *Tabaqat al-sufiyya*, ed. J. Pederson (Leiden, 1960). For a thorough analysis of the sources given in the text, see A. Schimmel, *Mystical Dimensions of Islam* (Chapel Hill, 1975), 84–92.
9. See W. M. Watt's Translation of al-Ghazali's *al-Munqidh min al-dalal, The Faith and Practice of al-Ghazali* (Chicago, 1982).
10. On Suhrawardi, see H. Corbin, *Shihaboddin Yahya Sohravardi Shaykh al-ishraq: L'Archange empourpre* (Paris, 1976).
11. A. M. Mackeen, "The Early History of Sufism in the Maghrib Prior to al-Shadhili (d. 656/1256)," in *Journal of the American Oriental Society*, 91:3, July-September 1971, 400.
12. A. Mustafa, *al-Bina' al-ijtima'i li'l tariqa al-shadiliyya* (Alexandria, 1982) 9.
13. Mackeen, "The Early History," 408.
14. A. H. Mahmud (d. 1978), former rector of the Azhar university, bases his account of the early life of al-Shadhili on Ibn al-Sabbagh's biography. See A. H. Mahmud, *al-Madrasa al-Shadhiliyya al-haditha wa-imamuha Abu al-Hasan al-Shadhili* (Cairo, 1969) especially 38–45.

15. E. H. Douglas, "Al-Sahdhili: A North African Sufi According to Ibn al-Sabbagh," in *The Muslim World* 38 (1948) 260.

16. A. M. Mackeen, "The Rise of al-Shadhili (d. 656/1256)," in *Journal of the American Oriental Society*, 91:4, October-December 1971, 484. Mackeen elaborates on this thesis by saying that

> The real birthplace of the Shadiliyya was certainly Egypt. Here it grew into a self-conscious body with a definite step towards theoretical expansion. The contrast in character between the Tunisian and Egyptian phases of its development found a typical Sufi portrayal in the form of a Divine command that reminded al-Shadhili that his days of *mihan* (persecution) have been replaced in Egypt with those of *minan* (Divine favors). (485)

17. Al-Shadiliyya is a major Sufi order in contemporary Islam. The following bibliography is intended to introduce the reader to the major books written about the order. It is known that the founder, Abu al-Hasan al-Shadhili (d. 656/1258), left no books behind him. Neither did the second shaykh of the order, Abu al-'Abbas al-Mursi (d. 686/1287). 'Abd al-Halim Mahmud wrote a good biography of Abu al-'Abbas which is included in his book, *al-Madrasa al-Shadhiliyya*, cited in note 14. The first important writer of the Shadhiliyya is Ibn 'Atta Allah (d. 709/1309–10), the second shaykh of the order. His work, *Lata'if al-minan*, edited by 'Abd al-Halim Mahmud (Cairo, 1974), is the first biography of both al-Shadhili and al-Mursi. Another major work by al-Iskandari is *al-Hikam al-'Atta'iyah*, which is a collection of proverbs and is available in the Western languages. The English translation of this book is rendered beautifully by the late Victor Danner in *Ibn 'Ata'illah's Sufi Aphorisms*. A comparable solid French translation is by Father Paul Nwyia, *Ibn 'Ata' Allah et la naissance*, cited in note 1. Many commentaries on this book by major Shadhili shaykhs have appeared throughout the ages. For this purpose see the following:

1. Ibn 'Ajiba, *Iqaz al-himam fi sharh al-hikam* (Cairo, 1915);
2. Ahmad Ibn Zarruq al-Fasi, *Qurat al-'ayn fi sharh hikam al-'arif bi-Allah Ibn 'Ata Allah al-Iskandari* (Cairo, 1972); and
3. Ibn 'Abbas al-Rundi, *Ghayth al-mawahib al-'aliyya fi sharh al-hikam al-'ata'iyya* (Cairo, 1970).

A good book on al-Rundi as a Sufi thinker is by Nwyia, *Ibn 'Abbad de Ronda* (Beirut, 1961). Another major biography of the Shadhiliyya is by Ahmad Ibn 'Ayyad, *Kitab mafakhir al-'aliyya fi'l ma'athir al-Shadhiliyya* (Cairo, 1961).

A major Shadhili thinker in sixteenth century Egypt is 'Abd al-Wahab al-Sha'rani. His work, *al-Tabaqat al-kubra*, documents the lives of the major Shadhili shaykhs. A recent book published in English about this important thinker is

Michael Winter's, *Society and Religion in Early Ottoman Egypt: Studies in the Writings of 'Abd al-Wahab al-Sha'rani* (New Brunswick, 1982).

One of the modern Shadhili shaykhs is the Algerian Shaykh al-'Alawi. Martin Lings has documented his life and thought in *A Sufi Saint of the Twentieth Century* (London, 1971).

A good bibliography on various books of Sufism is provided by A. Schimmel in *Mystical Dimensions in Islam* (Chapel Hill, 1975).

18.   Mackeen, on the basis of *Tabaqat* literature, maintains that

> The Ghumara were a large Berber tribe who. . . . belonged to the Baranis family of the Berbers. They had occupied a vast mountainous tract in Northern Morocco forming part of the Rif—later to acquire the name *bilad Ghumara* after them. The group has been variously divided into a number of clans dispersed in different Berber kingdoms, but the tribe, as a whole, preserved a sense of geographical unity. Living as an isolated community, they were rather slow in comprehending the new faith, but their acceptance of Islam, at any rate, was followed by a conscious reaction, at once religious and political, tending toward Kharijite anarchy and pagan liberalism. They favorably disposed to the Kharijite creed which they adopted in the second/eighth century and pledged their support to the rebellion of Maisarah, claimed as the first Berber revolt in the Muslim Maghrib. (Mackeen, "The Rise," 478).

19.   *Qutb* is one of the highest titles of Sufism. According to al-Qashani, the Prophet of Islam assumes the title of *qutb al-aqtab* (pole of poles or the major polestar). This title is given to Muhammad because of his "unique brand of perfection: no one may become the Seal of the Saints and the Pole of Poles, except by virtue of the inner aspect of the Seal of Prophethood." A. R. al-Qashani, *A Glossary of Sufi Technical Terms*, tr. by N. Safwat (London, 1991) 97. Ibn al-Sabbagh tells us that al-Shadhili attained the rank of *qutb* in Egypt.

20.   Douglas, "Al-Shadhili," 269.

21.   Mackeen, "The Rise," 479.

22.   Mahmud, *al-Madrasa*, 29.

23.   Ibid., 38.

24.   Mackeen, "The Rise," 485.

25.   Ibn 'Ata' Allah, *Lata'if al-minan*, 37.

26.   See Ibn 'Ata' Allah, *The Book of Wisdom*, tr. V. Danner (New York, 1978).

27.   Mackeen, "The Rise" 486.

28.   Mahmud, *al-Madrasa al-Shadhiliyya*, 55.

29.   See chapter seven of M. Lings's, *Symbol and Archetype: A Study of the Meaning of Existence* (London, 1992).

30.   See chapter four of this translation.

31.   Douglas, "Al-Shadhili" 272.

32. M. Lings, *Symbol and Archetype*, 68.
33. W. M. Watt, *The Faith*, 60.
34. Ibid., 62.
35. S. H. Nasr, *Sufi Essays*, (Albany, 1991) 43–44.
36. Ibid., 45.
37. Ibid., 89.
38. Ibid., 37.

Author's Introduction

1. In Sufi terminology, the *qutb*—an axis, pivot, or pole—refers to the highest in the hierarchy of saints. Some hold that there is only one *qutb* at any one time: some say there can be two, and some others say four. He is unknown to the world while alive. Other members of the Sufi hierarchy are *ghawth*, helper; *awtad*, pegs; *anwar*, lights; *akhyar*, good men; *shuhada'*, martyrs; *abdal*, substitutes; and *khulafa'*, successors. For more information, see A. Qashani, *A glossary of Sufi Technical Terms*.

2. A *ghawth* is a helper. It is generally considered that there is no fundamental difference between the *qutb* and the *ghawth*, except that he is called a *ghawth* only when someone seeks refuge in him. See Dozy, *Supplement aux Dictionnaires Arabes* (Leiden, 1881) 230, and al-Jurjani, *Kitab al-ta'rifat* (Leipzig, 1845) 169, 293.

3. References to Ibn al-Sabbagh occur in Brockelmann, *Geschichte der Arabischen Litteratur and Supplmentband* (Leiden, 1898) 804, where he is mentioned as Muhammad ibn Abi al-Qasim b. al-Sabbagh al-Himyari, author of this work; and Sarkis, *Dictionnaire Encyclopedique de Bibliographie Arabe* (Cairo, 1928) 142. The author's name is given as Muhammad b. Abi al-Qasim al-Hamidi, or al-Humaydi.

4. *Bast* and *qabd* are two mystical states of exaltation and depression, joy and sorrow.

5. Here, it is claimed for al-Shadhili that he is a descendant of Muhammad through al-Hasan, son of 'Ali b. Abi Talib, and of Fatima, daughter of the Prophet of Islam. The claim of al-Shadhili's connection with al-Hasan does not necessarily imply that he shared Shi'i views. However, al-Hasan, as well as his brother al-Husayn, is considered by Sufis as one of their spiritual ancestors. Al-Hujwiri asserted that he was profoundly versed in Sufism. See Hujwiri, *The "Kashf al-Mahjub," The Oldest Persian Treatise on Sufism* (London, 1911) 75. It appears also that the Sharifs particularly favored saint veneration and the development of the religious brotherhoods in Morocco after the time of al-Shadhili.

6. Al-Shadhili had a son called by the same name.

7. Al-Maghrib, or Morocco, is the land of the West. Geographers differ in delimiting this territory. It is generally agreed that the northern limit is

the Mediterranean Sea, the western limit is the Atlantic Ocean, and the southern
limit the sands of the Sahara. At the time of our writer, the eastern limit was
probably near Bijaya in Algeria. For more information, consult A. M. Mackeen,
"The Early History of Sufism in the Maghrib Prior to al-Shadhili (d. 656/1258),"
in *Journal of the American Oriental Society*, 91:3, July-September 1971, 398.

8. Ifriqiya included what is now Tunisia and part of Algeria, or possibly only
northern and central Tunisia. De-Goeje, in *Bibliotheca Geographorum Arabicorum*
gives the spelling Ifriqiya. See also Z. M. al-Qazwini, *Athar al-bilad wa akhbar
al-'ibad* (Beirut, n.d.) and S. G. Miller, *Disorienting Encounters* (Berkeley, 1992) 83.

9. *Khalifa* means vicegerent or successor. Among Sufis, he is the
representative of the head of a religious order, or the inheritor of the spiritual
power of the founder of an order. It is probably in this latter sense that the term
is used here—and continues to be used. For modern usage, see Sadler, "Visit
to a Chishti Qawwali," *The Muslim World*, October 1963, 290f. The assumption
of the title by al-Shadhili implied that he was the recognized head of the order.
That this text does not relate of whom he was a successor leads to the suggestion
that the title may have been bestowed upon him by adherents of his order after
the latter had undergone considerable development.

Chapter One

1. Ghumara is the name of a Berber tribe that resided in Northern Morocco,
south of Tangier and Ceuta. Al-Bakri did not consider these two cities as lying
within its boundaries (*E.I.*, II, 160f). It is also the name of the territory inhabited
by this tribe. It is described by S. Idrisi, *Description de l'Afrique et de l'Espagne*
(Leiden, 1866), 81, 170.

2. Abu al-Fath al-Wasiti is mentioned in Brockelmann; Brock. *Supp.* 781,
as having died in Alexandria about 589/1184 and as being the author of *Irshad
al-salikin fi manaqib al-Shaykh 'Ali al-Rifa'i*, the latter being his teacher. If we
assume this date to be correct, this person cannot have been the one mentioned
in our work, because al-Shadhili was born after this date. On the spread of the
Rifa'i order to Egypt, see J. S. Trimingham, *The Sufi Orders in Islam* (London,
1971) 39, 48.

3. 'Abd al-Salam Ibn Mashish is mentioned in Brockelmann 440 and
Brockelmann *Supp.* 787, as pupil of Abu Madyan and teacher of al-Shadhili.
He died in 625/1228, the year in which al-Shadhili went to Tunis. He was buried
on Jabal Alam (*E.I. rev.*, I, 91f). See also T. Burckhardt, "The Prayer of Ibn
Mashish," *The Islamic Quarterly*, nos. 1, 2 (1978) 68–75.

4. The term *wilaya*—sometimes written *walaya*—meaning friendship or
sainthood, and the power of saints to perform *karamat*, were discussed at length

by al-Hujwiri in *The "Kashf al-Mahjub,"* 210–220. Implied in the term is the idea of legal power or divine authority.

5. Bab al-Manara, one of the city gates just below the Qasba.

6. The meaning is that the coin was counterfeit. The Moroccan coin was lighter than others. See E. W. Lane, *Arab-English Lexicon* (London, 1863–1885) 876; and *E.I.*, 2, 1010ff on "Kimiya."

7. A *burnus* was an outer garment commonly worn by men.

8. The Great Mosque, or Mosque of the Olive Tree, was founded in A.D. 732. See *E.I.* 4, 838.

9. A legendary character who frequently visited with the saints by translevitation, he is also called *al-Khidr*. Ibn Qutayba reported a similar tradition from Abu al-Aswad in *The 'Uyun al-Akhbar of Ibn Qutayba*, tr. L. Koph, ed. F. S. Bodenheimer (Leiden, 1949). See also G. D. Newby, *The Making of the Last Prophet: A Reconstruction of the Earliest Biography of Muhammad* (Colombia; S.C., 1989), 182–189.

10. Abu Sa'id al-Baji was born in Baja al-Qadima, a village situated on the outskirts of Tunis, in 551/1156. He became a pupil of Abu Madyan, died in 629/1231, and was buried at Jabal al-Manar, near ancient Carthage. See Guide Bleu, *Algerie-Tunisie* (Paris, 1930) 367.

11. These two canonical festivals celebrated sacrifice and breaking of the fast. On both occasions, communal prayer is observed. See *E.I. rev.*, 3, 1007f.

12. A "revealer" is one who is able to see into the intimate thoughts of another. The term applies also to God's revelation or disclosure to man. Al-Sarraj explained three kinds of *mukashafa*. See A. al-Sarraj, *Kitab al-luma' fi'l tasawwuf*, ed. R. A. Nicholson (leiden, 1914) 70.

13. See note 5 of Author's Introduction.

14. Mount Zaghawan is a short distance south of Tunis. It is also pronounced *Zaghawan*. Al-Idirisi (in De Goeje, 119) described it as being very high with its slopes well-watered, fertile, and covered with grain fields and pastures. In various places were found Muslim hermitages.

15. For Balat, see *E.I. rev.*, 1, 978.

16. He was possibly from the modern city of Bijaya in Algeria. See *E.I. rev.*, 1, 1204, H. A. R. Gibb, *Travels of Ibn Battuta* (Cambridge, 1958) 44.

17. With the fall of the Fatimid dynasty, the ascendancy of Salah al-Din in Cairo in 1171, the increasing strength of the Sunni Almohads throughout North Africa, and the appointing of the Hafsid Abu Zakariya as governor of Ifriqiya (or Sultan, according to our text), the accusation of being a Fatimid would naturally be serious. Perhaps he had in mind some particular agitator.

18. Ibn Khaldoun, *Histoire des Berberes*, vol. 2, 298ff.

19. The shaykh is accustomed to receiving guidance in some supernatural way. He indicates this experience by such expressions as "It was said to me," or "I was inspired," or "'Lo, the summons," without stating the source of his

inspiration. There are instances in which he "sees" and talks with his spiritual guide. Somrtimes birds impart to him information, or he "sees" the Prophet, or the medium is a dream. However, the reader is generally left with no indication as to the source. One might say that it was the inward communication, the inner voice, or the subconscious.

20. 'Arafat is the name of a hill near Mecca where a sermon is delivered and special prayers are recited during the pilgrimage (*E.I. rev.*, 1, 604). For a description of the *wuquf* ceremony at 'Arafat, see R. F. Burton, *Personal Narrative of a Pilgrimage to el-Medinah and Meccah* (New York, 1856) chap. 28, and A. G. Sheikh, "From America to Mecca on Airborne Pilgrimage," in *The National Geographic Magazine*, July 1953, 1–60.

21. The Sultan was probably Kamil Muhammad. See S. Lane-Poole, *The Mohammadan Dynasties*, 77.

22. Ibn Battuta recorded that Alexandria had four gates, one of which was the Gate of the Lotus Tree where the road from the Maghrib ended. Another was the Green Gate which was opened only on Friday and through which the inhabitants went out to visit the tombs. See *E.I.*, 2, 536.

23. It might read *bab al-hadid*. This appears to be better grammatical construction, but probably *Jadid* is correct for, to modern times, the name *Bab Jadid* has been maintained.

24. The covenant (*'ahd*) may refer to the engagement consented to by a novice on becoming a recognized follower of the teacher, here symbolized by the giving and receiving of the garment. See R. Dozy, *Supplement*, 2, 185. Or it may be interpreted according to the Sufi conception of the "eternal covenant," man's pledge to love God before the creation of time. See E. J. W. Gibb, *Ottoman Poetry* (London, 1958–63) xxx; R. A. Nicholson, *Studies in Islamic Mysticism*, 206, n.69; and 214, n. 156; idem, *Literary History of the Arabs*, p. 398, n. 1; A. J. Arberry, *The Mystical Poems of Ibn al-Farid* (Dublin, 1956) 80f, 95, 122. Al-Qushayri described the conditions under which the *'ahd* between shaykh and novice may be made (*al-Risala*, 316), and he wrote, "If anyone has been a companion of a certain shaykh and then raises objections to him in his heart, he violates the ahd of companionship" (*al-Risala*, 258). He also said, "It is of great importance to a novice to keep his *'ahd* with God" (*al-Risala*, 323), and he wrote about violating one's *'ahd* with God (*al-Risala*, 315).

25. In the absence of other indications, this may be considered to be the Damanhur al-Wahsh, which is 104 miles from Cairo on the Desert Rim Route to Alexandria (*E.I. rev.*, II, 105f; W. Popper, *Egypt and Syria under the Circassian Sultans*, vol. 15 (Berkeley, 1955) 46 and map 4.

26. The reference is to the Mongols who, after several decades of threats to the Muslim empire, took Baghdad under Hulagu in A.D. 1258, the year of the death of al-Shadhili (*E.I.*, 4, 700f; S. Lane-Poole, *The Mohammadan Dynasties*, 74–83).

27. The Green Gate is one of the wall towers.

28. See A. Kamal, *The Sacred Journey* (New York, 1961) 92–95.

29. The *hijr* is the area enclosed within the wall of Hatim on the north side of the Ka'ba, and contain the burial place of Isma'il (Hughes, *A Dictionary of Islam* 337).

30. *Badal*, or the plural *abdal*, means *substitute*. The idea of the *badal* is contained in the Sufi doctrine that the cosmic order is upheld by a certain number of saints of varying grades. When one dies, his place is immediately filled by a substitute. The number of *abdal* varies from seven, according to Ibn 'Arabi, to three hundred, according to al-Makki. See V. Vacca's excellent article on *abdal*, called "Social and Political Aspects of Egyptian and Yamani Sufism," in the *Journal of the Pakistan Historical Society*, vol. 8, part 4, October 1960, 233–260, and Lane *Lex.*, 168.

31. The *lahd* is an oblong excavation in the side of a grave where the body is placed.

32. Al-Misran (oblique case M-s-r-y-n) is usually mentioned by Arab geographers with reference to Kufa and Basra. Here, however, the context suggests a place near Tunis.

33. Berbers were the indigenous population of North Africa from the dawn of historic times. See *E.I. rev.*, 1, 1173ff.

Chapter Two

1. The soldier-saints may be the Muslim army on the frontier confronting the crusaders. Al-Tirmidhi, who wrote before the Crusades began, explained, among other meanings, that the term *soldier* referred to difficult deeds demanding resolution and struggling, and related the soldier to God's army, of which the *Qur'an* contains many references, especially Q. 37:173 and 74:34 (*Khatm*, 146f). Elsewhere, he mentions the "soldiers" about the throne (*Khatm*, 330).

2. The metaphor of the beggar in king's garb is common in Sufi literature. Jalal al-Din Rumi, Persian poet and mystic, said, "The man of God is a king 'neath dervish cloak." See R. A. Nicholson, ed., *Divan-i-Shams-i Tabriz* (Cambridge, 1961). The Arab poet Abu al-'Atahiya also said in his *Diwan*, "If thou would'st see the noblest of mankind, behold a monarch in a beggar's garb," (R. A. Nicholson, *A Literary History of the Arabs* [Cambridge, 1930] 297f).

3. On *ishan*, see, Schimmel, *Mystical Dimensions of Islam* (Chapel Hill, 1975) 98–186.

4. *Shuhud* and *'iyan* are almost synonymous in this context, meaning the "mystical vision of God," "face to face," or "consciousness of being in God's presence. See Affifi, *The Mystical Philosophy*, 107; *Kashf*, 356, 370, 373; J. W. Redhouse, *A Turkish and English Lexicon* (Constantinople, 1890) 1332.

5. *Dhat* is commonly used reflexively, as in "the man himself." In this work, however, it usually refers to the essence or reality of a thing, person, or God. Al-Sarraj defined *dhat* as "the thing that subsists in itself," and he differentiated it from the names, descriptive epithets, and attributes that are its distinguishing marks. See *Luma'*, 351.

6. P. Nwyia (*Ibn 'Abbad de Ronda*, 126) states that this place is near Qayrawan. R. Brunschwig (*La Berberie Orientale sous les Hafsides* (Paris, 1947), 1, 304, note 1) cites al-Masruqin as one of the toponymes persisting to the present day in the region of Qayrawan. The author is from that locality. Ibn Maryam, writing on a first-century man named Masruq, explains that he was thus-called because, as an infant, he had been stolen.

7. Al-Zallaj, or Jallaz, a cemetery in the southeastern part of Tunis, was sacred to the memory of al-Shadhili who lived in that region in the first half of the thirteenth century (*E.I.*, 4, 840). It is now called the Cemetery of Sidi Belhassan, or al-Sayyid Abu al-Hasan.

8. This is knowledge that has come directly from God by way of inspiration or intuition without the help of intermediaries. Al-Ghazali wrote a treatise entitled *al-Risala al-Laduniya* in which he discusses at length this type of knowledge. A translation of which by Dr. Margaret Smith is found in *Journal of the Royal Asiatic Society*, April and July, 1938, 177–200, 353–374.

9. *Bada'* means "appearance." The *ahl al-bada'* here mentioned are evidently those Sufis who, although abiding by the decrees of God—as did the prophets, messengers, and saints before them—claim possession, by a special dispensation of God, of a knowledge of the mystical sciences and other sciences, and of the gift of extraordinary powers. Being of the elect, they are entitled to these divine favors unknown to and inexperienced by the common people. These favors come according to the good pleasure of God. The whole argument is a defense of Sufi beliefs, practices and experiences.

10. The presence (*hadra*) signifies the mystical experience of the heart's presence with God. Of similar meaning is *ghayba*, which denotes absence from self or from all save God. Al-Hujwiri discusses the relative value of the two words (*Kashf*, 248ff).

11. This may be taken metaphorically or literally. By "mother" might be intended "Mother of the Scripture" (*umm al-kitab*), the original of the Qur'an enscirbed on the "preserved tablet." Or it might mean the "clearly expressed" verses mentioned in Q. (3:5) (*E.I.*, 4, 1012); or the *Fatiha*, first chapter of the Qur'an. On *Umm al-Kitab* see, F. Rahman, *Major Themes of the Qur'an*, (Minneapolis, 1980) 135, and F. Rahman, "Islam's Attitude toward Judaism." *The Muslim World*, 72:1, January 1982, 1–13. In mystical terminology it might be the "first intelligence." See al-Naqshbandi, *Jami' al-usul*, 93; or the meaning of *umm* could here be nontechnical. It could be *abika*, (your father), instead of *ummika*. Thus, the sense of the phrase would be simply, "If you are not sufficiently

advanced to understand spiritual things, then be content with what you learn from your father or mother about the duties of Islam." It is notable that the secret of God is said to be in the mother (A. M. M. Mackeen, "The early History of Sufism in the Maghrib before Muhammad," in *Journal of the American Oriental Society*, July 1971, 407). Al-Tirmidhi, mystic of the third century after the Hijra, divided the heart into four parts, or stations (N. Heer, "A Sufi Psychological Treatise," *The Muslim World*, January 1961, 25ff).

12. *Jam'*, (union) and *farq*, (separation), are two terms that have been discussed at length by Sufi masters and that have received various interpretations. In general, it appears that *jam'* is applied to the mystical union with God in which the person loses consciousness of his own acts, even the acts of religious devotion. This experience is considered to be a free gift of God that cannot be acquired by human actions. *Farq*, on the other hand, denotes a state in which the person is conscious of his own actions, although these actions be of a religious character. Both experiences are indispensable lip expressions of sentiments of religious devotion and internal witness to the reality of God. For a detailed discussion of *jam'* see Qashani, 12–13. The term *'ayn al-jam'* is one of several terms for tawhid (*Luma'*, 372; *Kashf*, 252–260; *Risala*, 59–61).

13. See E. J. Jurji, *Illumination in Islamic Mysticism* (Princeton, 1936) 108.

14. Christian mystics expressed similar feelings. See (E. Underhill, *The Mystics of the Church* [New York, 1926] 217).

15. Al-Mahdiya is a coastal city about 135 miles south of Tunis, founded by the Fatimids in the early tenth century (*E.I.*, 3, 130f). Al-Idrisi describes it as an important port city given over to trade with other countries (Idrisi, 108f).

16. Qabis, or Gabes, is situated on the southern coast of Tunisia, about 225 miles from Tunis. It is noted in Idrisi, 106, and M. J. de Goeje, *Bibliotheca Geographorum Arabicorum*, 8, 346f. The person here mentioned probably came originally from this city.

17. This took place at 'Arafat. In view of what follows, the writer may have Mecca in mind.

18. Barqa is the district on the North African coast lying between the Gulf of Sidra and the Egyptian border, the ancient Cyrenaica. Geographers agree in describing it as a land whose ground is covered with a fine reddish dust that clings to the clothes. Barqa is also the name of a city in this region. About fifteen miles inland, east of Benghazi, it was founded as a Greek colony in 540 B.C. It is now called Madinat al-Marj (A. F. Mehren, *Manuel de la Cosmographie du Moyen Age* (Copenhaguen, 1874) 329; Idrisi, 136; al-Ya'qubi, *Kitab al-Buldan* (Leiden, 1892) 32; and Ibn Khaldun, *Histoire des Berberes* (Algiers, 1852–1856) 164.

19. Al-Tustari, d.896. See Brock. *Supp.*, 1, 333; R. A. Nicholson, *Literary History of the Arabs*, 392.

20. "He who truly fears anything flees from it, but he who truly fears God, flees unto Him. Fear, to the Sufi, was no mere dread of material consequences,

but of separation from God....In proportion to the mystic's nearness to God
is his fear of being cut off from Him" (M. Smith, "The Path of the Soul in Sufism,"
The Aryan Path, vol. 6, June 1935, 367f).

21. The foundations or sources are probably the *Qur'an* and *Sunna*, the first
two of the commonly recognized four sources of Muslim jurisprudence (*E.I.*, 2,
101; 4, 1054ff; J. Schacht, *An Introduction to Islamic Law* (Oxford, 1964) 60, 114).
The science of the derivatives, "branches" [*furu'*], pertains to the study of positive
law (*E.I. rev.*, 2, 889). However, here the terms *usul* and *furu'* may have a purely
Sufi connotation. Al-Sarraj discusses the various theories on the origins of Sufism
in his *Kitab al-Luma'*, 217f, and, on 410, he states that, to Sufis, the *furu'* are
decorum, morals, mystical stages and states, deeds, and words.

Chapter Three

1. Because the *Qur'an* is God's word, all Qur'anic expressions of praise to
God are in reality God's self-laudation. A Prophetic tradition, attributed to 'Ali
b. Abi Talib and recorded by al-Ghazali in his *Ihya'*, contains a lengthy expression
of God's self-glorification. See A. Jeffery, *Reader on Islam* (The Hague, 1962) 103f.
The mystic cannot reckon the praise due to God. A Prophetic tradition reads,
"I cannot reckon the praise that is Thine" (*Risala*, 243; *Luma'*, 113; al-Kalabadhi,
Kitab al-ta'arruf li madhhab ahl al-tasawwuf [Cairo, 1934] 125).

2. According to al-Ghazali (d. 1111), all believers would eventually be saved
from the fire. See D. B. Macdonald, *Muslim Theology, Jurisprudence, and Constitutional Theory* (New York 1926) 307. This was essentially the position of al-Ash'ari
(d. 935).

3. These are the "mysterious letters" which occur frequently in the Qur'an.
See *E.I.*, 2, 1072.

4. According to al-Tirmidhi, all saints are in need of the "seal of the saints"
for His intercession, as all prophets need Muhammad the Prophet for the same
purpose. See *Khatm*, 421. A similar idea is expressed in *Khatm*, 344, with regard
to the day of judgment. The world is never left without some of God's agents
who assume responsibility to defend the saint of God.

5. The expression *huwa huwa* has philosophical and mystical connotations.
See S. Afnan, *Philosophical Terminology in Arabic and Persian* (Leiden, 1964) 121f.

6. Al-Hasan and al-Husayn are two sons of the fourth caliph 'Ali. Their
mother was Fatima, daughter of the Prophet.

7. The *Hizb al-Bahr* is the most famous of litanies attributed to al-Shadhili.
Various translations, in part or in whole, exist. See C. Padwick, *Muslim Devotions*
(London, 1961) 23f, 98, 170; Rinn, 229f; and *Voyages*, I, 40–44.

8. These letters with no known significance introduce *Sura* 19 of the Qur'an
which records the divine favors on Zacharia, Moses, Ishmael, Idris, and Mary,

the mother of Jesus. See *Shorter E. I.* (Ithaca, 1961) 281f, 15; and A. Jeffrey, "The Mystic letters of the Koran," in *The Muslim World*, 1924, 247ff. An example of the possibilities in speculation on the value of letters of the alphabet within the Bektashi dervish order of Turkey, which originated in the seventh/thirteenth century, may be found in J. K. Birge, *The Bektashi Order of Dervishes* (London, 1937) 206ff.

    9. The *Torah* represents the Scriptures of the Jews, and the *Injil*, or Evangel, those of the Christians.

    10. *Umm* undoubtedly refers to *umm al-kitab*, interpreted often as the *Fatiha*, or first chapter of the *Qur'an*, although other meanings are possible. See *E.I.*, 4, 1012. The sovereign verse is said to be the Throne verse (Q. 2:256).

    11. An injunction frequently quoted by mystics is "Serve thy Lord until the certainty comes to thee" (Q. 15:99). The term *'ubudiya* comes from the Arabic root from which the words *servant, slave, humanity, worship, worshiper,* and *adoration* are derived. It is often associated, by antithesis, with "lordship." The service performed may be religious or menial. Among the many relative comments are "Servantship is more perfect than worship, then service, then adoration;" "Servantship is renouncement of personal choice, whatever divine decrees may befall;" "servantship is clearing oneself of the power and strength that rightly belong to God alone;" and "Servantship is embracing what has been commanded you and avoiding what has been held back from you." See *Risala*, 154.

    12. *Qaf* is the twenty-first letter of the Arabic alphabet, title of the fiftieth chapter of the *Qur'an*, and one of the "mysterious letters." The mystery surrounding *Qaf* leaves room for considerable speculation and various interpretations by Qur'anic commentators and mystics. See *E.I.*, 2, 614ff; H. Mustaufi, *Nuzhat al-qulub*, tr. G. Le Strange (London, 1919) 182, 188.

    13. Qur'an 68:1; 96:4. The *qalam* (pen) as used for writing was created by God for man, and is the instrument for recording God's decrees. See *E.I.*, 2, 675f.

    14. *Huduth* is a verbal noun meaning "beginning," or "the process of coming into existence," or "origination of something that previously had no existence." *Hadith* is "new" or what is "in process of coming into existence." Because *huduth* cannot be attributed to God the Eternal, the mystic would also be without that quality, relying solely on God's will for all things. To Shaykh Ahmad al-'Alawi, *huduth* is ephemeral existence, or existence of other than God. See M. Lings, *A Sufi Saint of the Twentieth Century* (London, 1971) 183.

Chapter Four

    1. The term *akhlaq*, meaning traits of moral character in man, has come to be applied to the science of moral philosophy. Al-Ghazali wrote of the beloved being near to God and possessing the most noble characteristics, which are divine

characteristics (*Ihya'*, 4, 296). Al-Hujwiri quoted Nuri as saying that Sufism consisted in morals rather than ceremonial practices (*Kashf*, 42). Cf. D. M. Donaldson, *Studies in Muslim Ethics* (London, 1953), especially chapters 6–9; and A. M. Wickens, tr. *The Nasirean Ethics* (London, 1964).

The author provides no explanation of the expression *al-takhalluq bi-akhlaq Allah*. Al-Ghazali's understanding of it occurs in *al-Maqsad al-asna* (Beirut, 1971), 42ff. He explained that there are several ways to understand and interpret expressions: with the physical senses; with animal sense; as a child, literally; as a theologian, as a saint, and so on. The mystic interprets this expression according to his understanding of God's attributes derived from revelation and contemplation. To him, God's attributes are perceived not through the physical senses but inwardly. He has an intense desire to acquire these attributes through drawing near to them, not spatially but psychically, as do the angels who draw near to God. There must be a serious effort to acquire these attributes, to be characterized by them and to be adorned with their charms. Thus, the servant becomes Lordly, that is, near to the Lord, and partners with the heavenly angels. Later in the *Maqsad* (162ff) al-Ghazali safeguarded his identification. He affirmed that the real essences of the divine names are God's attributes, that none but God can possess them, but that man can obtain something that is akin to and conformable with these qualities. To illustrate, he commented that one says that a pupil acquires the knowledge of his master, though the master alone can possess his own knowledge. So the pupil gained knowledge similar to that of the master.

2. *Hijab*, curtain or veil, is of *Qur'anic* usage (7:44, 33:53; 41:4; 44:50, and so on). Among mystics the *hijab* intervenes between man and God and prevents revelation (*Kashf*, 22, 149, 236, and more); *E.I.*, 3, 300. *Hijab* is defined as that which intervenes between the seeker and the thing sought (*Luma'*, 352). Attributed to Sari al-Saqati (third/ninth century) is the request, "God, with whatever Thou mayest punish me, do not punish me with the humiliation of the veil" (*Risala* [Cairo 1966], 18).

3. A sharp distinction is made between *ma'rifa* and *'ilm*. The former is mystical knowledge, received by direct experience, especially certain knowledge of the Truth or Reality as it is experienced by Sufis. It is divine knowledge of which al-Ghazali wrote. *'Ilm* is knowledge received by cognition, through intellectual processes. Sufis consider *ma'rifa* to be the higher form. Yet *'ilm* is not discredited. It is highly commended as a necessary means for the development of the religious life. With al-Shadhili, the term *'ilm* seems to have been limited to the various branches of religious knowledge, such as the traditions, the *Qur'an* and canon law.

4. Mystics refer to the Qur'anic statement that God is the Watchful or Watcher (Q. 4:1; 35:52) in relation to the practice of *muraqaba*. Someone explained, "*Muraqaba* is the servant's knowledge that the Lord is thoroughly informed about him, and his persistence, because of this knowledge, in watchfulness toward his

Lord" (*Risala*, 148). Another commented, "*Muraqaba* is keeping the eye on (shepherding) the inner soul for the purpose of beholding the True One" (*Risala*, 150).

5. *Kashf*, meaning uncovering or disclosure, is an intuition of or insight into what is hidden to the rational understanding. See *Luma'*, 346.

6. Ibn 'Ata' Allah (d. 1309) in his *Hikam* says; "There is not a breath that you breathe but that He has the determining in you of its going forth." A commentator adds that, at every breath, the "traveler is going toward his Lord. Some of the teachers say that the way to God is in the enumeration of the creature's breathing. The number of breaths in a day and a night, he says, amounts to twenty-four thousand. Thus, the servant's respect for his Lord is registered in his breathing" (R. L. Archer, *Muhammadan Mysticism in Sumatra*, 53).

7. Both *ta'til*, divesting God of attributes, and *tashbih*, anthropomorphism, are considered to be heresies. In this passage, divesting one's self of acts of self-mortification is also contrary to the divine law. See *E.I.* 4, 685, 702; *Kashf*, 200ff.

8. *Tawba* and *inaba* seem to be used synonymously for repentance or turning to God. Yet, writers make a difference. *Inaba* implies a turning away from doubts, worldly things, and heedlessness to God. J. A. Subhan says that *inaba*, conversion, must be preceded by *tawba* (*Sufism: Its Saints and Shrines* [New York, 1970] 72. A writer on 'Abd al-Qadir al-Jilani distinguished between the two by saying that *tawba* is the property of one who repents through hope for reward. *Inaba* also has the meaning of formally renouncing the world and entering into a dervish fraternity (Redhouse, 206). Al-Makki, in one place, defined *inaba* as repentance and turning to God (*Qut*, 1, 75). Elsewhere, he distinguished between the two, explaining that *inaba* implies the working of the heart while *tawba* is turning toward or approaching the Master (*Qut*, 2, 81). For al-Trimidhi, *inaba* is turning to God in the beginning of one's career before God's guidance (*Khatm*, 416). Cf. *Risala*, 79.

9. *Wajd* and *faqd* are used with diverse significations. Al-Junayd used *faqd* in the sense of *fana'*, *dhahab*, and *ghayba*, terms denoting the mystical "passing away" in union with God (*Luma'*, 91, 146/338). "*Wajd*," he says, "is everything that the heart finds of sorrow or joy" (*Luma'*, 310, Arabic). *Wajd* is also said to consist in revelations from *al-Haqq* (ibid.). Al-Hujwiri explains that, in both states, one is overpowered (*maqhur*), bereft of one's own volition (*Kashf*, 368). Another definition of *wajd* is "that which alights upon the heart and comes to it without personal effort or cultivation; and it is said that it is flashes of light that gleam and then quickly subside. See *Risala*, 58.

10. Al-Hujwiri defines the *fawa'id* as "the apprehension by the spirit of what it cannot do without (*Kashf*, 384).

11. *Haba'* is sometimes translated "atoms." Shaykh Ahmad al-'Alawi said, "Thou seest us among men, but we are not as thou seest" (Martin Lings, *A Sufi Saint of the Twentieth Century*, 28).

12. The *wird*, plural *awrad*, is the time devoted to private devotion, in addition to the five stated prayers, and the formula itself recited on this occasion (*E.I.*, 4, 1139). With the development of religious brotherhoods, each congregation had its own particualr *wird*. The shaykh is employing the term to signify self-imposed daily obligations. Al-Ghazali described seven *awrad* for the daytime and five for the night, among which were practical duties (*waza'if*) such as visiting the sick, attending funerals, working at trades for a livelihood (*Ihya'*, I, chap. 10, 300ff). See C. Padwick, *Muslim Devotions*, 20–22; *Qut*, 7, chap. 24, 122, and *Luma'*, 419.

13. Sufi writers describe in various manners *'ilm al-yaqin, 'ayn al-yaqin, and haqq al-yaqin*. With al-Qushayri, with whose ideas al-Shadhili was familiar, the first is science that is contingent on proofs, and belongs to the intellectuals. The second pertains to clarification which, according to the commentator, signifies revelation and bestowal, and belongs to the men of the sciences. The third comes under the ephithet of clear evidence, and is the property of the men of intuition (*ashab al-ma'arif*) (*Risala* [Cairo, 1966] 74). In the philosophy of Ibn 'Arabi, *'ilm al-yaqin* is knowledge derived from logical proof that does not admit of defect or doubt. *'Ayn al-yaqin* is knowledge derived from mystical contemplation. *Haqq al-yaqin* is knowledge of the real significance of what is observed. See Affifi, 147.

14. *'Illiyun* is one of the names of Paradise, or the highest place there to which the souls of the believers ascend. See Q. 83:18, 19; Lane *Lex.* 2147; *E.I. rev.*, 3, 1132. Among the Ikhwan al-Safa it is the realm of the divine Being, above the hierarchy of lower beings (S. H. Nasr, *An Introduction to Islamic Cosmological Doctrines*, 71).

15. The metaphor of the cup and intoxication, which is commonly used to express the mystical union with God, is also found among Christian mystics. St. Augustine prayed; "O that I might repose on Thee. O that Thou wouldst enter into my heart, and inebriate it, that I may forget my ills, and embrace Thee, my sole good!" (E. B. Pusey, *The Confessions of Saint Augustine* [New York, 1932] 3). See *Kashf*, 184ff; 226f; *Luma'*, 340, 344; A. J. Arberry, *The Mystical Poems of Ibn al-Farid* (Dublin, 1956) 81ff.

16. Al-Mansura was a town in Lower Egypt on the right bank of the Damietta branch of the nile (*E.I.*, 3, 257). This episode may be situated in A.D. 1250, eight years before the Saint's death. In that year, the Crusader army under Louis IX suffered defeat at al-Mansura after having taken Damietta. The paragraphs that follow may be understood in the light of the Crusader threat. The vision of the pavilion and the Saint's encounter with the Prophet reassured him. The date suggested is plausible in view of mention of 'Izz al-Din ibn 'Abd al-Salam, a celebrated jurist who died a few years later than the Saint. See P. Hitti, *History of the Arabs*, (New York, 1949) 654f.

17. Dhu'l-Hijja is the last month of the Muslim calendar. The year of this incident is not stated.

18. Traditions contain abundant references to pavilions or tents in Paradise. See I. Goldziher, *Muslim Studies* (London, 1967) 231, n.3, for later use of tents over graves.

19. On the allowableness and advantages of chanting, recitation, and singing to produce ecstasy opinions differ (*E.I.*, 4, 121). Al-Ghazali, who devoted book 18 of his *Ihya'* to this question, considered it allowable according to the law, but advised caution and moderation, maintaining that the evil lay in the emotions being aroused in such a way as to lead persons to perform unlawful acts (*J.R.A.S.*, 1901, 220, 235ff). Al-Hujwiri, writing a generation before al-Ghazali, devoted a whole chapter to *sama'*. He believed the sense of hearing to be superior to sight in fulfilling religious obligations, and the most beneficial hearing to be that of the *Qur'an* recited. The hearing of poetry, also, was permissible. The effects of hearing may be good or evil according to a person's temperament (*Kashf*, 393–413). Al-Sarraj, writing still earlier, also devoted several chapters to the subject (*Luma'*, 69–77, 267–300). Cf. Al-Attas, *Some Aspects of Sufism as Understood and Practised among the Malays* (Singapore, 1963) 69f, for modern expression of *sama'*; H. A. R. Gibb, *Mohammedanism, A Historical Survey* (London, 1953) 132.

20. Pompey's Pillar is mentioned by Ibn Battutah (*Voyages*, 7, 31).

21. Al-Jazira al-Qibliya was undoubtedly Cap Bon, the peninsula jutting eastward from Tunis, called al-Watn al-Qibli.

22. This book was by Taj al-Din ibn 'Ata Allah al-Iskandari al-Shadhili who died in 709/1309.

23. Humaythira was a place situated in Upper Egypt, in the desert of Aidhab, mentioned by Ibn Battutah (*Voyages*, 7, 40, 109; 2, 253) and by Idrisi, 27.

24. The theme of phantom and dream visitation of the beloved is familiar in mystical poetry. Cf. A. J. Arberry, *The Mystical Poetry of Ibn al-Farid* (Dublin, 1956) 56, 57, 61, 96, 104, 117.

25. Taj al-Din ibn 'Ata Allah wrote; "Divine Reality is veiled from you only by His extreme nearness to you. He is veiled because of the intensity of His manifestation; and He is hidden from sight only because of the greatness of His light" (Maxims 243, 244, 245 of *al-Hikam al-Atta'iyah*, in R. L. Archer, *Muhammadan Mysticism in Sumatra* 74). Cf. P. Nwyia, *Ibn 'Ata Allah et la naissance de la confrerie sadilite* (Beirut, 1972), maxim 155, 150–153.

26. Bab al-Salam is one of the doors on the west side of the Mosque of the Tomb in al-Madina (*E.I.*, 3, 91).

27. Suq al-Balat was the commercial quarter or market place contiguous to the Masjid al-Balat in Tunis.

28. Qaysariya was the name of this edifice. For such a structure in Cairo, see E. W. Lane, *The Arabian Nights* (New York, 1927) 1053, n, 18.

29. Al-Husayn was the grandson of the Prophet by 'Ali and Fatima.

30. While the saint cannot claim the prerogative of the Prophet in being sent as an apostle "to" men for the purpose of being a "mercy," he fulfills the same

function while "among" men. Al-Tirmidhi emphasized the Prophet's mission as a "mercy" to mankind (*Khatm*, 321).

31. He was a celebrated canon lawyer of Cairo who, according to al-Sha'rani, suffered the enmity of the scholastic theolgians, as did al-Shadhili himself, and was accused of infidelity. He died in A.D. 1262, four years later than al-Shadhili (R. A. Nicholson, *A Literary History of the Arabs*, 461).

32. Ibn Hayara was first disciple in the village of Shadhila.

33. A *murabit* is a Muslim recluse; or a partisan of the Almoravid dynasty which ruled in North Africa from 1056 to 1147.

34. The Turks here mentioned may be the Mamluks, slaves of the Egyptian courts, most of whom were Turks, who seized authority in A.D. 1250, eight years before the death of al-Shadhili (S. Lane-Poole, *A History of Egypt in the Middle Ages*, 243ff).

35. Another way to express "changed in disposition" is "becomes irritated." See D. B. Macdonald, *The Religious Attitude and Life in Islam*, 275.

36. The image of the clouds of illumination may derive from Q. 2:159; 24:40, 43; 30:47; or 35:10 in which the formation and movement of clouds are "signs" of God's working. Ibn 'Ata Allah likened the mystical experience to a cloud (P. Nwyia, *Ibn 'Ata Allah et la naissance de la confrerie Sadilite*, 170f).

37. One of the meanings given by Baydawi (in *Anwar al-tanzil* [Cairo, 1925] 567) on the verse quoted is that they will strike or afflict you with the eye ('*ayn*). Traditions support the reality of belief in the power of the eye. See J. Chelhod, *Les Structures du Sacre chez les Arabes* (Paris, 1964) 155f.

38. The *witr* is the "odd" service of worship performed during the night, after the evening worship and before that of the earliest dawn. Traditions do not agree on the most effective time for the act, nor on its being of an obligatory nature. See E.I., 4, 1139f; E. E. Calverley, *The Worship in Islam*, 193–96. According to Malikite law, the latter part of the night is recommended as preferable for the *witr* (L. Bercher, *La Risalah* (of al-Qayrawani) [Algiers 1945] 70f).

39. Al-Sarraj explained that freedom is the ultimate that the Sufi can reach in his servantship to God. Nothing in this world has power over him. One is free when he is a slave to God. One Sufi exhorted another; "God created you free. So be as He created you." Al-Junayd said: "The last station of the mystic is freedom." Another said; "The Servant is not truly a servant so long as he gives ear to anyone except God" (all from *Luma'* 373). Al-Sarraj has a short chapter on false ideas of freedom (*Luma'*, 420f). See also al-Sulami, *Tabaqat al-Sufiyya*, 94.

It is said that freedom means that the servant is not in bondage to creatures and is not subject to the power of created things (*Risala*, 170f). It is also said that the real meaning of freedom lies in perfect servantship for, if one's servantship is sincere to God, his freedom is without admixture of bondage to others (*Risala*, 171).

Al-Qushayri closes his short chapter on freedom with several pithy sayings, some of which are the following:

"The major part of freedom is in service to the poor."

"Whenever you see a beggar, be a servant to him."

"The lord of the [Sufi] people is the one who serves them" (a prophetic tradition).

"The noble and free man leaves this world before he leaves it [at death]."

"Have companionship only with free and noble men who listen without speaking." (All from *Risala*, 172).

40. Abu Hurayra related a saying of the Prophet; "I should like to be killed in the way of God, then be made to live, then be killed, then be made to live, then to be killed, then be made to live, then be killed" (related in M. Ali, *A Manual of Hadith* [Lahore, 1951] 261f). The idea in post-*Qur'anic* thinking is that the *shuhada'*, martyrs, had the possibility of returning to life several times to continue the *jihad* (*E.I.* 4, 259ff).

41. The Qur'anic verses referring to the lawfulness of game especially during the pilgrimage, are 5:6 and 5:95ff. The argument here, judging from the context, seems to be the superiority of mystics to the ordinary jurists by virtue of their divinely bestowed capacities. The *Minhaj al-talibin* of al-Nawawi stipulates the licitness of game killed by the dog of a Muslim (E. C. Howard, tr. *Minhaj al-talibin* [London, 1914] 472). According to the Malikite rite, game killed by a hunting dog that had been sent by his (Muslim) master is lawful (L. Bercher, *La Risalah* [Algiers, 1945] 158f).

42. *Kasb*, similar in meaning to *iktisab*, acquiring or earning, denotes human agency as opposed to the absolute working of the divine will and to the principle of trust (*tawakkul*). In the theology of Al-Ash'ari, although everything has been predetermined by God, man has the power to "acquire" those actions that have already been predestined for him. See *E.I.*, 2, 785f; *Kashf*, 225, 254.

43. *Fana'* and *baqa'* two technical terms common in Sufi usage, signify "passing away" and "remaining", two states that may refer to God or the world. Definitions vary. With al-Qushayri *fana'* is "the decline of blameworthy qualities," while *baqa'* is "the ascent of praiseworthy qualities" (*Risala*, 61).

In the poetry of Ibn al-Farid, they are the survival of the divine attributes after passing away from the human attributes (A. J. Arberry, *The Mystical Poems of Ibn al-Farid* [Dublin, 1956] 72, n. 42). See *Kashf*, 241–245; *Luma'*, 213, 341, 344; *E.I. rev.*, 1, 951. P. Nwyia refers to the two phenomena as "*l'instase apres l'extase*" (*Ibn 'Abbad de Ronda* [Beirut, 1961] 165).

44. E. J. Jurji, *Illumination in Islamic Mysticism*, 65; Redhouse, 1294f. F. Jabre comments that, in the thought of al-Ghazali, *'irfan* is synonymous with *ma'rifa*, *wijdan*, and *dhawq* (*La Notion de Certitude selon Ghazali* [Beirut, 1958] 146).

45. Here follows a succinct exposition of the order of God's bringing into being of the cosmos, including man. The Neoplatonic order of the system is recognized, all proceeding from the Godhead; but, instead of emanation, the

process is one of manifestation, a theophany, similar to the *tajalli* of Ibn 'Arabi and al-Jili (See R. A. Nicholson, *Studies in Islamic Mysticism* [Cambridge, 1921] 125ff). It is a process of God becoming conscious of Himself through His creation, and the individualization of His attributes in the created world. God, with His attributes, "confronts" nonbeing, and sees Himself as in a mirror. Man, the microcosm, unites within himself the qualities of being and nonbeing. He has being by virtue of his descent from the Godhead, or by god having implanted in him of His *sirr* or life. His aim is to become free from nonbeing and thus entirely reunited with the godhead. The mystic circle consists in the descent of the soul through various stages of self-revelation, to man, and then a return to its source through mystical experience. These stages vary in Sufi literature according to current cosmological theories. See E. J. W. Gibb, *A History of Ottoman Poetry*, vol. 1 (London, 1958–1963) 18–20; 34–46; 52–59.

Chapter Five

1. Bonah was the modern city called 'Anaba on the Mediterranean coast of Algeria.

2. Ibn 'Ata' Allah was the author of *Lata'if al-minan* (Cairo, 1974), and successor of al-Mursi as leader of the Shadhiliyia movement. See P. Nwyia, *Ibn 'Abbad de Ronda* (Beirut, 1961) lviii ff.

3. This possibly refers to *Tahdhib al-akhlaq* (*Training of Morals*), by Ibn Miskawayh (d. 1030); or part of book 32 of al-Ghazali's *Ihya' 'ulum al-din*; or other similar work.

4. The text does not indicate the nature of these supplications, but a manual of prayer, *Ahzab wa Awrad* (Cairo 1347/1928–1929) by Ahmad al-Tijani, 63ff, 72, contains ten familiar invocations, some Qur'anic and others non-Qur'anic, with instructions to repeat them seven times, and denoted *musabba'at*, which are known to the elect and commonalty alike. Also Constance Padwick, in her *Muslim Devotions* (London, 1961) 85ff, treats their origin in the *Qur'an* and traditions. Al-Makki related that al-Khidr reveived them from the Prophet (*Qut*, 1, 10).

5. This village was sixty-eight miles from Cairo on the Middle Route to Alexandria. See W. Popper, *Egypt and Syria under the Circassian Sultans* (Berkley, 1955) vol. 15, 46 and map 4.

6. Babal-Sidra was one of the gates of Alexandria (*E.I.*, 2, 536).

7. The *Risala* was the well known mystical work of al-Qushayri (d. 1074).

8. Abu Madyan died in 1198 (*E.I. rev.*, 1, 137). He was the teacher of 'Abd al-Salam ibn Mashish, teacher of al-Shadhili (1:14–18 *supra*). See J. J. S. Barges, *Vie du celebre Marabout Cidi Abu-Medien* (Paris, 1884).

9. Ibn Maryam recorded that al-Mursi related that Abu Madyan possessed seventy-one sciences, was one of the four *awtad*, (lieutenants), and head of the seven *abdal*, (substitutes). The source of this information was Ahmad Baba, *Nayl al-Ibtihaj bi-tatriz al-dibaj* (Cairo, 1908) 109, 125, 169, 346. For *awtad* and *abdal*, cf. 1, 95 and 4, 304 *supra* and notes. For Ibn Maryam see *E.I. rev.*, 3, 865. For life and works of Ahmad Baba, see *E.I. rev.*, 1, 279f.

10. The sciences are not detailed in this work. An idea of the possiblities may be gained by reading al-Ghazali's views on the subject in Gardet and Anawati, *Introduction a la theolgoie musulmane*, 113ff; A. J. Arberry, *The Doctrine of the Sufis* (Cambridge, 1935), chap. 31, 82ff for views of al-Kalabadhi; *Khatm* (Beirut, 1965) 419; *Luma'*, 378f. The first section of Ibn 'Arabi's *al-Futuhat al-makiyya* treats the sciences under seventy-three headings.

11. The meaning of this concise passage, with neither vocalization nor commentary, is uncertain. It is somewhat clarified, however, by Ibn 'Ata' Allah is *Latai'f*, 61, where the subject seems to be the importance of a generous person for the welfare of a people. There Abu al-'Abbas is reported to have commented; "The important thing is not who possesses [wealth]. The matter of importance is who possesses [it] and possesses [it] in order to allow [others] to possess [it]." He then makes the statement regarding himself, with slight variation, that occurs in the text. His wealth, of course, consists in his being unveiled before God and His throne. It may also imply authority in spiritual matters, or the "great dominion" mentioned elsewhere. 'Abd al-Halim Mahmud places this sentence in the context of trust, without further explanation in (*Abu al-Hasan al-Shadhili* [Cairo, 1969] 141).

12. The "seven" may be the seven *abdal* (substitutes) in the Sufi hierarchy (Rinn, *Marabout et Khouan* 56; *E.I. rev.*, 1, 94f), one of the grades below that of *qutb*. Abu Madyan was considered head of the seven.

There are other possibilities, however. According to Ibn 'Arabi (d. 1240), the mystic receives his knowledge from the spirits of the seven spheres. These spirits are the prophets of the past, such as Moses, Joseph, Adam, Jesus (Affifi, 110). From previous statements in the text, it is certain that the sciences to which allusion is made here are not those of the philosophers, but of the mystics. They have a divine source. Real knowledge is that of the Apostle, advanced Sufis, and saints. The metaphor "stars of knowledge" occurs frequently, suggesting a celestial origin. It is knowledge divinely supplied. The Saint once explained that, early in his career, his teacher was Ibn Mashish, but that, as a mature Sufi his mentors were five Adamic and five spiritual, such as angelic, a view that is consonant with that of Ibn 'Arabi which has been previously expressed. The number *seven* has mystical rather than mathematical significance. Furthermore, considering the time lapse, it may be reasonable to assume that the theories of Ibn 'Arabi would be better known to al-Mursi (d. 1285) and his followers, from whom the author received much of his information, than to al-Shadhili (d. 1258). Ibn 'Arabi mentions seven sciences that are special to the people of God.

13. Water, one of the four elements composing the sublunary world, surrounds the earth globe (S. H. Nasr, *An Introduction to Islamic Cosmological Doctrines* [Cambridge, 1964] 140).

14. Shihab al-Din was the son of al-Shadhili. It is assumed that the eulogizer is al-Mursi.

15. He was a contemporary with the author Ibn al-Sabbagh. See *E.I.*, 4, 841.

16. Bab al-Bahr was the "Gate of the Sea."

17. Al-Kumi was possibly descended from the Kumiya tribe of the Maghrib (*E.I.*, 2, 1117). Shaykh Muhammad al-Kumi is referred to as a companion on Abu Marwan and Abu Madyan in Muhammad al-Bahli al-Nayyal, *Al-Haqiqa al-ta'rikhiya li al-tasawwuf al-Islami* (Tunis 1384/1965) 211, note 1, and the information is added that the location of his tomb is known in the Zallaj Cemetery in Tunis. This may be the same al-Kumi to whom reference is made here.

18. This probably was Abu 'Abd Allah Muhammad ibn Sultan.

19. *Rawda* is the garden by the Prophet's tomb in Madina, now included in the Mosque of the Prophet. See *E.I.*, 3, 90.

20. This was accomplished by translevitation. The implication is that God is able to supply man's needs, and concern about them is unnecessary. Also, the saint, although dead, is empowered to perform a *karama*, such as levitation, to meet the crisis. See E. W. Lane, *The Customs and Manners* (London, 1917) 237.

21. The mosque Jami' al-Muhriz stands in that locality today opposite a *zawiya* of the same name. See *E.I.*, 4, 839.

22. Supposedly, this was Abu 'Abd Allah ibn Sultan.

23. Simjum a village near Tunis situated beside the salt marsh bearing that name.

24. Cf. E. E. Calverly, *The Worship in Islam* (London, 1957) 97; W. McKane, *Al-Ghazali's Book of Fear and Hope* (Leiden, 1962).

25. He was a servant of al-Shadhili, and brother of Abu 'Abd Allah ibn Sultan. The only tutor mentioned in the text is Abu 'Abd Allah Muhammad, brother of al-Mursi, teacher of boys in Alexandria. So the person here designated as "Ibn al-Mu'addib could very well be the nephew of al-Mursi, and considerably younger than Madi.

26. Obviously, the father of the author was much younger than Abu 'Abd Allah and his brother Madi. The author lived in al-Masruqin and had opportunity to know Madi and his brother intimately—a fact that is corroborated by many allusions in this chapter, and one which may substantiate the authenticity of much of what was attributed to al-Shadhili, al-Mursi, and other persons mentioned in this work.

27. This is possibly an allusion to the incident of Moses who desired to see the Lord (Q. 7:139). The Lord did not reveal Himself to Moses, but He did reveal

Himself to the mountain. Therewith, the latter changed to dust. The point is that, with the Lord's self-revelation, there is no assurance of the fixity of anything. What appears to be immutable, such as a physical defect, can change.

28. See James Robson, *Mishkat al-Masabih* (of al-Baghawi), vol. 2, 419, 424, on sharing with others during the fast month. Several traditions are noted in Wens. *Concor.*, 3, 456–458, and 5, 169.

29. According to al-Tirmidhi (The third century of *Hijra*), the *sadr* is the place where the *nafs* receives its impulses toward evil (N. Heer, *Bayan al-farq* [Cairo, 1957] 35, 40, and M. Lings, *A Sufi Saint of the Twentieth Century* (London, 1971) 52.

30. Bab al-Jazira was below Bab Jadid toward the lake, and is known by that name in modern times.

31. The author is narrating here. Near ancient Carthage, there is an archeological site named "Damus al-Karita," and 87 miles from Tunis on the route to Tabarqa there is a Jabal Damus, or Damus. On the east coast of Tunisia, eight or ten miles southwest of Monastir, is a small village called Damus.

32. The phenomenon of illumination arising from graves of saints is not uncommon. See L. Massignon, "La Cite des Morts au Caire," *Opera Minora*, 3, 259, 261.

33. Repetition of this formula prevents error, or indicates that no error has been made.

34. A.H. 668 is A.D. 31 August 1269 through 21 August 1270. On 25 August 1270, Louis IX King of France died at Carthage while conducting the Second Crusade (de Joinville, *Memoires of the Crusades*, tr. F. T. Marzials [New York, 1958] 324).

35. That is, he followed the teachings of the religious order represented by al-Shadhili and al-Habibi. The author recorded this incident more than a half century after the death of the shaykh.

36. The Muslim calendar year, having twelve lunar months, is approximately eleven days shorter than the solar year.

37. Add to this quote, "And therefore shall not suffer misfortune." Al-Tirmidhi, in *Sahih*, manu. 26, related a tradition. "The fire will not touch a Muslim who has seen me or who has seen someone who has seen me."

38. This refers to the author Ibn al-Sabbagh. Here is a play on the name *Jamal* (beauty) with the verb *jammala* that follows and means to beautify.

Bibliography

Affifi, A. *The Mystical Philosophy of Muhyid Din-Ibnul 'Arabi* (Cambridge: Cambridge University Press, 1939).

Afnan, S. *Philosophical Terminology in Arabic and Persian* (Leiden: Brill, 1964).

Ali, M. *A Manual of Hadith* (Lahore: Muhammad Ashraf, 1951).

Arberry, A. J. *The Doctrine of the Sufis* (Cambridge: Cambridge Univeristy Press, 1935).

———. *The Mystical Poems of Ibn al-Farid* (Dublin: Emery Walker, 1956).

Archer, R. L. *Muhammadan Mysticism in Sumatra* (Singapore: Royal Asiatic Society, 1937).

al-Attas, S. N. *Some Aspects of Sufism as Understood and Practiced among the Malays* (Singapore: Malasian Social Research Institute, 1963).

Baba, A. *Nayl al-ibtihaj bi-tatriz al-dibaj* (Cairo: Babi, 1908).

Barges, J. J. S. *Vie du Celebre Marabout Cidi Abou-Medien* (Paris: Ernest Leroux, 1884).

Baydawi, I. *Anwar al-tanzil fi asrar al-ta'wil* (Cairo: Babi, 1925).

Bercher, L. *La Risalah* (of al-Qayrawani) (Algiers: Jules Carbonel, 1945).

Birge, J. K. *The Bektashi Order of Dervishes* (London: Luzac, 1937).

Bodenheimer, F. S., ed. *The 'Uyun al-Akhbar of Ibn Qutayba*, tr. L. Koph (Leiden: Brill, 1949).

Brockelmann, C. *Geschichte der Arabischen Litteratur and Supplementband* (Leiden: Brill, 1898).

Brunschvig, R. *Le Berberie orientale sous les Hafsides des origines a la fin du XV siecle* (Paris: Maisonneuve, 1947).

Burckhardt, T. "The Prayer of Ibn Mashish," *The Islamic Quarterly*, nos. 1, 2 (1978) 68–75.

Burton, R. F. *Personal Narrative of a Pilgrimage to el-Medinah and Meccah* (New York: Tyleston, 1856).

Calverley, E. E. *The Worship in Islam* (London: Luzac, 1957).

Chelhod, J. *Les Structures du Sacre chez les Arabes* (Paris: Maisonneuve et Larose, 1964).

Corbin, H. *Shihaboddin Yahya Sohravardi Shaykh al-ishraq: L'Archanae empourpre* (Paris: Fayard, 1976).

Danner, V., tr. *Ibn 'Ata'illah's Sufi Aphorisms* (Leiden: Brill, 1973).

De Goeje, M. J., ed. *Bibliotheca Geographorum Arabicorum*, 8 volumes (Leiden: Brill, 1870–1894).

De Joinville, V. *Memoires of the Crusades*, tr. F. T. Marzials (New York: Scribners, 1958).

Dermenghem, E. *Le Culte de saints dans l'Islam maghrebien* (Paris: Gallimard, 1954).

Donaldson, D. M. *Studies in Muslim Ethics* (London: SPCK, 1953).

Douglas, E. H. "Al-Shadhili: A North Africarn Sufi, According to Ibn al-Sabbagh." *The Muslim World*, 38 (October 1948): 257–279.

Dozy, R. *Supplement aux Dictionnaires Arabes* (Leiden: Brill, 1881).

Encyclopedia of Islam (Leiden: Brill, 1913).

Encyclopedis of Islam Revision (Leiden: Brill, 1961).

al-Fasi, A. I. Z. *Qurat al-'ayn fi sharh hikam al-'arif bi-Allah Ibn 'Ata' Allah al-Iskandari* (Cairo: Dar al-Kutub, 1972).

Gardet, L. and G. Anawati. *Introduction a la theologie musulmane* (Paris: J. Vrin, 1948).

al-Ghazali, A. H. *Ihya' 'ulum al-din* (Cairo: Babi, 1918).

———. *al-Risala al-laduniya* (Cairo: Babi, 1934).

———. *al-Munqidh min al-dalal* (Damascus: Dar al-Ma'rifa, 1959), tr. W. M. Watt, *The Faith and practice of al-Ghazali* (Chicago: Kazi Publications, 1982).

———. *al-Maqsad al-asna fi sharhi ma'na asma' Allah al-husna* (Beirut: Dar al-Turath, 1971).

Gibb, E. J. W. *A History of Ottoman Poetry*, 6 vols. (London, 1958–63).

Gibb, H. *Travels of Ibn Battuta*, 2 vols. (Cambridge: Cambridge University Press, 1958).

Gilis, C. *La Doctrine Initiatique du Prelinage a la Maison d'Allah* (Paris: Les Editions de L'Oeuvre, 1982).

Goldziher, I. *Muslim Studies*, 2 vols. (London: Luzac, 1967).

Guide Bleu, *Algerie-Tunisie* (Paris: Vrin, 1930).

Heer, N., ed. *Bayan al-farq* (Cairo: al-Dar al-Misriyya, 1958).

Heer, N. "A Sufi Pyschological Treatise," *The Muslim World*, January 1961.

Hitti, P. *History of the Arabs* (New York: St. Martin's Press, 1949).

Howard, E. C., tr. *Minhai al-talibin* (London: Luzac, 1914).

Hughes, T. P. *A Dictionary of Islam* (London: SPCK, 1896).

al-Hujwiri, A. *The "Kashf al-Mahjub," The Oldest Persian Treatise on Sufism*, tr. R. A. Nicholson, Gibb Memorial Series, no. 17 (London: Cambridge University Press, 1911).

Ibn 'Ajiba. *Iqaz al-himam fi sharh al-hikam* (Cairo: Babi, 1915).

Ibn 'Arabi. *al-Futuhat al-makiyya* (Beirut: Dar Sadir, 1968).

Ibn 'Ata' Allah. *al-Hikam al-'Atta'iya* (Cairo: Silsilat al-Buhuth, 1969).

———. *Lata'if al-minan*, ed. A. H. Mahmud (Cairo: Matba'at Hassan, 1974).

———. *The Book of Wisdom*, tr. V. Danner (New York: The Paulist Press, 1978).

Ibn 'Ayyad, A. *al-Adhkar al- 'aliyyah wa'l asrar al-shadhiliyyah* (Alexandria: al-Dar al-Qawmiyya, A.H. 1288).

———. *Kitab al-mafakhir al-'aliyya fi'1 ma'athir al-Shadiliyya* (Cairo: Halabi, 1961).

Ibn Khaldoun. *Histoire des Berberes*, 4 vols. tr. M. de Slane (Algiers: Jourdan, 1852–1856).

Ibn Miskawayh. *Tahdhib al-akhlaq* (Beirut: al-Jami'a al-Amerikiyya, 1969).

Irdrisi, S. *Description de l'Afrique et de l'Espagne* (Leiden: Brill, 1866).

Jabre, F. *La Notion de Certitude selon Ghazali* (Beirut: l'Universite Libanaise, 1958).

Jeffrey, A. "The Mystic Letters of the Koran," *The Muslim World*, April 1950.

Jeffery, A. *Reader on Islam* (The Hague: Mouton, 1962).

al-Jurjani, A. *Kitab al-ta'rifat* (Leipzig: Vogelii, 1845).

Jurji, E. J. *Illumination in Islamic Mysticism* (Princeton, N.J.: Princeton University Press, 1936).

al-Kalabadhi, A. B. *Kitab al-ta'arruf li madhhab ahl al-tasawwuf*, ed. A. J. Arberry (Cairo: al-Matba'a al-Misriyya, 1934), tr. A. J. Arberry, *The Doctrine of the Sufis* (Cambridge: Cambridge University Press, 1935).

Kamal, A. *The Sacred Journey* (New York: Sloane and Pearce, 1961).

al-Kharraz, A. *The Book of Truthfulness*, ed. and tr. A. J. Arberry (London: Oxford University Press, 1937).

Lane, E. W. *Arab-English Lexicon* (London: Williams and Norgate, 1863–1885).

———. *The Customs and Manners of the Modern Egyptians* (London: Murray, 1917).

———. *Arabian Nights* (New York: Tudor, 1927).

Lane-Poole, S. *The Mohammadan Dynasties* (Westminster: Constable & Co., 1894).

———. *A History of Egypt in the Middle Ages* (London: Methuen and Co., 1925).

Lings, M. *A Sufi Saint of the Twentieth Century* (London: Allen and Unwin, 1971).

———. *Symbol and Archetype: A Study of the Meaning of Existence* (London: Quinta Essentia, 1991).

Macdonald, D. B. *Muslim Theology, Jurisprudence, and Constitutional Theory* (New York: Scribner, 1926).

Mackeen, A. "The Early History of Sufism in the Maghrib Prior to al-Shadhili," *Journal of the American Oriental Society*, 91:3 (July–September 1971): 398–408.

Mackeen, A. "The Rise of al-Shadhili," *Journal of the American Oriental Society*, vol. 91(4) (October–December 1971) 477–486.

Mahmud, A. H. *al-Madrasa al-shadhiliyya al-haditha wa-imamuha Abu al-Hasan al-Shadhili* (Cairo: Dar al-Kutub al-Haditha, 1969).

al-Makki, A. T. *Qut al-aulub fi mu'amalat al-mahbub*, 2 vols. (Cairo: Al-Babi, 1893).

Massignon, L. *Opera Minora*, 4: vols., ed. Y. Moubarac (Beirut: The Catholic Press, 1963).

McKane, W. *Al-Ghazali's Book of Fear and Hope* (Leiden: Brill, 1962).

Mehren, A. F. *Manuel de la Cosmographie du Moyen Age* (Copenhaguen: Knogelige bibliotek, 1874).

Michon, J. L. *Le Soufi marocain Ahmad Ibn 'Ajiba et son Mi'raj* (Paris: Vrin, 1973).

Miller, S. G., ed. and tr. *Disorienting Encounters: Travels of a Moroccan Scholar in France in 1845–1846: The Voyage of Muhammad As-Saffar* (Berkeley: University of California Press, 1992).

Mustafa, A. *al-Bina' al-ijtima'i li'l tariqa al-shadhiliyya* (Alexandria: Matba'at al-Ma'arif, 1982).

Mustaufi, H. *Nuzhat al-qulub*, tr. Le Strange (London: SPCK, 1919).

al-Naqshabandi, A. D. *Jami' al-usul fi al-awliya'* (Cairo: al-Babi, 1910).

Nasr, S. H. *An Introduction to Islamic Cosmological Doctrines* (Cambridge: Harvard University Press, 1964).

Nasr, S. H. *Sufi Essays*, rev. ed. (Albany, N.Y.: State University of New York Press, 1991).

al-Nayyal, M. B. *al-Haqiqa al-tarikhiyya li al-tasawwuf al-Islami* (Tunis: Dar Tunis, 1384/1965).

Newby, G. D. *The Making of the Last Prophet: A Reconstruction of the Earliest Biography of Muhammad* (Colombia: University of South Carolina Press, 1989).

Nicholson, R. A. *Studies in Islamic Mysticism* (Cambridge: Cambridge University Press, 1921).

———. *The Idea of Personality in Sufism* (Cambridge: Cambridge University Press, 1923).

———. *A Literary History of the Arabs* (Cambridge: Cambridge University Press, 1930).

———, ed., and tr. *Divan-i-Shams-i Tabriz* (Cambridge: Cambridge University Press, 1961).

Nwyia, P. *Ibn 'Abbad de Ronda* (Beirut: The Catholic Press, 1961).

———. *Exegese coranique et langage mystique* (Beirut: Dar el-Machreq, 1970)

———. *Ibn 'Ata' Allah et la naissance de la confrerie sadilite* (Beirut: The Catholic Press, 1972).

Padwick, C. *Muslim Devotions* (London: SPCK, 1961).

Palacious, M. A. "Sadhilies y alumbrados." *Al-Andalus*, vol. 9 (1944).

Palacios, M. A. *The Mystical Philosophy of Ibn Masarra and his Followers*, trs. E. Douglas and H. Yoder (Leiden: E. J. Brill, 1978).

Popper, W. *Egypt and Syria under the Circassian Sultans* (Berkeley: University of California Press, 1955).

Pusey, E. B. *The Confessions of Saint Augustine* (New York: Scribner, 1932).

al-Qashani, A. R. *A Glossary of Sufi Technical Terms*, tr. N. Safwat (London: The Octagon Press, 1991).

al-Qazwini, Z. M. *Athar al-bilad wa akhbar al-'ibad* (Beirut: al-Risala, n.d.).

Qushayri, A. Q. *al-Risala al-qushayriya*, 2 vols. (Cairo: Babi, 1330–1912).

Rahman, F. *Major Themes of the Qur'an* (Minneapolis: Bibliotheca Islamica, 1980).

———. "Islam's Attitude Toward Judaism," *The Muslim World* 72:1, (January 1982): 1–13.

Redhouse, J. W. *A Turkish and English Lexicon* (Constantinople: Redhouse Press, 1890).

Rinn, L. *Maraboute et Khouan* (Algiers: A. Jourdan, 1844).

Robson, J. *Mishkat al-masabih* (of al-Baghawi), 4 vols. (Lahore: Muhammad Ashraf, 1965).

al-Rundi, I. A. *Ghawth al-mawahib al-'aliyya fi sharh al-hikam al-'ata'iyya* (Cairo: al-Fajalla, 1970).

Sadler, A. W. "Visit to a Chisti Qawwali," *The Muslim World*, October 1963.

Sarkis, J. E. *Dictionnaire Encyclopedique de Bibliographie Arabe* (Cairo: J. E. Sarkis and Sons, 1928).

al-Sarraj, A. N. *Kitab al-luma' fi'l tasawwuf*, ed. R. A. Nicholson (Leiden: Brill, 1914).

Schacht, J. *An Introduction to Islamic Law* (Oxford: Oxford University Press, 1964).

Sha'rani, A. W. *al-Tabaqat al-kubra* (Cairo: Matba'at 'Ali Sabih, n. d.).

Sheikh, A. G. "From America to Mecca on Airborne Pilgrimage," *The National Geographic Magazine* (July 1953): 1–60.

Schimmel, A. *Mystical Dimensions of Islam* (Chapel Hill: University of North Carolina Press, 1975).

Shorter Encyclopedia of Islam (Leiden: Brill, 1961).

Smith, M. "The Path of the Soul in Sufism," *The Aryan Path*, vol. 6, June 1935.

Smith, M. "'al-Risalah al-Laduniyah,' by al-Ghazali," *Journal of the Royal Asiatic Society* (1938): part 3.

Subhan, J. A. *Sufism: Its Saints and Shrines* (New York: Samuel Weiser, 1970).

al-Sulami, A. R. *Tabaqat al-sufiyya*, ed. J. Pederson (Leiden: Brill, 1960).

Swan, G. "Saintship in Islam," *The Muslim World*, vol. 5 (1915): 229–39.

al-Tijani, A. *Ahzab wa awrad* (Cairo: Dar al-Uns, 1347/1928–1929).

al-Tirmidhi, A. M. *Sahih* (Cairo: Babi, A.H. 1292).

al-Tirmidhi, H. *Khatm al-awliya'* (Beirut: al-Dar al-Lubnaniyya, 1965).

Trimingham, J. *The Sufi Orders in Islam* (London: Oxford University Press, 1971).

Underhill, E. *The Mystics of the Church* (New York: Abingdon Press, 1926).

Vacca, V. "Social and Political Aspects of Egyptian and Yamani Sufism," *Journal of the Pakistan Historical Society*, vol. 8, part 4, October 1960.

Watt, W. M. *The Faith and Practice of al-Ghazali* (Chicago: Kazi Publications, 1982).

Wensinck, A. J. *Concordance et indices de la tradition musulmane*, 7 vols. (Leiden: E. J. Brill, 1933).

Wickens, A. M., tr. *The Nasirean Ethics* (London: SPCK, 1964).

Winter, M. *Society and Religion in Early Ottoman Egypt: Studies in the Writings of 'Abd al-Wahab al-Sha'rani* (New Brunswick: Transaction Books, 1982).

al-Ya'qubi. *Kitab al-Buldan*, ed. de Goeje (Leiden: Brill, 1892).

Index